To my dear Mother

May you have a very happy
and blessed birthday.

September 1965.

My love,
Ruth

MOTHER OF THE QUEEN

MOTHER
OF THE
QUEEN

The Life Story of Her Majesty
Queen Elizabeth The Queen Mother

by

DAVID DUFF

FREDERICK MULLER LIMITED
LONDON

First published in Great Britain 1965 by
Frederick Muller Limited
Printed by C. Tinling & Co. Ltd.
Liverpool, London and Prescot

To Doreen

Author's Note

FOR EVENTS in the life of Her Majesty Queen Elizabeth the Queen Mother since her marriage reference has been made to the newspapers and magazines of the time. Acknowledgment is made to the following for descriptions of particular occasions: the engagement and wedding of Prince Albert, Duke of York, to Lady Elizabeth Bowes-Lyon—*Morning Post, Daily Mail,* and *Nottingham Guardian;* the visits of the Duke and Duchess of York to Belgrade (1923) and Berlin and Oslo (1929)—*Morning Post, Daily Sketch* and *Sunday Graphic;* the births of Princess Elizabeth (1926) and Princess Margaret Rose (1930)—*Morning Post* and *Daily Express;* the weddings of the Duke of Kent (1934) and the Duke of Gloucester (1935) —*Morning Post;* the Jubilee of King George V and Queen Mary (1935)—*The Times* and *Morning Post;* the death of King George V (1936)—*Morning Post, Daily Telegraph, Daily Express, Daily Mail, Star,* and *Evening News;* the abdication of King Edward VIII (1936)— *The Times, Daily Mail* and *Daily Express;* the Coronation of King George VI and Queen Elizabeth (1937)—*Sunday Times, Daily Express* and *Evening Standard;* the Victory celebrations (1945 and 1946)—*The Times, Sunday Express* and *Evening Standard;* the wedding of Princess Elizabeth (1947)—*Daily Telegraph, Daily Express* and *New York Herald Tribune;* the illness, death and funeral of King George VI (1952)—*The Times, Observer, Daily Telegraph, Evening News* and *Evening Standard;* the death of Queen Mary (1953)—*Sunday Express* and *Evening Standard;* the Coronation of Queen Elizabeth II (1953)—the *Daily Telegraph* and the *Daily Express;* the weddings of Princess Margaret (1960), the Duke of Kent (1961) and Princess Alexandra (1963)—*Sunday Times, Daily*

Telegraph, Daily Express, Evening News and *Evening Standard*; the death of Sir David Bowes-Lyon (1961)—*Daily Telegraph* and *Daily Express*. Special Numbers for royal occasions published by *The Field, The Sphere, The Illustrated Sporting and Dramatic News, Vogue, Weekly Illustrated, The Illustrated London News* and *The Queen* have also been consulted.

For the visits of the Duke and Duchess of York to East Africa in 1925 and to New Zealand and Australia in 1927 I have relied, in the main, on the detailed description of Mr. Taylor Darbyshire; and for Their Majesties tour of South Africa in 1947 on that of Mr. Dermot Morrah. In the sphere of memoirs and reminiscences I have consulted those of Mabell, Countess of Airlie, Mr. Cecil Beaton, Lady Cynthia Colville, Lady Diana Cooper, Mr. H. T. Cozens-Hardy, Mr. John Dean, Mr. Norman Hartnell, Princess Marie Louise, Mrs. Eleanor Roosevelt, Lord Sysonby, M. Gabriel Tschumi, and the Duke and Duchess of Windsor. Among biographies of, and studies upon, members of the Royal Family, reference has been made to those of Lady Cynthia Asquith, Mr. Hector Bolitho, Major J. T. Gorman, and Miss D. M. Stuart dealing with the lives of King George VI and Queen Elizabeth up to 1937; those of Sir George Arthur, Mr. John Gore and Sir Harold Nicolson upon King George V; those of Mr. James Pope-Hennessy, Mrs. Kathleen Woodward upon Queen Mary; and those of Brigadier Stanley Clark, Mr. Richard Dimbleby, Miss Dorothy Laird and General Sir Leslie Hollis upon Queen Elizabeth II and Prince Philip. The debt to Sir John Wheeler-Bennett's life of King George VI, a masterpiece in accuracy and detail, is acknowledged in full. These, and all other works consulted, are listed in the bibliography.

DAVID DUFF

Contents

Acknowledgments

I AM grateful to Messrs. Macmillan & Co. Ltd. for permission to quote from *King George VI: His Life and Reign*, by John W. Wheeler-Bennett; to Messrs. John Murray Ltd. for permission to quote from *Queen Adelaide*, by Mary Hopkirk; to Messrs. Cassell & Co. Ltd. for permission to quote from *A King's Story* by H.R.H. the Duke of Windsor and from *The Second World War* by Sir Winston Churchill; to Messrs. Rupert Hart-Davis Ltd. for permission to quote from *The Light of Common Day* by Diana Cooper; to Messrs. Evans Brothers Ltd. for permission to quote from *Crowded Life* by Lady Cynthia Colville and from *Silver and Gold* by Norman Hartnell; to the Hutchinson Publishing Group for permission to quote from *The Royal Family in Africa* by Dermot Morrah and from *Queen Elizabeth* by Lady Cynthia Asquith; to Messrs. William Kimber & Co. Ltd. and Messrs. Curtis Brown Ltd. for permission to quote from *Royal Chef* by Gabriel Tschumi; to Messrs. Robert Hale Ltd. for permission to quote from *The Glorious Years* by H. T. Cozens-Hardy, and from *H.R.H. Prince Philip* by John Dean.

Illustrations

ILLUSTRATIONS

*Acknowledgment is made to the following for their co-operation in
supplying some of the photographs used in this book: Cecil Beaton
(the jacket and frontispiece), and Baron Studios (the lower photograph facing page* 160).

I *Introducing . . .*

ELIZABETH Angela Marguerite Bowes-Lyon was born on 4th August 1900. On the morning of that day Queen Victoria sat at her window in Osborne House as H.M.S. *Australia* came into the Bay. Soon, as her tired head sunk in prayer, the guns thundered out over the Isle of Wight in salute to the dead Duke of Edinburgh and Saxe-Coburg, her second son. He was a Naval officer. He was fifty-six. He was a victim of cancer and had died quietly in his sleep. The blinds were drawn at his London home, Clarence House, St. James's.

Fifty-two years later died another second son of a Sovereign, King George VI. He also was a Naval officer. He was fifty-six. He was a victim of cancer and he died quietly in his sleep. Clarence House was the home of his daughter and son-in-law, the Duke of Edinburgh. Thereafter it was to be the home of his widow.

In that half century of time, at the close of which a page of royal history repeated itself, the girl born in the last months of the life of Queen Victoria had come to be the leading lady in the land, and the outstanding woman of her country.

It is now for over forty-two years that her engagements, her activities and her movements have been chronicled. Only during the mourning period for her husband and during two illnesses of comparatively short duration, has she been off the stage. First as the Lady Elizabeth Bowes-Lyon, then as the Duchess of York, next as Queen Elizabeth and now as Queen Elizabeth the Queen Mother, she has become a part of the British day.

She has flown around the world, and she has sailed around the world. She is known in the big cities and remote places of Canada,

13

Australia and New Zealand. She has travelled Africa from Tunis to the Table Mountain. In New York and Washington she is the 'Queen Mum', a title that is hers alone. She has received ovation in the streets from Oslo to Rome. To the French she is a part of themselves, remembering always the beauty of her in the sun of Paris in 1938. She is a figure of world wide importance, beloved and respected.

Never, in those forty-two years, has there been criticism of her actions or activities. In this, for a woman in her high position, she is unique. No word has been spoken against her by those societies and sects which, in recent years, have considered it incumbent upon them to censor the doings of certain members of the Royal Family. Rather, in its place, has there been praise.

A religious woman, a firm believer in the sanctity of married life, she was fortunate in her husband, who shared her beliefs. He loved her beyond measure. Often, during his last illness, the nurses would fetch her so that he could touch her hand.

Unprepared, and undesirous of the burden, she moved into Queenship with a smooth tranquillity that was to amaze those around the Court. Not one false move did she make, or one false word did she utter. Within the next two years, as Europe tottered on the brink of a war that was inevitable, she made State visits to France, Canada and America, forging new bonds that were to hold fast through the years of struggle. It was she who turned the tide of American affection back to the British Throne.

As a wife, she knew the full handicap of the impediment in her husband's speech, and also the limitations on his strength that his early medical history imposed. She knew that the strain of war would sap him to the end and drain away his years—their years together. Loyalty and courage are in her to as large a degree as they were in Queen Mary, her mentor. In vivid contrast with Queen Victoria, she has not allowed death to interfere with public engagements.

She has always regarded herself as a member of the royal team, and, as such, has given of her best. Yet, in her personal life she is an individualist, complete in herself. Gardening and fishing have been her spare time occupations. She is able to lose herself in the pleasure and preoccupation of the moment, the thrill of a horse-race, the water round her feet, the magic of music, ballet and opera. She is able to leave the world behind in the make-believe of charades, and she knows the simple ways of children and dogs, and is accordingly adored by both.

Friendship with her is a treasured thing, and lasts the full course. For chance acquaintances, years do not slow the recognition or dim the memory. The Queen Mother can adjust herself to types of people, ages of people, differing races of people, in an instant. There is always the freshness of the moment about her engagements, always she seems to be taking bouquets as if it were for the first time. She can convey upon a bazaar at Sandringham the importance of a Commonwealth tour. People who meet her feel, within a few moments, that they know her. Herein lies one of the elements of her success. They do know her. The image and the woman are the same. The charm, the smile and grace are integral parts of her.

Her courtesy and her manners are a byword throughout the world. She never leaves an aircraft or a royal train until she has thanked the crews. She always remembers the photographers. She moves to a point where the background is suitable, smiles at the right second, waits patiently until the pictures are taken.

Born into a slow and peaceful world of vastly differing social structure, a world of carriages and afternoon calls, of oil lamps and lessons from a governess, when the seasons and the feast days were the milestones of the year, she has moved into a fast moving, democratic age with an easy grace, and adopted it as her own. Yet it was in her childhood, under the guidance of a brilliant mother, that the foundations for the role that she plays today, were laid.

It was the atmosphere pervading her childhood that instilled into her the peace and charm that has persisted. That atmosphere was noted by a Labour statesman, Mr. J. R. Clynes, and it had a deep and lasting impression upon him. As Home Secretary, it was his duty to be at Glamis for the birth of Princess Margaret. The Princess was over a fortnight late in arriving, and in the interim Mr. Clynes stayed nearby as the guest of Mabell, Countess of Airlie. He was entertained at many of the great houses of Angus, where live four families allied to the Royal Family. One day, as he drove away from

Glamis, he said to Lady Airlie: 'What a different atmosphere you find in these great houses where families have lived for generations from those which have just been put up by some millionaire.' Time and time again he said to her: 'I have seen things up here which I shall remember as long as I live.'

From the historical viewpoint Queen Elizabeth the Queen Mother has been responsible for introducing a number of breaks with royal tradition. Her wedding in Westminster Abbey was the first occasion of a marriage there of the son of a reigning Sovereign since 1269. The birth of her children brought to an end the custom of the Home Secretary being in attendance at such occasions. She was the first commoner bride of a Prince in direct line to the Throne for over two hundred and fifty years, since James, Duke of York, later James II, married Anne Hyde, daughter of Lord Clarendon, in 1660.

For so long had the British Sovereigns chosen their brides or grooms from the courts of the mainland of Europe that the announcement of the engagement of Prince Albert, Duke of York, to Lady Elizabeth Bowes-Lyon was considered to be revolutionary. In the event it was but a return to standard practice, long delayed. In early centuries, it was the custom of the Sovereign to give the hand of a son or daughter in marriage to one of the great families, such as the Nevills, the De La Poles, the Tudors or the Mortimers. They owned vast estates and had a strong hold over those who lived on them. Tied to the Throne by matrimony, they brought with them to the Court not only power, but riches. But religious differences, internecine strife, particularly in Scotland, foraging, pilfering away of family fortunes, these things, helped by royal jealousy, broke the power of the great nobles. By the fifteenth century marriages between the Royal Family and the aristocracy were becoming fewer, though there was one outstanding example. In May 1464 Edward IV, three years a king, married Elizabeth, daughter of Sir Richard Widville. The only subsequent cases of the Sovereign marrying a commoner came with the matrimonial extravaganza of Henry VIII fifty years later. His alliance with Anne Boleyn, daughter of Sir Thomas Boleyn, produced a situation much in keeping with the royal situation today, in that their daughter ascended to the throne as Queen Elizabeth. Henry also married Jane, daughter of Sir John Seymour, Katharine,

Elizabeth and David

Elizabeth at the age of two

In the garden at Glamis

Lady Elizabeth Bowes-Lyon on 'Bobs' at St. Paul's Walden Bury

daughter of Lord Edmund Howard, and Katharine, daughter of Sir Thomas Parr. Thereafter, with the exception of James II's secret marriage to Anne Hyde, the problem of recognized marriages between Royalty and commoners did not arise until the early days of the reign of George III, when two of his brothers took commoner brides. The Duke of Gloucester married Maria, Countess Waldegrave, and the Duke of Cumberland, the Hon. Anne Horton. The King had personal objection to these two ladies on social and political grounds. He took steps to ensure that Princes and Princesses, present and future, should not embarrass the Sovereign by unsuitable marriages. In 1772 the Royal Marriage Act was passed. The restrictions which it imposed made it necessary for special steps to be taken before Prince Albert, Duke of York, could marry Lady Elizabeth Bowes-Lyon.

From the time that she became Duchess of York in 1923 until 1965, her sixty-fifth year, the Queen Mother has ceaselessly and cheerfully carried out a programme of home duties, the total of which is beyond count and exceeds that executed by any member of the Royal Family in history. Already well beyond the retirement age for women, she continues her programme of engagements with unflagging zeal. Her first care has been for the young and for the sick. Hospitals owe her a debt only fully known to them. As Chancellor of London University she has become an expert in the sphere of education. The Services, in particular her own regiments, have treasured her many visits and she is a staunch supporter of associations caring for ex-Servicemen. A lover of the opera and the ballet, her many appearances there have strengthened their general appeal and enriched charity performances.

On occasions in all the fields of our national life, the presence of Her Majesty, the Queen Mother, ensures the stamp of success.

2   *The Princess of St. Paul's*

HER Majesty Queen Elizabeth the Queen Mother arrived at St. Paul's Walden Bury in time for the seventeenth birthday celebrations of her elder sister, Mary. She was the ninth child of Lord and Lady Glamis, and she joined five brothers and two sisters. The first-born, a girl, had died seven years earlier. The boys ranged from sixteen-year-old Patrick, Master of Glamis, through John, Alexander and Fergus, to Michael aged seven. Sister Rose was ten. The gulf in time left Elizabeth alone in her nursery world. But she had not long to wait for company. In the spring of 1902 a 'darling bruvver', arrived and his name was David. The Bowes-Lyon ménage was complete.

When Elizabeth was four her grandfather died. Her father became 14th Earl of Strathmore and Kinghorne, Viscount Lyon and Baron Glamis, Tannadyce, Sidlaw, and Strathdichtie, in Scotland; Baron Bowes, of Streatlam Castle, in the co. Durham, and Lunedale, in the co. York, in the United Kingdom. Elizabeth inherited the courtesy title of Lady. But to certain of her parents' friends she was known as Princess Elizabeth from the time that she could toddle. It was a game. They would bend the knee to her, and she hold out her hand to be kissed. It just came naturally. Whilst her sisters had Mary and Rose familiarized into May and Rosie, the baby was accorded the full regality of Elizabeth.

St. Paul's Walden Bury lay in the then rustic silence of Hertfordshire, Hitchin to the north and Welwyn to the south. Two centuries had weathered its brick to the soft tincture of a rose, and honeysuckle and magnolia clung to its walls. A friendly hotchpotch of a house, low over the porticoed front door and flanked by a square tower with bow windows. Chimney pots everywhere and, lording it among them, a belfry. It was as if four or five houses had been pushed together to form a family settlement, the sort of house of which children never tire.

Outside were all the things that go into a child's heaven, a harness room and stables, a tumble-down barn where the hens laid, a dairy, garden temples, fountains, statues green from the moss and the rain, and a giant oak looking down on hawthorn clipped to the likeness of peacocks.

The grounds and the gardens were the wonder of St. Paul's. Here was the influence of André Le Nôtre, the great designer responsible for the gardens of Versailles. *Allées* cut through a wood, each ending with a statue or an arresting view, gave a sense of size. Nearer to the house were neat yew hedges screening the roses, and a rock garden. There were mulberries to suck and limes to smell. There was sufficiency for a child within the gates.

It is nearly thirty years since the Queen Mother recalled for Lady Cynthia Asquith her memories of St. Paul's in the days of King Edward VII. They are words which the years cannot dim.

'At the bottom of the garden, where the sun always seems to be shining, is THE WOOD—the haunt of fairies, with its anemones and ponds, and moss-grown statues, and the BIG OAK under which she reads and where the two ring-doves, Caroline-Curly-Love and Rhoda-Wrigley-Worm, contentedly coo in their wicker-work "Ideal Home".

'There are carpets of primroses and anemones to sit on, and she generally has tea either in the shadow of the statue of Diana or near another very favourite one called the "Running Footman" or the "Bounding Butler" (to grown-up people known as the Disc-Thrower). These statues live in cut-out grassy places, and sometimes there are wild strawberries around them, sometimes bee-orchises.

'Whenever—and this is often—a dead bird is found in this enchanted wood it is given a solemn burial in a small box lined with rose-leaves.

'Her small brother David is always with her and usually a tiny Shetland pony called "Bobs". Bobs will follow her into the house and even walk up and down long stone steps, and she has to be very careful that he does not tread on her little brother's toes.

'Now it is time to go haymaking, which means getting very hot in a delicious smell. Very often she gets up wonderfully early—about six o'clock—to feed her chickens and make sure they are safe after the dangers of the night. The hens stubbornly insist on laying their eggs in a place called the FLEA HOUSE, and this is where she and her brother go and hide from Nurse.

'Nothing is quite so good as the FLEA HOUSE, but the place called the HARNESS ROOM is very attractive too. Besides hens there are bantams-whose-eggs-for-tea-are-so-good. Also Persian kittens and tortoises . . .'

Elizabeth had the same nurse, Clara Cooper Knight, from the time she was a few weeks old until she was eleven. Then, fifteen years later, she became nurse to the baby in the next generation, Princess Elizabeth.

The nursery was a wide, comfortable room, well rubbed by those who had used it before. Favourite pictures from story books, framed by the gardener, hung on the walls. A screen was a jigsaw of scraps, and a high brass fender kept crawlers out of the hearth. Toys passed down from hand to hand were none the less loved because of signs of wear. Some were still there when the time came for Princess Elizabeth and Margaret Rose to play in that same room.

Lady Strathmore herself undertook the early education of Elizabeth and her 'darling bruvver' David. Nina Cecilia Cavendish-Bentinck, as she was before her marriage, was a cousin of the Duke of Portland, and a great granddaughter of the famous third Duke, who was twice Prime Minister, 1783 and 1807–1809. So St. Paul's had its strong link with mighty Welbeck Abbey in the Dukeries of Nottinghamshire, where reigned the immaculate Duchess, Mistress of the Robes to Queen Alexandra.

Lessons were simple, basic, artistic. Most of the stories of history and the Bible were known by the time they were seven. Emphasis was on dancing, drawing and music, all of which came easily to Elizabeth. Dancing was taken a step further when the children went to the Sun Hotel at Hitchin for private lessons.

Her mother made for her a long, red dress, copied from a Velasquez. It was hooped and touched the floor. In this, in the candlelight, Elizabeth would show off the steps that she had learned, lifting the hem to show her twinkling feet, her face lit with smiles below the gold cap that graced her jet black hair.

There were too many in the family for peace to remain perpetual at St. Paul's. On occasions brothers and sisters would differ over rights of possession or privilege, and battle commenced. Then a thousand years of feuding and skirmishing in the Lyon story showed itself in the raw in the peaceful Hertfordshire countryside. Teeth and nails, fists and feet went into action until the flame of anger blew out. Love, and the handicap of size, always left Elizabeth and David as allies in these dangerous moments. They planned together for mutual safety and mutual gain. Their schemes covered a wide field of opportunity, how to obtain particular titbits between meals, how to extract tips and presents from relations and visitors, and, probably most important of all, how to avoid lessons.

When wearied of the schoolroom and the task their mother had prepared for them, they had a most cunning means of escape. They would sneak down to the 'Flea House', a ruined building once used for brewing, the place where the hens laid. A ladder reached up to its grimy attic and up this the imps would clamber. This ladder was in the last stages of decay, and no sane adults would entrust their safety to its rungs—certainly not Nurse Knight. The children lay silent in their eyrie. At last the searchers and the pursuers grew weary. Their voices died away. The hunt was over. Then, in the shadows of the attic, the business of the day began. Here were hidden stores enough to withstand a siege. Apples and oranges, tins of sweets and bars of chocolate shared a box with, awful to confess, matches and Woodbines.

But 'the Benjamins', as the two youngest Bowes-Lyons were called, did not win every round against authority. The moment of retribution came. Elizabeth cried her heart out when a stick was taken to David, but she could have saved her tears. He was too lovable to allow of enduring anger, and throughout the proceeding never stopped laughing. The experience had little effect.

As the car began to oust the horse, chauffeurs, more accustomed to reins, had a horror and an ignorance of bangs and clatters emerging from the internal combustion engine. The children thought up a splendid idea. When the chauffeur brought the car round to the front door, unnoticed they jammed an inflated football bladder under one of the front wheels. The Earl and Countess emerged. They took their places on the back seat and the rug was wrapped round their knees. The chauffeur let in the clutch. The resultant bang echoed round the *allées* of Le Nôtre. The alarm engendered was a delight to see. From their hiding place the children rocked with glee.

Most children occasionally indulge in strange, unaccountable acts of destruction. May be it is an act of defiance against grown-ups, may be an attempt to see how far they can go and yet escape the corner or the slipper. Young Elizabeth had such a moment of aberration. She cut a pair of new sheets into strips with the nursery scissors. She owned up, and got away with the crime.

Animals were the great love in Elizabeth's life. The love has remained constant through all the years. Not for any particular type of animal or bird, but for practically everything that breathes.

No. 1 love was 'Bobs', the Shetland pony that was part of the landscape of St. Paul's. A fat little man, with a mane down over his eyes. He followed Elizabeth everywhere, round the garden, up the steps, even into the house if he could get there. A charming photograph was taken of Bobs and his owner. They posed on the wide lawns of St. Paul's. The backdrop was the square, clipped yew hedges, the 'Bounding Butler' on his stone plinth, and the avenue of tall trees that the children called 'the Cloisters'. She was side-saddle and wore a long habit, and a wide hat. The day might be anywhere in three centuries of time.

Dogs were everywhere, and 'the Benjamins' seldom played alone. There were her father's dogs, her brothers' dogs, her own dog. When the cameras came out the collie and the cocker had to be there too.

Bobby was a bullfinch. Throughout the baby years he strutted the nursery table, helping himself as desired from the contents of Elizabeth's plate. He was an institution. Then a cat got Bobby. The realization that the tiny, limp form would never move again brought tears welling to the blue eyes. David had a pencil box made of cedarwood. He sacrificed it for a coffin. A little cortège snuffled away to the wood. There, in a deep grave, Bobby was buried, as the future

Queen of England intoned, on and on, a funeral service of her own devising.

Goats, rabbits, tortoises, canaries, kittens, hens, all had their halcyon days of favouritism and special diet. But it was with the pigs that another chapter of tragedy came to be written. Lucifer and Emma were Berkshires and black. Daily Elizabeth and David made their pilgrimage to the sty to feed them apples and scratch their backs. One morning they arrived to find only one pig in the sty. Lucifer had gone. Urgent enquiries around the back door produced the information that he had been sent to a local charity bazaar as a prize for the raffle. Matters had gone too far for him to be returned.

Off ran Elizabeth and David to the place where the bazaar was being prepared. Here they learned how many tickets had been printed for the raffle. Back they hurried, deep in consultation, for they planned to corner the raffle. Mathematics, painfully executed, told them how much cash would be needed to ensure the safe return of Lucifer. There began a hectic shaking of money boxes, urgent demands on the staff for loans, and the searching of pockets and purses.

When the total sum available was counted, it was found that they had enough to buy half the tickets. It was even money on Lucifer being back in his sty that night. But the luck that, many years later, robbed the Queen Mother of winning the Grand National, worked against her that afternoon of the bazaar. The number that was at last called out as the winning ticket was not among the wad that she clasped in a perspiring hand.

In such a world of relative values 'the Benjamins' were self-sufficient and never bored. The confines of organized games did not appeal to them. They were happy in a world of make believe, in houses up the trees and on the fascinating line where the water of the pond met the bank. They had their own names for insects and birds, buildings and pools, statues and trees. It was their world and they walked alone with its secrets. And on wet days there was the endless fun of dressing up. In the trunk was a wide choice, relics of the eight elders or passed down through history. Some strange characters walked that nursery floor.

As soon as she could read, the world changed for Elizabeth. In those long dark evenings of winter, before the flick of a switch could turn on canned interest ready made, she would lie on the floor, her chin cupped in her hands. Faster and faster she read as the months passed. Scottish history and fable she liked best, and she learned it so well that Queen Mary was astonished at her deep knowledge when first they met.

An outstanding point in the character of this lovable but ordinary, healthy, happy Elizabeth was in her dealings with grown-ups. She was a hostess by the time she was three. She was completely unshy with visitors. She would gracefully meet callers at the door and lead them upstairs, conversing the while, when she was so small that she had to have two feet on a step before she could surmount the next.

Friends called and Lady Strathmore was unavoidably detained for a while. When she came down she found that her youngest daughter had already rung for tea and was doing the honours completely undisturbed.

To a house like St. Paul's there came many visitors, not all expected. It was the custom of the day. But there came moments when light conversation dragged, when pleasantries had been exchanged. Then Elizabeth was sent for, from the nursery or the garden. The crisis passed as she entered the room. She not only held the floor but she had the gift of making the impression that, when the moment for parting came, it had come too soon. Even when, in reality, it was a blessed relief.

It was this gift that led adults who met Elizabeth as a child, and later cast back their minds to remember the moments, to lean towards panegyrics. They, of course, knew the girl who stood smiling by the teapot in the drawing room, and not the one who kept Wood bines in the attic in the 'Flea House'. Thus Lord Gorrell, author and editor:

'To every lover of children she had about her that indefinable charm that bears elders into fairyland. In the simplest and most unconscious way she was all-conquering. In addition to the charm of especially winsome childhood, she had, even then, that blend of kindliness and dignity that is the peculiar characteristic of her family. She was small for her age, responsive as a harp, wistful and appealing one moment, bright-eyed and eager the next, with a flashing smile of appreciative delight, an elfin creature swift of movement . . . quick of intelligence, alive with humour, able to join in any of the jokes, and touchingly and sometimes amusingly loyal to her friends.'

On the other side of the baize door 'the two Benjamins' were equally loved, but in this description of them by Mrs. Thompson, housekeeper to the Strathmores for thirty years, written after Lady Elizabeth had become Duchess of York, may be seen, between the lines, the fruition and effect of certain plans hatched in the 'Flea House' attic.

'They were the dearest little couple I have ever seen, and the Duchess always took the lead. She would come tripping down the stairs and it would be: "Mrs. Thompson, have you any of those nice creams left for us?" and she would herself open the cupboard and help herself to what she liked best.

'I remember the Duchess inviting me to play cricket with them. She had great fun at me as I could not send the ball anywhere near the wicket. . . . I can see her now coming outside the window of the housekeeper's room with her pony Bobs, and making him beg for sugar, and often she would come up by herself and pop her head up suddenly and make us all jump, at which she would have a good laugh. She had a very happy childhood, and always good health to enjoy it.'

Treats for Elizabeth meant trips to London. There her father had an Adam house in St. James's Place. Being handy to the Park Nurse Knight could take 'the two Benjamins' there and let them race to tiredness on the grass and under the trees much as they did at home. Each year there was a visit to London after Christmas and then came the most important of all occasions, the visit to the pantomime at Drury Lane. There were parties, too, and fancy dress dances. Costumes out of history suited Elizabeth best. Little boys tumbled for her and forgot the ice cream and the fruit salad. It was at a party given by Lady Leicester that she was introduced to a boy called Bertie. Prince Albert of Wales was just ten. He did not see her again until 1918, but he never forgot her.

Advantage was taken of the visits to London to add some professional polish to Elizabeth's accomplishments. She attended

Madame D'Egville's dancing classes (report: 'graceful and intelligent') and began her musical instruction with Madame Matilde Verne, an association that was to last until her marriage. Round to the Pianoforte School, hand in hand, went Elizabeth and David, so small that they had to be lifted on to the stools. Yet within six months Elizabeth was taking the star role in a pupils' concert.

London was also the start point for the greatest adventures in the lives of 'the two Benjamins', visits to their maternal grandmother, Mrs. Scott, who lived in Florence.

Lady Strathmore's mother was Caroline Louisa Burnaby before her marriage to the Rev. Charles Cavendish-Bentinck in 1859. She was his second wife. He died in 1865 and five years later his widow married Harry Warren Scott, third son of Sir William Scott of Ancrum. Widowed again in 1889, Mrs. Scott made her home at the Villa Capponi looking out over Florence.

The children were fortunate indeed to have had the chance to travel abroad so young, for war was to blank out their teenage years. Memories of the cross-Channel trip, the long train winding through the night, the cypress trees, the Florentine picture, the blue sky and the sun were to stay as clear in their minds as the pictures in a story book.

Queen Elizabeth II has said that the sun always seemed to have been shining when she was a child. It shone for her mother too.

3 Benjamin on the Battlements

WITH the earldom that Lady Elizabeth's father inherited in 1904 came two castles, Glamis, in Angus, Scotland, and Streatlam in County Durham. So, taking into account their London house, the Bowes-Lyon children were in much the same position as the Royal Family. And they moved from one residence to another with much the same regularity.

To 'the two Benjamins' each house had its own special place in the scheme of their life. London stood for treats. Streatlam was associated with visits. Glamis meant holidays. St. Paul's was home.

This width of home life was a strong factor in the making of the character of the young Elizabeth. She would have been perfectly happy to spend all of her time at St. Paul's, searching for eggs, burying birds, dressing up and scrounging for cream buns. But her parents were infiltrating into her a far broader vista. London was giving her grace, fashions and the arts, Glamis tradition, Florence beauty and culture, St. Paul's a love of the country ways, and Streatlam[1] a sharply contrasting view of another side of life. And all the time she was meeting people of very different types.

The Queen Mother is widely looked upon as being just Scottish, although her mother was English, she has French blood and was born in England, a point that she has often made. Yet there is no doubt that the age-old power and tradition of Glamis has become predominant in her.

Glamis Castle is twelve miles north of Dundee and four miles south of Kirriemuir. It is open to the public on certain days between May and September, and teas are served. It is cheaper if one only

---

[1] Streatlam Castle was later sold.

wishes to see the grounds, all of which would have come as a great surprise to 'Capability' Brown who laid them out. The old order has indeed changed mightily.

Glamis is one of the oldest inhabited dwellings in the United Kingdom. It stands where the Sidlaw hills slide into the Strathmore valley, the Grampian wall to the north. Poet Gray described it as 'rising proudly out of what seems a great thick wood of tall trees, with a cluster of hanging towers on the top'.

Said to be the scene of the murder of Duncan in 'Macbeth', fourteenth-century chronicler John of Fordun went further. He asserted that here Malcolm II, the grandfather of Duncan, was done to death.

One family has owned Glamis since the fourteenth century, when Sir John Lyon moved in after his marriage with Jean, daughter of Robert II of Scotland. Their grandson, Patrick Lyon, was sent to England as a hostage for the ransom of James I in 1424. He was released three years later. In 1445 he was created Lord Glamis, a peer of Parliament.

So Elizabeth stepped into over five hundred years of family history as, tired and excited, she left the London train and drove up to her Scottish abode. Let us then see Glamis as she saw it then, not that the passing of sixty odd years has made much difference to such a memorial, the pointed turrets of which recall the days when the *Garde Ecossaise* garrisoned many of the castles of the Loire.

She looks up at the central staircase tower, crowned by a great clock. On the drive to the right stands an old cannon. The doorway is small, for it is part of the ancient building and a restricted entrance had its advantages in defence. And then, above her head, appears the inscription proclaiming that the castle was built by Patrick, Lord Glamis and Dame Anna Murray, his wife. Their monograms are on the wall, with the date 1606.

It was Patrick, first Earl of Kinghorne, who changed much of Glamis and his grandson carried on the work between 1670 and 1689. It was in this century that the south-east wing was built, old work coming down to make room for it.

Elizabeth climbs up the circular staircase of stone, slowly, a step at a time, as slowly as the men who carried the still body of Malcolm II that way after the battle of Hunter's Hill in 1034—a legend long believed but now in doubt. She looks up at the board where the bells hang, the tell-tale name beneath each—Duncan's Room, Old Armoury, Hangman's Room, Prince Charlie's Room, King Malcolm's Room.

She peeps into Scott's Room. Here twenty-year-old Sir Walter spent the night in some trepidation. The bed is still covered with the Scott tartan, for visitors to Glamis always slept beneath their own plaid.

Others slept uneasy there. The Hangman's Room is so named as the last person to occupy it hung himself. Prince Charles Edward also had a disturbed night. When the English came after him he fled leaving his spare clothes behind and his watch ticking under the pillow.

Elizabeth walked in an atmosphere steeped in the love of the Stuarts. Here the old Pretender was entertained by the sixth Earl, and beds were made up for all the retinue of eighty. In a picture of Jesus Christ there is a distinct look of Charles I, a work of art which upset Cromwell considerably.

There were so many places that a little girl and a smaller brother could explore—the great banqueting hall, with its windows recessed in walls eight feet thick and its vaulted ceiling, a masterpiece in plasterwork executed in 1620, and the Chapel with a priest's hole behind the wainscoting, and secret staircases, and a dark well communicating with the crypt far below.

Beyond the walls there was a wide and wonderful world for 'the two Benjamins' to play in, lovely gardens, broad terraces, tall trees, leading back to the heathered hills. Here was the famous sun dial, upon which two lions of the house sit proudly with dials in their paws. There were no less than eighty-one dial faces to count.

It was only natural that the history of the place, the legend that was all about, had an effect upon the children, particularly their games. A favourite one, very unpopular at the receiving end, was 'repelling raiders'. This entailed climbing to the roof with a supply of 'boiling oil', in this case plain cold water, and pouring it over visitors unfortunate enough to pick this time for standing by the main door.

Another game was connected with ghosts. Now no home in the British Isles is more associated with spectral appearances than Glamis. It is no new belief. After Sir Walter Scott had stayed there he wrote: 'I was conducted to my apartment in a distant part of the building. I must own that when I heard door after door shut, after my conductor had retired, I began to consider myself too far from the living and somewhat too near to the dead. . . .'

When 'the two Benjamins' were young the interest in ghosts was mostly confined to visitors. But on the announcement of the engagement of Lady Elizabeth Bowes-Lyon to the Duke of York, when every fragment of information about the royal bride became news, the belief that there was a grim secret behind the walls of Glamis became of paramount interest. It was said that the Strathmores did not mind how many ghosts were supposed to walk their home, for the more there were said to be, the easier it was to hide the real secret.

There are certainly tales of the usual run of ghosts. Unseen hands continually open and close the door of a certain room. Earl Beardie, a medieval knight, walks the passages, probably for the benefit of children. Then there is the Grey Lady. She is a beautiful and smiling apparition. Nobody minds seeing her as she only appears when good luck is on the way.

There are many Bowes-Lyon ancestors who qualify to drift round the rooms they knew so well, during the still night hours. Strange and violent deaths have come to many of them. One was killed in a duel. One was burned at the stake as a witch. Two were tortured on the rack. Two fell in fights with neighbouring families. One fell at the battle of Sherriffmuir. One was murdered in India by the Nabob of Bengal. And the tenth Earl died suddenly and inexplicably only a few hours after he was married.

The secret of the real ghost is closely guarded. When the eldest son reaches the age of twenty-one, it is believed that he is let into the secret. Then only he, his father and the estate factor know what the true story is.

There is the story of the room lost for ever centuries ago.

The dice were rolling one Saturday night. Lord Glamis and a neighbouring nobleman were deep in a duel of chance. Piles of gold and silver crossed the table, and came back again. Broad acres were lost and won.

An old retainer knocked at the door and entered. He reminded Lord Glamis of the lateness of the hour and that the morrow was the Sabbath. But the dice still rolled.

At five minutes to midnight the servant came in again. He touched his master's shoulder and pointed to the time. 'I care not what day of the week it be,' roared Lord Glamis. 'If we have a mind to, we shall play on until Doomsday!'

Twelve began to chime on the Castle clock. Scotland slept. Yet still the dice were thrown. As the last note echoed out among the towers, the door opened silently and a cold breeze blew into the room. The players swung round in surprise. Standing in the doorway was the tall, slim figure of a man dressed all in black. As he stood staring down at them, the colour drained from their cheeks. Then the stranger spoke.

'I will take your Lordship at your word,' he intoned. 'Doomsday has come for you.'

The apparition faded. The door closed. Lord Glamis jumped up to chase the intruder but stopped, frozen with terror. The walls were closing in. The room was growing ever smaller. Recovering themselves the noblemen raced for the door, but already it was too small for them to pass through. They turned to the window, but it had shrunk to the size of a peephole. Their wild screams were muffled. When the old retainer returned, he could not even find the room.

That is one version of the ghostly secret of Glamis, the house in which Princess Margaret was born on a wild night of thunder and lightning.

There is another candidate, a spectre that one might well expect to meet in the early hours. She is Janet, widow of the sixth Lord Glamis and one of the most wronged women in history.

Janet was one of the hated Douglas Clan, a granddaughter of the notorious Earl of Angus who was known as 'Bell the Cat'. James V of Scotland detested and feared her. Several times he tried to have her arrested on false charges, and each time he failed. Then a distant relative told the King that she was plotting against his life with poison and witchcraft. She was seized and taken to Edinburgh. With

31

her went five so-called accomplices. They were Archibald Campbell, her second husband; John Lyon, a kinsman; her sixteen-year-old son, Lord Glamis; an old priest; and Alexander Makke, who was said to have made up the poisons.

They went to the rack. None spoke, except one. He was the young Lord Glamis. At the sight and sound of all that dreadful agony, he broke down. He cried out that his mother was guilty.

On 17th July 1537 Janet Douglas, Lady Glamis, was led out on to Castle Hill. She was tied to the stake. Beautiful and silent to the end, the flames devoured her. Innocent, she suffered the fate of a traitor.

And the others? Her husband was imprisoned in Edinburgh Castle awaiting his execution. A rope was smuggled in to him. During the night he managed to squeeze through the bars of his cell. He tied the rope fast and lowered himself into the abyss below. He reached the rope's end, but still his feet touched nothing. There he hung until his hands could grip no longer. He fell, and was smashed on the rocks below.

John Lyon and the old priest were hanged. Alexander Makke had his ears cut off. Young Lord Glamis was kept in prison and his estates declared forfeit. Then, conscience-stricken, the accuser confessed that he had made up the story to get his revenge on Lady Glamis. But the King only laughed.

A third theory was put out by the late Mr. G. W. E. Russell. He was of the opinion that there was once a feeble-minded heir born in the family. He was kept locked in a secret room so that none should know that the son who took the title was not the rightful owner. The prisoner lived on for nearly a hundred years, and strange stories were put about so that the real truth should not be discovered.

This ties in with the local story of the slater. He was making repairs to the castle roof. Suddenly he raced down the ladder and, with ashen face, began to tell his workmates of a terrible sight that he had chanced upon. At that moment the estate factor rushed on to the scene and hurried the man away. It is said that the slater was sworn never to repeat what he had seen, was given a pension and sent to Australia.

The ghosts and the grim secrets did not frighten Elizabeth at all. In fact she and her 'darling bruvver' exploited them for their own

The dancing lesson

The Countess of Strathmore and Lady Elizabeth with convalescent soldiers at Glamis

Elizabeth at the age of twenty-one

amusement. Before guests arrived there was urgent activity with the dressing-up box and the red ink. On their arrival they were given the softening up treatment, being warned to watch out for Earl Beardie and his friends. It took quite a lot of courage to walk past a still, knifed form in a dimly lit corner and to stare unmoved at a spectral apparition in the bed.

But there was little ghostly about the rooms in which the family lived. This was a wing built in the last century, light and airy, looking out over the Dutch garden.

A great attraction about the summer stays at Glamis was that all the family was together, the boys being on holiday from school and university. With enough brothers to make half a team, and relations and guests to complete it, cricket occupied many of Elizabeth's days. She and David were persistently pointing out that it was their turn to bat. There was tennis too, a game at which she was later to become most proficient. There was a family pride to be upheld on the court, for her 'Uncle Pat'[1] had been the Wimbledon doubles champion in 1887 with H. W. W. Wilberforce. In three years at Cambridge he had won eight out of his nine singles matches against Oxford.

There were long, tiring days when 'the Benjamins' struggled after the guns and the grouse, picnic days with wild flowers to be picked, stonecrop and speedwell, herb-bennet and bugle, marjoram and myrrh.

There was also a substitute for Bobs, the Shetland. This was an aged donkey with ideas of its own. With Elizabeth on board it trotted on, taking its own course, faster than the attendant retinue liked. And if it saw water it went straight for it, to Elizabeth's delight.

The people of Glamis remember clearly the childhood days of the Queen Mother. As a woman journalist wrote a few years ago: 'They don't make much of a song and dance about anything in this quiet Scottish village. But mention "the Lady Elizabeth" and they will almost burst into verse as they tell you stories about her girlhood.'

They may remember being tied up to the railings with string, waiting to be scalped by a minute Red Indian chief and his squaw,

[1] The Hon. Patrick Bowes-Lyon, 1863–1947.

or recall two fearsome figures decorated with feathers of blackcock and grouse and howling war cries, raiding dairy or kitchen and demanding milk or biscuits. Many of the schemes of 'the Benjamins' had their fruition in the satisfying of the inner self.

It is mainly to her childhood days at Glamis that the Queen Mother owes one of her greatest gifts—that of the common touch. The gift has seldom been better demonstrated, and never left her. Deep south of the Border the relationship between laird and his servants and tenants has been misunderstood and misjudged since the days of the Stuarts and beyond. The Marquis of Huntly summed it up in 'Auld Acquaintance' when dealing with the misunderstanding about the relationship of Queen Victoria and her ghillie, John Brown. 'Most families in Scotland are fortunate in having around them dependants whose forbears have been for long periods connected with them by service, and who are proud of the almost hereditary association. The "retainer class", as it may be called, is probably diminishing in numbers, but it is not extinct, and for length of service the Scottish retainer takes the premier place in the world.'

Elizabeth learned early that each person and each job was as relatively important as any other person or any other job, a theory exemplified by a head gardener who remarked, after the laird had asked for the hot-house key on three days running, that he supposed that his master would be asking for his own key shortly!

Thus we see the young Elizabeth greeting the estate factor: 'How do you do, Mr. Ralston? I haven't seen you look so well, not for years and years, but I am sure you will be sorry to know that Lord Strathmore has got the toothache.'

There were touches of the old splendour for the child to see, moments of tradition that were to last for ever. Such as the two pipers marching round the great table as dinner ended, and the silence when they had gone. And the excitement of the Forfar ball.

It was at the time of this ball in 1905 that Lady Cynthia Colville, for thirty years Woman of the Bedchamber to Queen Mary, first met Elizabeth. She was fascinated by her, and never forgot her. She was more fascinated still a few years later when she discovered that the dark-haired girl had a fan mail from several young boy friends and kept up quite a correspondence.

To fan the interest, marriage was in the air. Elizabeth was only eight when she was first a bridesmaid, and the news of the part that she was to play was announced to everyone she met. The wedding of her eldest brother, Lord Glamis, and Lady Dorothy Osborne, daughter of the Duke of Leeds, took place at the Guards' Chapel, Wellington Barracks. She had a frock of white muslin and lace and carried a bouquet of pink roses. 'Darling bruvver', in blue silk, was a trainbearer.

They repeated the performance two years later when her eldest sister, Mary, married Lord Elphinstone. This time she was a Romney maiden.

Two great interests were instilled in the Lady Elizabeth at Glamis —gardening and Scottish history. When the Castle became their home Lady Strathmore set about making a new garden, and it held everyone's attention until it was completed in 1910. It was a formal garden that she designed, enclosed by a clipped yew hedge. A fountain was its central point, blue tiles reflecting the blue of the sky. Around was an herbaceous border, its flowers so chosen that there was colour throughout the seasons. Semi-circular stone steps led to a terrace, and stone vases stood sentinel on a low wall. Lady Strathmore planned bays in the yew hedge, each bay to contain a statue of her children. When it was all done a plaque was put up bearing the names of all the craftsmen who had helped in its creation. So, throughout Elizabeth's childhood, there was always the growth of the garden to watch, and flowers to learn about. It was to stand her in good stead when she married a man whose horticultural knowledge was, to say the least of it, sketchy.

For historical knowledge she only had to pay a visit to Mr. Stirton, the minister at Glamis, and later of Crathie and Chaplain to the King when at Balmoral.

The Minister had many historical treasures that his little caller could handle and enquire about, but always her eyes would return to a picture on the wall. It was of a handsome young man. He was the dream man of the moment. He was Prince Charles Edward.

But there was one historical relic that she was not allowed to see. She begged in vain. She wanted to go down and see the vault where her ancestors were buried.

4 Growing Up With War

WHEN Elizabeth and David were old enough to be classified as 'schoolroom' rather than 'nursery', governesses began to arrive and lighten, or otherwise, the burden of Lady Strathmore. At first they were French, and the language of France was the order of the day. It came easily to Elizabeth and by the time she was ten she was fluent. The success of the ladies varied. Their elder pupil summed up the situation, tersely and completely, in an essay under the seemingly irrelevant title of 'The Sea'. She wrote: 'Some governesses are nice and some are not.'

At nine the experiment of school was tried upon her. She attended a day establishment in London. The experiment lasted but two terms. Maybe the call of the 'Flea House' and the *allées* of St. Paul's was too strong to admit of city regimentation. But she did have the satisfaction of taking away with her at least one prize. And she did carry on with her dancing and music lessons in London.

Then came a moment of sadness, the end of a chapter of sunshine, the first taste of loneliness. David came of an age when he must go away to school. She missed him very, very much. Another change came with the nationality of the governess. A Fräulein came from Germany, heavier in body and mind than the Madamoiselles who had preceded her. Some differences of opinion seem to have arisen between her and David during the school holidays. She returned to the Fatherland, to the relief of those who could already hear the rumble of war. She was replaced by a home product whose strong line was tennis, very useful to a girl who was to marry a Wimbledon player. Elizabeth passed her Junior Oxford, and was educationally advanced for her age.

She also grew in social stature. She was an aunt before she was ten. By the time she was fourteen she had two nieces and two nephews. Strangely enough she was nearer in age to them than she was to the top layer of her own brothers and sisters. Her first touch of real tragedy came when she lost one of them. Her brother Alexander died unmarried in 1911.

It was in the early days of the reign of King George V that Elizabeth experienced a freedom with anonymity that was to prove unique in her life. At the end of each term David returned home more of a man, more self-assured. Brother and sister were allowed to go out together in London, to sample the thrill of the theatre. The choice was restricted, but yet here was adult licence, queuing for the cheap seats and shuffling forward grasping limited silver.

When David came back from school at the end of the summer term of 1914 the grown-ups were talking of nothing but Bank Rate and Winston Churchill and the Fleet. Elizabeth was concerned with the theatre treat that she had been promised for 4th August, her fourteenth birthday. On that day came the announcement: '. . . his Majesty's Government have accordingly notified the German Government that a state of war exists between the two countries as from 11 p.m. to-day.'

She sat in the box of the great theatre, her family around her, the star of her evening, watching in the intervals and at the end, a scene of wild excitement, of intense patriotism, of frightening anticipation. It was an experience that seared right into the heart of the girl. She was never to forget. And later, as the light went out in her bedroom, Great Britain moved into war.

She awoke to a new world. Her four elder brothers were preparing to join the army. Three served in the Black Watch and one in the Royal Scots. In the few days before they left home there was so much to do. There was sewing and shopping, and the endless guess as to what would be needed and what not. The eldest of those young men was thirty and the youngest twenty-one. And their father, who was in his sixtieth year, put on uniform as well. As Lady Rose Bowes-Lyon, the only other sister at home, was training to be a nurse at a London hospital, much of the burden of the behind-the-scenes activities fell upon Elizabeth. Schoolroom routine was washed away. She became a woman overnight.

One by one they went away and there was a great emptiness in the house. But there was hardly time to notice it, for within a week of the declaration of war Elizabeth was off, in a packed train, for Scotland and Glamis. There preparations had already begun for turning the Castle into a convalescent hospital for the wounded.

It was all a great contrast with the August that had gone before. There were no clicks from the cricket bat, no friends to stay, no shooting parties. Already some of the men of the estate had left to join the local battalion and the women and the children were busy preparing for their comfort during the autumn and the winter ahead. Tables were piled high with wool and sheepskins, scarves and socks and gloves, and the future Queen of England sat on the floor crumpling up tissue paper and stuffing it into sleeping bags.

Yet for her there was no lack of family excitement and celebration, for in September two of her brothers married. On the 17th came the military wedding of Fergus to Lady Christian Dawson-Damer, daughter of the Earl of Portarlington, and on the 29th John was married to the Hon. Fenella Hepburn-Stuart-Forbes-Trefusis, Lord Clinton's daughter.

David went back to school. Elizabeth sat lonely by her high window in Glamis, trying to pick up the thread of lessons that had been so abruptly interrupted. In November the 5th Black Watch landed in France and very shortly there were to be many other duties to distract her.

In December the first car loads of wounded came over the Sidlaw hills from Dundee. The men had smashed shoulders, broken limbs, head wounds—the cure was time and peace. Some had been shattered by the tidal wave of war, and the quickly changing scenes of life. They had misgivings about convalescing in a Castle and being cared for by the Nobility. That was before the word got around that the best fate of the Great War was to stop a 'blighty' one and end up at Glamis.

Lady Strathmore always met arrivals at the door and introduced herself. Thereafter the men were guests of the family. This was particularly so when Lady Rose, her nursing training completed, arrived to take charge. There were sixteen beds neatly lined up round the walls of the big dining room. The crypt became the men's dining hall. Suitable as it was for the purpose, there were some among the convalescents who found the antlers, the cold armour, the fiercesome axes, rather a contrast with the kitchen at home. They also had the run of the library and the billiard room, the table there proving a blessing beyond compare.

And so Christmas came, the first that Elizabeth had ever spent at Glamis. It was unforgettable. A great tree stood in the crypt. There were presents on it for everybody, wounded, staff, servants, family. To the men far from home those presents became treasured things. In time they found their way back to their own families and stayed as mementoes through the years. There were whist drives and competitions and prizes. And the sing-song at the end was as unlicenced as if they had been in barracks or their particular public-house.

At first new arrivals were puzzled how to treat the fourteen-year-old girl with blue eyes, a title and a fringe over her forehead. She soon put them wise, as she called them by their Christian names, chided them, comforted, teased. They saw in her a look of their daughters, or a girl friend far away. Two of them, attempting to carry a tray of dishes before they were strong enough to do so, dropped the lot. Their eyes turned fearfully, guilty from the fragments on the floor towards the Lady Elizabeth. She was leaning against a pillar, rocking with laughter.

She pulled their legs unmercifully. David came back from school. She dressed him up as a lady of great importance. The clothes were easy to find and he was padded in the right places. Make-up was applied and a large hat went over his golden hair. So attired Elizabeth led him into the ward, serious, subservient. She took the important visitor from bed to bed. The visitor asked all the right things, the men made all the usual replies. Their remarks when they later learned who had carried out the inspection were not so polite.

Elizabeth would frighten them out of their wits by racing round the garden on her bicycle with her eyes shut. This feat of daring usually ended with her upside down in a flower bed. It seemed to amuse her immensely.

She would come down to the ward when her lessons were over and

39

spend the evening with the men. She learned to play whist, her face wrinkled up with concentration. A series of quick wins cast doubt on the authenticity of the rules that she was following. And then she would write the letters home for the men with injured hands and arms, tactfully helping with the halting, dictated words.

She would sit at the piano and play for them the tunes that they had sung in France. Sometimes she would be persuaded to sing herself, songs of the olden days that she had been taught in London and at St. Paul's. The freshness of 'I have a song to sing O', had a magic all its own in the great room amid the beds and bandages. It was a long, long way from Ypres.

There were no 'troubles' among the men at Glamis. They disciplined themselves. If they tried to run before they could walk, Elizabeth would stand before them, stamp her foot and tell them not to be silly. The only occasions when signs of antagonism appeared was when a soldier appeared to be getting more than his fair share of Lady Elizabeth's time. She had to be most careful what table she sat down at to play whist.

Lady Strathmore took it upon herself to see that her patients were supplied with tobacco and cigarettes. Elizabeth did the shopping in the village. If she saw a man with an empty pipe in his mouth, she would ask: 'Why are you not smoking? Have you no tobacco? Why didn't you tell me?'

Yet the Earl was far from a rich man, in the superlative sense. There were few luxuries for Elizabeth. A young officer's wife who met her at tennis parties during the war years was struck by her simple charm and a complete lack of outward show of wealth. Her racket looked as if at some time it had been used for fishing and her shoes as if they had been passed down from an elder sister.

The dark months of the first winter of war dragged on. For the men fit enough there were visits to the movies and pantomime in Forfar and Dundee and walks down the long avenue to the village. Castle life was enlightened by rat hunts in the crypt or fires in the chimneys, unaccustomed to the furnaces that the men piled up. The 'postie' became an important person, and each morning Elizabeth was at the door to meet him. The distribution of the mail became the most eventful moment of the day to both family and patients.

Summer came. Once more there was cricket on the lawns, picnics in the hills. In July Elizabeth became an aunt again when a daughter was born to the wife of her brother Fergus. And in the middle of September Captain Fergus Bowes-Lyon, of the 8th Battalion, the Black Watch, was able to snatch a short leave at Glamis. He said his good-byes at the Castle on the evening of Monday, 20th September. On the 25th the battle of Loos began. Two days later Captain Bowes-Lyon was killed at the Hohenzollern Redoubt. The men in the ward sent a letter of condolence to Lady Strathmore, and the crypt and the dormitory were silent. But she would not allow her sorrow to interfere with the work of recuperation, and the gramophone began again. But now war had a different meaning to Elizabeth and the post and telegram a greater significance. And there was the sadness of the partings.

There was always a lump in the throat when one batch of convalescents left and the cars that took them away brought another batch in over the hills. There was the last night party, the speeches, the photographs, the presents for each man. And next day, before they left, the ceremony of writing their names in the visitors' book. And into the hand of Lady Elizabeth they pressed souvenirs that they had treasured, so that she would remember them. She always did. Troops came to Glamis from overseas, mainly New Zealand and Australia. On her overseas tours, as Duchess, Queen and Queen Mother, people have speculated when she moved over to a man in the crowd, shook his hand and began laughing and talking with him. What was she saying to him? Probably something like, 'Do you remember that rat in the crypt, Charlie?' The 'old boys' of Glamis are widely spread and have evergreen memories.

Lady Elizabeth did not confine her attention solely to the men in the neat beds in the dining room. She also took an active part in the local life. She was keen on the Guide movement and on one occasion her girls were inspected by Princess Mary. A friendship grew between the two that was to have far-reaching results.

She was a girl of village, not the daughter of the Castle. When the time came for her to be confirmed, she could, by right, have had the Bishop of Brechin come to Glamis and carry out the ceremony in the private chapel. But she would have none of it, and took her place in anonymity among the lassies in the classes at St. John's Church, Forfar.

In May 1916 Lady Elizabeth moved up a step in Castle importance. In that month her sister, Lady Rose, married the Hon. William Leveson-Gower, R.N., at St. James's Piccadilly. Elizabeth was a bridesmaid, in pink with a Dutch bonnet. When she returned it was as the other right hand of her mother.

She was soon to get a chance to show the authority of her adult role. It was December, and David had come home from Eton. The convalescent men had been sent to the cinema in Forfar, and Glamis was silent. Elizabeth, from the garden, saw smoke coming from the top of the central Keep, ninety feet high. She raced for the telephone.

The wind caught the flames and there were several outbreaks on the roof by the time the local fire brigade arrived. But hopes that these men would be able to cope were soon destroyed. The only available water supply was the river Dean, which flowed by several hundred yards away. This distance, plus the height, was far beyond the reach of the parochial hoses. There was an agonizing wait until the men of Forfar arrived. They found themselves in a similar predicament.

It was then that Lady Elizabeth announced: 'The Dundee fire brigade will be here soon, for I telephoned them when I called the local brigade.' It was fortunate indeed that she had done so, or Glamis might well have gone.

A crowd had gathered on the lawns. Above them, in the darkening sky, the pinnacles of the towers were half-hid in the swirling smoke and flames that raced across the roof like wild clouds in a blood-red sunset. The outline of the Castle was shown in strange relief. Here was a thousand years of history going up in a holocaust. And then the tank went.

The lead storage tank under the roof collapsed under the intensity of the heat. The spiral staircase became a waterfall. It threatened the drawing room and all the treasures that lay therein. Elizabeth raced for the stairs, David and volunteer helpers behind her. Armed with brushes and whatever implements they could lay hands on they swept away at the water, turning the stream from the drawing room and on down the stairs to the stone vaults below where little damage could be done. When the flow ceased Elizabeth called for further helpers and along a line of thirty of them the treasures of the Castle were passed to a place of safety.

Then the Dundee brigade arrived after its journey over the hills. Soon the water of the Dean was harnessed. Ice cold, it turned to clouds of steam as the rainbow of it touched the roofs. One by one the flames went out. Darkness fell before the firemen ceased their task. And more than ten years were to pass before the damage done that December evening was put to rights.

Lady Elizabeth had won her spurs. Everywhere it was being said that it was her quick reaction, her calmness, her determination and courage that were, in the main, responsible for the saving of Glamis.

Those years of 1916–1918 were particularly testing for Lady Elizabeth, for she bore a heavy burden for one of her years. Lady Strathmore, who described herself as looking more like a grandmother than a mother to her youngest daughter, was feeling the strain. She had lost one son, and another had been wounded. The threat of another telegram haunted her. It came in the early weeks of 1917, before Glamis had recovered from the shock of the fire. Michael was dead.

'Reported dead.' There was no body to confirm the news. No one had seen him die. It was assumed that he was dead. David was brought home to bring a ray of light into the darkness of his mother and his sister. But David would wear no mourning. When asked why not by the minister of Glamis, he said that his brother was still alive. He had seen him in a dream, lying in a house surrounded by trees and a white cloth round his head.

In the spring of that year the sun suddenly shone brilliantly on the Castle of Glamis. Captain Michael Bowes-Lyon was reported as being in a prison hospital in Germany, suffering from a severe head wound. It was still serious news, but so much better than the other.

It was now realized that Elizabeth, at seventeen, should see more of life than the somewhat narrow confines of Glamis. She began to make trips to London and stay with her married sister. She took up music lessons again and attended concerts and lectures.

But there was still a testing time ahead. In the summer of 1918 Lady Strathmore became seriously ill and the task of looking after her and at the same time attending to the many points arising from the convalescent hospital fell squarely on eighteen-year-old Elizabeth. Someone who saw her at the time noted the tiredness on her face and the lack of the usual sparkle.

The Armistice, and the relief of it, did not mean the end of the war for her. Perhaps it was marked more clearly on that February afternoon when she hurried to the station to meet the brother returning from the prison camp. Perhaps the end came for her as the last convalescent soldiers signed the visitors' book at Glamis and went their ways, just five years after the first wounded had come over the hills from Dundee.

For all her formative years Lady Elizabeth had been hand in hand with war. She had seen close tragedy and suffering. She had learned of tact and authority, restraint and kindness, courage and hard work. It was an apprenticeship that was to stand her in good stead twenty years on from there.

5 Enter a Prince

LADY Elizabeth Bowes-Lyon did not plunge into the wildly-eddying waters of London's social life in the post-war years. Rather she paddled in, testing the temperature, letting the ripples come slowly up. From the plethora of anecdotes on her past that appeared when she made the great headlines in 1923 it would appear that she took Mayfair by storm. Although she was a very good dancer, the rest simply was not true.

For her there had been no sudden break with girlhood as comes with the end of years in a boarding school. The communal way of life had not disturbed her privacy in the growing time. The regimentation of the form room and the crocodile were unknown. For her not the sudden change from the gym slip to the long frock, and the rush down the stairs to whirl into the medley of the music and the gay adventure. She was already grown up. If outward sign was needed, the plait had gone and her hair was tied in a knot behind her head.

Men she knew in an adult way. She had met so many hundreds, of all ranks, and seen them in their weaker moments. But always to them she had been a very special person—the chatelaine minor of Glamis. And there was still work for her to do in Scotland. Even when the wounded had left there was the task of helping those whose experiences had left them unsuited for civilian life, of finding jobs for those who were discovering that the paradise of peace was not all that they had expected. In addition there were the demands of the Forfarshire Girl Guides. She was District Commissioner of Glamis and Eassie Parish and she put all her enthusiasm and energy into the job.

She came to London, and to St. Paul's again. She visited David at Eton. She went to dances, chaperoned by her mother or a sister. She visited country houses. She was at Ascot, in white lace, to be inculcated with a thrill beyond the dresses, the top hats and the strawberries. And she was a bridesmaid again, this time at the wedding of her friend, Lady Lavinia Spencer, to Lord Annaly. It was a friendship for a lifetime, for right up to the time of Lady Annaly's sad death the Queen Mother was climbing the high stairs to her Knightsbridge flat to talk long hours with her. Friendship with the Queen Mother has always meant a true, unbreakable bond.

In 1920 the Earl of Strathmore parted with his London home in St. James's Place and bought 17, Bruton Street, which leads out of Berkeley Square. It was an address that was to ring round the world when Princess Elizabeth was born there. But before the family could move in there was much alteration and redecoration to do, and Lady Elizabeth was kept very busy.

On her London visits she was seeing more and more of Princess Mary, being invited to the Palace to chat, mostly on Guide affairs. She also met another member of the Royal Family. At a dance given by Lord Farquhar she was re-introduced to the King's second son, Prince 'Bertie'. He had just been created Duke of York. It was fifteen years since she had given him the crystallized cherries from her slice of Christmas cake at the children's party at Montague House. The event was duly recalled.

The Duke was twenty-four. He had shaken royal circles by arriving on 14th December 1895. The 14th of December was the death date of Prince Albert the Consort. Queen Victoria reserved it entirely for his memory. As on the same day of the same month her eldest son had been snatched from the jaws of death in 1871 and her daughter Alice had died in 1878, she had, and with good reason, come to look forward to the 14th with foreboding. In passing on the news, with some trepidation, the boy's father expressed regret that the birth should have taken place on such a sad day. But the Queen took a surprisingly optimistic view. She wrote: 'I have a feeling it may be a blessing for the dear little boy, and may be looked upon as a gift from God!'

At twenty-four the Duke was apt to be shy and reserved. He had an impediment in his speech and he was subject to moods of gloom. He was keen on history, civic problems and the betterment of the lot of poor boys. He was good at games, particularly tennis, a trier at everything and basically as nice and sound a character as any to appear in the history of the Royal Family.

He suffered from being brought up in the shadow of the 'great ones', who in their omnipotence granted little boys an intelligence quotient no higher than puppy dogs. Queen Victoria ran it close with God. Then there was the vaunting Kaiser, the Empress Frederick with her guttural 'r's and Grandpapa, reigning un-challenged in the 'Big House' at Sandringham. His own parents, loving as they were, had little idea of the necessity of levity in small boys' lives. The slightest misdemeanour meant a visit to father's study in the evening. There the mottoes for a life's creed hung threateningly upon the wall.

In the schoolroom 'Bertie' found himself playing second fiddle to his elder brother David and his sister Mary, who was up to every prank.

Prince 'Bertie' went to Osborne and the Royal Naval College, Dartmouth. He became a midshipman in 1913. He served in the battle of Jutland and was mentioned in despatches. His health broke down, and the effect of an operation prevented him from pursuing his naval career. He joined the Royal Naval Air Service, was on the Western Front in 1918, and qualified as a pilot. In 1919 he entered Trinity College, Cambridge, taking a course in economics, history and civics. He then devoted his interest to industrial relations and the setting up of a holiday camp for poor boys in Kent. He was being groomed as a future Governor-General of one of the Dominions. His mother, usually most reticent on such matters, had already primed him on the advisability of looking round for a suitable wife.

It was in the autumn of that year that the Duke saw Lady Eliza-beth again. He motored over from Balmoral for a short stay at Glamis. Princess Mary, who was staying with Lady Airlie nearby, was a visitor too. For two young people both interested in history, there was so much to talk about, so many expeditions to make. One was to Kirriemuir, 'Thrums' to the readers of Sir James Barrie.

That Christmas was spent at St. Paul's and it was just like the days

47

before the war except that it was not now she and David who hung up their stockings, but a tribe of nephews and nieces. Shortly afterwards Lady Elizabeth made her first acquaintance with Paris. She was a close friend of Diamond,[1] daughter of Lord Hardinge, British Ambassador in Paris, the two girls being within a few weeks of the same age. During her stay at the Embassy there was all the thrill of a ball, a new and broadening experience. There were sightseeing excursions to *palais* and *château*. But, perhaps more important, there were rambles round the side streets and along the Left Bank. Elizabeth fell in love with Paris and the next year she was back.

In the summer of 1921 Lady Strathmore again fell seriously ill and her youngest daughter took over role of nurse and hostess at Glamis. It was in the latter capacity that she received the Duke of York when he paid his second visit to the Castle in the autumn. The impact was being felt. He wrote to his mother: 'It is delightful here & Elizabeth is very kind to me. The more I see of her the more I like her.'

The next regal step was the arrival of Queen Mary, escorted by Princess Mary. Lady Elizabeth received them, entertained them and led them on a tour of the Castle. Queen Mary was a stickler for historical accuracy. But as she listened to the uninterrupted flow of data and anecdote covering the pages of Scottish history, she was astonished at the knowledge in the head of the demure little brunette. A respect and friendship was founded that day.

Then came the announcement of the engagement of Princess Mary to Viscount Lascelles. Because she was the Forces' Sweetheart of the First World War, because she was marrying a commoner, public interest was immense. There were to be eight bridesmaids. Three were cousins of the bride, one of the bridegroom. Among the remainder was the name of Lady Elizabeth Bowes-Lyon. For the first time her name was in black type. For the first time her picture was on the front page.

On 28th February 1922 she went to Westminster Abbey, in a straight gown of cloth of silver, with a huge silver rose on her side. At the reception afterwards at Buckingham Palace she sat next to the Duke of York. When the guests went down to the forecourt to see Princess Mary and her husband leave, and to deluge them with

[1] Married, 1923, Major Robert Abercromby, M.C. Died 1927.

rose petals and silver horseshoes, the two stood together, side by side, a little apart from the others.

By this time it was generally known in Court circles that the Duke was very much in love with Lady Elizabeth. The doubt in people's minds was whether she would accept him. There was more to it than the exchange of the carefree, happy days with a close-knit family at St. Paul's and Glamis for the discipline, the routine, the constrictions of a royal life, with the spotlight ever upon her. The future of the Prince of Wales had to be considered. As he was the most sought-after bachelor in the world, it could be assumed that he would marry. If he married, it could be assumed that he would have children. If these two assumptions came to pass, then all would be well. But if accident or illness were to claim the Heir to the Throne, if he were to remain unmarried or marry and have no children, then the greatest of all responsibilities would fall, if not upon her husband and herself, then most certainly on their children. It was one thing to be a Duchess. It was quite another thing to be a Queen, or the mother of the Sovereign. There was also the health of 'Bertie' to be considered, and the existence of inherited weaknesses. He had already cracked up once, causing his withdrawal from the Navy, and his impediment was an obvious drawback in limelight affairs. She thought of everything, except for a word that the British did not know—abdication.

Anyway nothing could be done whilst her mother was ill, and it was not until the early summer of 1922 that Lady Strathmore recovered her health.

The Duke, on the other hand, was dead set on starting married life. He had seen the Bowes-Lyons in their country homes, and what he saw he liked. They were always happy, united, from the Earl at the pinnacle to the tribe of grandchildren at his feet. It was a contrast with his own home life. There he was often alone with his parents. His sister was married. The Prince of Wales was away on overseas tours much of the time and, when at home, was taking his own line. Prince Henry was with his regiment, Prince George with his ship. The King was subject to bursts of violent criticism. Ever a stern parent, he had become even more exacting since his riding accident in France during the war. And he felt the loss of Princess

Mary deeply. His frequent outbursts, coupled with the eternal tact and understatements of Queen Mary, were getting on the Duke's nerves. There was impatience in him too, or he would not have been a true grandson of the Duke of Teck, who had the terror of a temper.

King George did not relish the thought of gay young daughters-in-law flitting round his homes. As late as August 1922 he told Queen Mary: 'I must say I dread the idea and always have.' He was a man of habit. Each morning he rose at the same moment. He straightened his hair with the same brushes that he had used as a boy at Sandringham. Even the collar stud was the same (when it broke he had it mended). Breakfast was at nine, and that meant nine. He had it alone with his wife. It was better that way, as throughout the meal his parrot Charlotte roamed the table, sticking her beak into the sugar and marmalade. Ritual followed ritual. After breakfast was over he would light the cigarette in his holder and stride out through the front door. There, the captain on the bridge, he would scan the sky for weather portents. The parrot sat on his wrist. The Cairn stood at his heel. It was an inheritance from his grandmother, a reaction bred from the uncertainties of his father. It was a difficult stronghold for a daughter-in-law of the post-war era to enter with impunity.

But, unbeknown to her, Lady Elizabeth had already made her impression on the King. He was missing his daughter greatly. Here was a girl who had been Mary's friend for years, who shared the same interests, who had been bridesmaid at her wedding, a quiet, intelligent girl who did not blow smoke rings or toss back cocktails. When he was told of his son's plans to marry her, he so far gave himself away as to say, 'You'll be a lucky fellow if she accepts you.'

It was a troubled autumn. The public were wearying of the Coalition Government. In October Mr. Lloyd George resigned after six years as Prime Minister. The King sent for Mr. Bonar Law. Parliament was dissolved. At the election the Conservatives were returned. In December was born the constitution of the Dominion of the Free State of Southern Ireland. But the question that absorbed H.R.H. the Duke of York was whether, when the moment came, Lady Elizabeth Bowes-Lyon would say yes or no.

In January the Duke was asked to be a weekend guest at St. Paul's Walden Bury. He duly arrived on Saturday, the 13th. The King and Queen were at Sandringham. A telegraphic code word had been arranged to report on the success or failure of the mission.

On Sunday morning 'Bertie' and Elizabeth excused themselves from the church party. Instead they went for a walk, out beyond the 'Flea House' and into the wood. Here she had ridden so often on her Shetland pony. Here she and David had buried the torn body of Bobby the bullfinch in a pencil box of cedarwood. Every inch of it, every tree that made its magic, was wrapped to her childhood. There was the cold smell of winter, and open views that in the summer the leaves hid. They reached the tall avenue that she called 'The Cloisters'. They stood beneath the trees. He asked his question. For a minute she thought it over, pondered it out in the peace and the silence. Then she answered 'Yes'. They came back to the drawing room in the interval between the end of Church and Sunday lunch. They told their news. It was the greatest day in the story of St. Paul's. And of the moment Lady Elizabeth was to say: 'I'm not sure that I wasn't the more surprised of the two.'

That afternoon King George and Queen Mary were before the fire at York Cottage, Sandringham. A telegram arrived. It read: 'All right. Bertie.'

As yet there was no ring upon Lady Elizabeth's finger.

On Monday the Duke travelled to Sandringham. He arrived, with the Comptroller of his Household, after tea was over. The King and Queen, diplomatically ignoring the code telegraph, listened to their son's formal announcement of his engagement. Consent was given. Queen Mary commented: 'We are delighted and he looks beaming.'

The news went out immediately.

COURT CIRCULAR
YORK COTTAGE, Sandringham,
Monday.

'The Duke of York, attended by Wing Commander Louis Greig, has arrived at York Cottage.

'It is with the greatest pleasure that the King and Queen announce the betrothal of their beloved son the Duke of York to the Lady

Elizabeth Bowes-Lyon, daughter of the Earl and Countess of Strathmore, to which union the King has gladly given his consent.'

Next morning the Duke returned to London, his mission completed, whilst his fiancée regarded with astonishment the flood of mail that threatened to engulf St. Paul's. She had hoped for a few days of peace and privacy, time to find exactly where her feet were on the floor. She admitted that she felt dazed. But as she confided in a friend: 'The cat is now completely out of the bag and there is no possibility of stuffing him back.'

She drove to London. On every street corner the newspaper posters emblazoned the news of the engagement. Bruton Street was besieged.

In two short days she had rocketed from a girl whose name sometimes appeared in the social columns up to the peaks, among the most important women in the land. She had had no time to sort out the emotions and reactions that followed in the train of her walk in the wood. She had had no opportunity to learn how the threads ran in the tapestry of the regal way of life. And she had had no experience in dealing with the Press. Now, as she glanced through the pages that were full of her, she learned about herself: 'Lady Elizabeth is essentially unmodern—and that is her charm. She is like a picture by Sir Peter Lely. Her figure is that of a woman, not the flat, boyish outline so much admired today. She has wonderful skin and eyes and hair. But her greatest charm is her voice. It is like cream and honey turned into sound, and the listener is hypnotized by its musical quality. Although serenity is the keynote of Elizabeth's character, as with all the women of the Strathmore family, she has also a Scotch shrewdness. She is intensely home-loving. Perhaps that is one of her chief charms for her husband-to-be. From her mother she inherits the housewifely qualities of the Dutch.'

Lady Elizabeth was courteous to the Press, as she was always to be. She was wearing an evening dress of mauve, silver slippers and two ropes of pearls when she received the representative of the *Daily Mail*. 'I am blissfully happy,' she told him. 'I haven't got my engagement ring yet, but I have seen the one that I think I am going to have, and it's beautiful. It is a half-hoop made up of two diamonds and a sapphire—my favourite stone—in the centre. We haven't made any plans yet about the wedding, and I had no idea that there was going to be all this excitement over it. All those things will be fixed during my visit to Sandringham. Nor have we had time to think about where we are going to live, but it will have to be somewhere in or around London, as Prince Bertie's work will keep him in town a good deal.'

In due season the ring that she dreamed of arrived.

Another paper quoted the views of the bride's father: 'We are quite pleased, as H.R.H. has a high sense of duty, is a fine type of the young Englishman, and has been a devoted suitor for two or three years.'

One daily came out with a highly coloured description of Sunday's walk in the wood, in which it was said that the Duke had to ask Lady Elizabeth more than once before she gave her consent. H. T. Cozens-Hardy was then on the staff of *The Star* and editor Wilson Pope sent him round to Bruton Street to see if this was true. Cozens-Hardy tells the story in his memoirs, *The Glorious Years*.

'The Bruton Street butler did not give me a particularly warm welcome, and Lady Strathmore, who apparently was not surprised at so early a call from the Fourth Estate, came downstairs and seemed quite ready to assist the servant in his efforts to get rid of me. But just behind the countess was her daughter, with the most radiant face that the purlieus of Bond Street had ever seen, and the fugitive wisp of hair on her forehead which the predecessors of Cecil Beaton took care should be the fascinating feature of every photograph of the forthcoming bride.

' " Mother, leave this gentleman to *me*," she exclaimed as I was shown into the breakfast-room and the countess and the butler withdrew.'

This is an extract from the interview that Londoners poured over that evening:

' " I suppose," Lady Elizabeth began, "you have come to congratulate me? How very kind of you. I am *so* happy, as you can see for yourself." A pause, and then: "You ask where is the Duke? Well, Bertie—you know everybody calls him Prince Bertie—has gone out hunting and he won't be back until this evening, when, I've no doubting (*smiling*), I shall see him."

'Lady Elizabeth was seated at a little writing-desk, pen in hand and a pile of letters and telegrams before her. "I never imagined our engagement meant so much hard work. I think cablegrams must have come from all parts of the world, and I have been trying to answer them. I hadn't the remotest idea everybody would be so interested or so kind."

'Asked about her reported hesitation before accepting the proposal, she replied with the greatest composure. "It is true he proposed in the garden at Welwyn on Sunday. The story that he asked me two or three times amused me. It was just news. Now look at me. Do you think I am the sort of person Bertie would have to ask twice?"'

The interview had an interesting sequel. A few days later an Equerry travelled from Buckingham Palace to Bruton Street. The instructions that he carried were explicit. No further interviews were to come out of No. 17. It was the order of the King.

6 *Preparing for Westminster*

ON 20th January 1922 Lady Elizabeth Bowes-Lyon travelled with the Duke of York and Lord and Lady Strathmore to Norfolk to stay at York Cottage with the King and Queen. As the chill winds blew in from the Wash, she entered an estate that was very new and strange to her, both in location and tradition, yet one that was fated to be closely entwined in her future story.

At Buckingham Palace and Windsor the King ruled from the nation's homes for Sovereigns. The aura could be understood. Balmoral was but a seventy-year-old reproduction version of Glamis. There was a way of life that she knew well. But Sandringham was a private world, the childhood home of her fiancé, the place that King George loved best in all the world, the temple of Edward and Alexandra. Their names were linked in stone above the door of the 'Big House'. 'This house was built by Albert Edward Prince of Wales and Alexandra his wife in the Year of Our Lord 1870.' Everywhere, in stone, in custom, in tree, was the imprint of the builders. King Edward's chair still stood in the bar of the Feathers Inn, waiting to receive his ghost. And in the mansion that crowned the lawns his widow still lived, seventy-eight and her memory fading. Deep in her heart she still thought of herself as the nation's Queen. From her window Elizabeth could see burning the few lights that were enough for the needs of an old woman in her loneliness. Yet in the King's residence there was scarcely sufficient accommodation to cope with the influx of guests.

York Cottage had been given to King George as a wedding present by his father. Orignally known as 'Bachelors' Cottage', it had been used to take the overflow of male guests during the shooting parties. A maze of small rooms, it had been added to in differing styles. Passages and stairs wound around. When guests arrived, the staff had to move out. The King remarked that he did not know where they slept, but presumed that it was in the trees.

Lady Elizabeth arrived at Sandringham at a time of anniversaries. Thirty years had passed since the engagement of her future parents-in-law, since the then Duke of York proposed to May of Teck in a garden. Sixty years had flowed since Princess Alexandra of Denmark left Copenhagen to marry the Prince of Wales and set up house at Sandringham. Memories were running strong. But they were memories of days before Elizabeth was born, or too young to remember. Yet 'mother-dear', as her children called Queen Alexandra, was still lovely when Lady Elizabeth was taken up to the 'Big House' to be shown to her.

For the newly engaged couple the visit to Sandringham was more a time for fixing things than a romantic interlude. Even had there been time to spare, the setting was not attuned to lovers' ways. King George and Queen Mary had had no experience of romance and really did not know what the word meant, or have much patience with it. Queen Mary had originally been engaged to her husband's elder brother, the Duke of Clarence, a very odd young man. Six weeks after the announcement, in January 1892, he died. Fifteen months later she was engaged to his younger brother. She arrived, tired out, at York Cottage on her wedding night to find that her future home had been furnished throughout by 'the man from Maples', according to the utilitarian tastes of her sailor husband. Her mother-in-law refused to relapse her hold on 'Georgie' and would burst in at any moment. And only five minutes away the bedroom of her dead fiancé was being kept exactly as if he was alive. A fire burned, and there were flowers in the vases. His toilet items were left exactly as they were when he died. It was Albert all over again. Yet the two found great love together, but not in the accepted romantic way.

So the superlatives of love found no place in the Sandringham stay. 'Bertie' was again heartily informed that he was 'a lucky fellow'. His mother noted down that he was 'supremely happy'. 'Pretty, charming, engaging, natural' were in the bouquet passed to Lady Elizabeth. There must have been the ingredients of ordeal in that official introduction to her fiancé's parents, particularly as she had only been seven days engaged, and seven hectic days at that. But she came back from Norfolk with victory behind her. She had walked into the heart of a critical man, set in his ways and averse to daughters-in-law, and into the heart of a woman who gave her affections very sparingly.

There were now two pressing points to settle. The first was the date of the wedding. The King and Queen had been asked to pay an official visit to Italy in the spring and the Italians had not yet fixed the timings. Then the news came through that early May would be the most suitable. So Thursday, 26th April, was decided upon as the day for the marriage.

The other, and most vital point, was to make it legally correct for the Duke to marry a commoner.

Two hundred years before, the dual rule of England and Hanover had led to a tactful understanding between the Royal Houses of Germany and Britain that brides and bridegrooms should be selected from their own courts. George I had decreed, on his own authority, that royalties should only marry royalties. George III took the restriction a step further. Whilst he himself had given up the lovely titled girl after whom he hankered, to wed, in duty bound, a Princess in a poke from Germany, his brothers, the Dukes of Gloucester and Cumberland, had broken away from the ruling. They had both married home products, and the King had personal objection to their ladies on social and political grounds. Accordingly, in 1772, the Royal Marriage Act was passed. This enacted that 'no descendant of his late majesty George II (other than the issue of princesses married or who may marry into foreign families) shall be capable of contracting matrimony without the previous consent of his majesty, his heirs and successors, signified under the Great Seal. But in case any descendant of George II, being above 25 years old, shall persist to contract a marriage disapproved of by his majesty, such descendant, after giving 12 months' notice to the privy council, may contract such marriage, and the same may be duly solemnized without the consent of his majesty, etc., and shall be good except both Houses of Parliament shall declare their disapprobation thereto'.

This act had led to the odd situation whereby, in 1817, George III, despite his large family, had only one grandchild in line for the Throne.

The case of the Duke of York was the first time for over 250 years that a Prince in direct succession was to wed a commoner with royal consent. His predecessor had also been a sailor and a Duke of York. In December 1660 James—brother of Charles II and later James II —admitted to having married Anne Hyde, daughter of Lord Clarendon. Their daughters became Queen Mary and Queen Anne.

On 12th February a special meeting of the Privy Council was held. The King then signed the following document:

'Whereas by an Act of Parliament entitled "An Act for the better regulating of the future Marriages of the Royal Family", it is amongst other things enacted "that no descendant of the body of His late Majesty King George II, Male or Female, shall be capable of contracting matrimony without the previous consent of His Majesty, His Heirs or Successors, signified under the great Seal,"

'Now know ye that we have consented and by these Presents signify Our Consent to the contracting of Matrimony between His Royal Highness Albert Frederick Arthur George, Duke of York, and the Lady Elizabeth Angela Margaret Bowes-Lyon, youngest daughter of the Right Honourable Claude George, Earl of Strathmore and Kinghorne.'

There had, of course, been other marriages between Royalty and commoner in recent times, but in none of these cases had there been the same chance of offspring succeeding to the Throne. Only the previous year Princess Mary had married Viscount Lascelles. In 1919 Princess 'Pat' of Connaught had become Lady Patricia Ramsay. In 1889 Queen Victoria had given her blessing to the engagement of the daughter of the Prince of Wales, Princess Louise, to the Earl of Fife, and upped him to a Duke over the dining table. But Queen Victoria had really set the ball rolling when she agreed to the marriage of her own daughter Louise, to the Marquess of Lorne, son of the Duke of Argyll, in 1871. Admittedly the Princess, 'The Maiden all for Lorne' as she was known, had threatened to go into a convent if she did not get her way, but it was chiefly the wars in Europe, and the sabre rattling of Bismarck, that influenced the royal decision. The Prussian Royal Family took the deepest exception to this break with tradition. Worried, the Queen took Lord Lorne on one side and told him of the hostility in Berlin. Lorne answered: 'Ma'am, my ancestors were kings when the Hohenzollerns were parvenus.' The matter was settled. Fortunately in 1923 the Hohenzollerns were in no position to express opinions about who married who.

Another point to be settled was the future home of the royal couple. This was to be White Lodge, in Richmond Park, and Queen Mary got busy with the necessary alterations and improvements. She was making certain that there would be no repetition of what had happened to her when she reached her bridal home at Sandringham.

Except for short visits to York Cottage Lady Elizabeth spent much of the engagement period in London, where answering the mail and making arrangements for the wedding kept her busy the day through. But in March she and the Duke managed to fit in a short stay at Glamis. They spent a day in Edinburgh, where they visited the factory of McVitie and Price to settle details of the wedding cake. This was to be nine feet high and weigh 800 pounds. In four tiers, it was to carry the arms of the two families. Enough cake of the same mixture was to be made to allow of distribution to 100,000 children. In the afternoon they attended the England versus Scotland Rugby International and their presence diverted the attention of even the keenest fans.

The problem of wedding presents was taking up a great deal of the time of the Duke and Lady Elizabeth. They were pouring in from all parts of the world. Post Office vans were making special journeys to deliver them, and in some cases taking them back. It did not seem to be appreciated that presents could not be accepted by a royal couple unless the donors were known in Court circles, with the exception of certain societies and organizations connected with royalty.

The Palace is always anxious to avoid the acceptance of presents the motive behind which is publicity and advertisement. The ingenuity of publicity seekers can be amazing. Lord Lascelles had received an invention which, the sender said, would throw him out of bed at any time he required in the morning. All the inventor asked in return was a testimonial. Royal patience was nearly exhausted when Lady Elizabeth received a bottle of patent medicine four feet high.

In all, gifts to the value of over a quarter of a million pounds were returned by the Duke and his future Duchess. A courteous explanation of the guiding rules was sent with each. The greatest care had to be taken that no mistakes were made, for on one occasion that had happened to a foreign King, which had upset him greatly. When there was doubt, the Duke and Lady Elizabeth had to go into conference. Perhaps in some hospital ward one of them might have stopped to speak to a patient in the iron bed. In memory of that minute the invalid might have sent a small present, and the return of that would mean tragedy indeed.

Looking back to her war years at Glamis, some of the presents that pleased the bride most came from hospitals. The National Orthopaedic Hospital for Crippled Children, an organization in which she was deeply interested, was running a needlework competition to swell its funds. Lady Elizabeth agreed to accept the winning pieces as a wedding present. From the disabled men at the Blighty Works at Slateford arrived a set of shepherd tartan plaids. A cheque for £2,500 which came to the Duke was spent on providing entertainment for poor children in cities where unemployment was high.

The Needlemakers' Company sent a thousand needles with eyes of gold, the Worshipful Company of Gardeners the bouquet to be used at the Abbey, made up of the white roses of York and the white heather of Scotland. From Windsor came a grand piano and cutlery, from Worcester some of its most perfect china, from the City of London antique silver dishes. It was obvious that Lady Elizabeth was to be short of nothing in her married life and to be the owner of many treasures of high capital value.

Of all the flood of presents that of the City of Glasgow must be singled out. At the end of January the Duke had received the Freedom of the City and, in reply to the speech of the Lord Provost, he had said how glad he was that his first public appearance after his engagement was in Scotland as he had had 'the wisdom, the foresight, and the good fortune to have persuaded a Scottish lady to share his life.' Now from the Clyde came a clock of the most extraordinary achievements. Four times a day during the week it played a march, but on the Sabbath it was silent. As the working day marches were played there passed through a hole in the dial a procession of the Royal Family as they were in 1804, and then a troop of the Horse Guards appeared.

The presents[1] eventually all went on display at Buckingham Palace, the tables looking as if Aladdin's cave had been emptied.

One of Lady Elizabeth's presents could not go on display at the Palace. It was 'Half a moonlit night'. This was the traditional dowry

---

[1] Among the principal presents were:

The King to the bride: An ermine cape and a suite including a tiara, a necklace, a brooch, earrings, and hair ornaments of diamonds and pale Persian turquoises.

The Queen to the bride: A necklet of diamonds and sapphires with a bracelet, a ring, brooches, and pendant to match, and an old lace fan with mother-of-pearl frame and handle.

Queen Alexandra to the bride: A necklace of pearls and amethysts with a heart-shaped amethyst pendant set in brilliants. To the bridegroom: A very fine antique silver box.

The Countess of Strathmore to her daughter: A diamond and pearl bracelet and a diamond and pearl necklace to match.

The Earl of Strathmore to his daughter: A diamond and platinum tiara and a rope necklace of pearls and diamonds.

The bridegroom to the bride: A necklace of diamonds and pearls with pendant to match.

The bride to the bridegroom: A dress watch-chain of platinum and pearls.

Princess Mary and Viscount Lascelles to the bride and bridegroom: A quantity of finest bed linen.

Princess Royal and Princess Maud: Diamond and sapphire brooch.

The King and Queen of Spain: Gold cigarette case with the monogram 'A' engraved upon it.

Officers of the Royal Navy: The Order of the Garter in brilliants and enamel.

The American Ambassador to Lady Elizabeth: A sketch of the Duke of York.

Prince Paul of Serbia: Framed sketch of Lady Elizabeth by Sargent.

The Duchess of Norfolk: Tea-set of very delicate china in ornamental gold holders.

The Premier of Ulster and Lady Craig: Gold-mounted blackthorn walking-stick in a case.

The Members of the Cabinet: Silver inkwells, silver stamp boxes, and four very fine silver candlesticks for use on a writing-table.

A present 'For Elizabeth with our best wishes' was a case of gold teaspoons from 'Maud, Charles and Olav', the Queen, King and Crown Prince of Norway, while the same three donors sent 'For dear Bertie' a case of gold dessert knives with enamel handles.

A joint gift of a wonderful old clock bore the names of the Duke of Connaught, Princess Christian, the Duchess of Argyll, Princess Beatrice, the Marquis and Marchioness of Cambridge, Viscount and Viscountess Eltham, Lady Mary Cambridge, Colonel and Lady Evelyn Gibbs, Lord Frederick Cambridge, the Earl and Countess of Athlone, Lord Tremarton, Lady May Cambridge, the Marquis of Milfordhaven, the Dowager Marchioness of Milfordhaven, Lady Louise Mountbatten, the Crown Prince of Sweden, Captain and Lady Patricia Ramsay, Princess Helena Victoria, Princess Marie Louise, and the Marquis and Marchioness of Carisbrooke.

of the Lyon family to their daughters. Being interpreted, it meant that the menfolk used to go out on a moonlight night suitable for their purpose and devote themselves to raiding and plundering. On their return the spoil was counted and half the total went to the bride.

Meantime the editors of the women's pages were avidly waiting for a description of the wedding dress. This came in March. It was to be one of the simplest ever worn by a royal bride. 'A beautiful chiffon moire dress of old ivory colour, and of a simple medieval style embroidered with silver thread and pearls, with lace sleeves of specially-made Nottingham lace. The train is composed of beautiful old lace mounted on tulle, the lace graciously lent by her Majesty the Queen. The bride will wear a tulle veil with a wreath of orange blossom.'

Queen Mary also lent the old *Point de Flanders* veil. As for her trousseau, Lady Elizabeth chose colours of a light hue and much of the work of making them was done by a skilled seamstress who had been in the service of the Strathmores for many years.

There were to be eight bridesmaids. Queen Victoria had had this number and the precedent had been followed. At Queen Mary's wedding they had all belonged to the Royal House, but in the case of her daughter the limitation had been taken away. Lady Elizabeth was to be attended by six girl friends and two young nieces. Three of her friends had been with her at the Abbey wedding of Princess Mary. They were Lady Mary Cambridge, daughter of the Marquis of Cambridge, Queen Mary's elder brother; Lady May Cambridge, daughter of Princess Alice, Countess of Athlone, Queen Mary's younger brother; and Lady Mary Thynne, daughter of the Marquis and Marchioness of Bath. The other three were Lady Katharine Hamilton, daughter of the Duke and Duchess of Abercorn; Miss Diamond Hardinge, with whom Lady Elizabeth had stayed in Paris in 1921 and 1922; and Miss Betty Cator, daughter of a former High Sheriff of Norfolk. The nieces were Cecilia Bowes-Lyon and Elizabeth Elphinstone, both eleven.

At the Faculty Office the marriage licence was engrossed. This was done by Mr. Bull, a clerk who had been writing licences for ordinary folk, and engrossing them for royalty, for fifty years. He wrote in old English lettering with black ink. It was reported that for three days, in a locked room, he stooped over a roll of parchment a yard square, and that he used twenty quill pens of varying thickness.

On the evening of the 25th April Lady Elizabeth Bowes-Lyon went to Buckingham Palace. There she had a long talk with Queen Mary.

7 Wedding Story

ON Thursday, 26th April, the bells of Westminster Abbey pealed for three and a half hours. A million people came to see the bride and groom, the first son of a reigning Sovereign to marry at Westminster since Edmund Crouchback, Earl of Lancaster and son of Henry III, was wedded to Aveline, daughter of William de Forz, Count of Aumale, in 1269.

At Buckingham Palace the King, as was his wont when breakfast was over, inspected the weather. It was still raining. It had been raining most of the night. To his relief the deluge petered out at half past nine. The relief was even greater to the crowds in the Mall seeking shelter under the wedding editions of the morning newspapers, and only then could the finishing touches be put to those decorations on the processional route that were most vulnerable to water.

Guests were due to be seated in the Abbey by ten o'clock. Mr. Lloyd George and Mr. Asquith arrived at the same time, but not together. 'Margot', sinuous in almond green, meekly followed her husband. Mr. Baldwin looked noble and satisfied. The Prime Minister walked in with Lord Curzon. The two Mr. Chamberlains were impressive. Mr. Winston Churchill arrived last—and late. Lady Diana Cooper was looking her loveliest. Also present was the huntsman of the Pytchley in pink, and a contingent of Boy Scouts and boys from the industrial centres in which the Duke had already showed such a lively interest.

On one count the day was robbed of a break with tradition and an even wider audience. The B.B.C. had applied for permission to broadcast the service. The Dean of Westminster was in favour, but the Chapter considered it to be a too revolutionary step.

The coach arrived for Lady Elizabeth at eleven o'clock. She walked confidently across the pavement with her father, but she had forgotten one thing, her gloves! Six thousand people were jammed around Bruton Street and every window and balcony was full.

Queen Alexandra left Marlborough House. Beside her sat the Dowager Empress Marie of Russia. Close behind followed the Duchess of Portland. This was a memorable day for the Cavendish-Bentincks.

At eight minutes past eleven the King and Queen left Buckingham Palace in the Glass Coach. Before them sat Prince George. They were followed five minutes later by the Prince of Wales, in the uniform of Colonel of the Welsh Guards, the Duke of York in the full dress of the Royal Air Force and Prince Henry in the crimson and gold of the Hussars. The Prince of Wales was in the role of 'chief supporter', the closest thing to a 'best man' allowed to a royal bridegroom. It is a relic of the days when there was often rivalry among the King's sons as to which should succeed to the Throne. Appointment of a 'chief supporter' ensured that the only priority that applied was one of age.

In the Abbey waited the Archbishops of Canterbury and York, the Bishop of London, the Dean of Westminster and the Primus of the Episcopalian Church of Scotland.

The King and Queen passed up the nave to take their places on the right of the Sacrarium. On the King's left sat Queen Alexandra, in purple and black, with an ermine coat, still graceful, still slender, and with her inevitable umbrella. On their arrival both the Duke of York and the Prince of Wales kissed her and whispered in her ear.

The bride and her maids came in by the west door. She was leaning on the arm of her father, in uniform of scarlet, and carried a small Prayer Book, the gift of her fellow confirmation candidates at Forfar. She paused by the grave of the Unknown Warrior and laid upon it her bouquet of white roses and heather. She moved on towards the Altar, to the music of 'Lead us Heavenly Father, lead us'. Then it happened—the moment that so many people were always to remember. As if at the touch of a spot light's switch the sun broke through the April clouds, pouring from a patch of bright blue sky over the Abbey wet with rain. Bars of brilliance pierced the high window, flooding the north transept and the Sacrarium and wiping out the candlelight. It flashed on the silver and the gold and the jewels of the guests, it floodlit the bride, it gave a majesty to the building that was beyond compare.

His Royal Highness the Duke of York and Lady Elizabeth stood side by side at the steps of the Sacrarium, listening to the words of the Dean of Westminster. The Primate took on the service. He came to the marriage vows. Few heard the response of the Duke, but the bride's 'I will' was sweet and clear. With sword clanking, the Prince of Wales stepped smartly to his brother's side. He produced the ring, rather to the relief of the Duke, it seemed. The wedded pair moved to the High Altar, and out of view of most in the Abbey.

The Archbishop of York gave the address. He said: 'Will you take and keep this gift of wedded life as a sacred trust? Sacred it must be, for your love, and God's love, are within it. With all our hearts we wish that it may be happy. But you cannot resolve that it shall be happy. You can and will resolve that it shall be noble. You will think not so much of enjoyment as of achievement. You will have a great ambition to make this one life now given to you something rich, and true and beautiful.'

The King, two Queens and an Empress went into the Vestry with the bridal pair, the Prince of Wales and the Earl and Countess of Strathmore. The two of them came out hand in hand, and smiling. An observer remarked that her eyes were as bonny a blue as ever laughed roguishly under a glengarry.

The 'Wedding March' filled every corner of the Abbey. Slowly the tide of colour ebbed away. The last guests made their way to the cars and the carriages. And behind them, in the silence, they left the ghost of two hours of majesty and love that was to haunt other marriages in the years to come.

The new Duchess of York was welcomed into London's Streets with an acclamation and a cheering such as had not been heard since Armistice night. At places the crowds were a hundred deep. Inevitably their procession got behind time. Particularly vociferous was the throng that packed that part of the route which the Duke and Duchess covered alone. While the rest of the Royal Family and the guests went straight down the Mall to the Palace, the bride and groom turned right at Marlborough Gate, then via St. James's Street, Piccadilly and Constitution Hill. Flags and handkerchiefs at the windows looked like wind blowing through a flowerbed. Street musicians were playing Scottish airs. Confetti was as thick as snow flakes. And the sun was still shining when they reached the Palace.

Ten minutes later they were on the balcony. The King and Queen joined them. The Dowager Empress of Russia came out, to taste again the roar of a happy crowd, and the Princess Royal with Princesses Victoria and Maud. Then they all drew back but the Duke and Duchess, allowing them to be alone to savour a great moment in their day.

If there was a snag to the wedding day it was the length of the breakfast. The Duke and Duchess had to sit at the table for an hour and a half before the toasts came and they could escape. When the time came for the then Queen to arrange the wedding breakfast for her daughter, Princess Elizabeth, she said firmly: 'We won't have anything like that this time!' Elizabeth and Philip got fish, meat with beans and new potatoes, and ice-cream—*Filet de Sole Mountbatten, Perdreau en casserole,* and *Bombe glacée Princess Elizabeth.* The consumption time was twenty minutes.

King George V was determined that only the very best was good enough for the charming daughter-in-law who was entering his family. His thoughts went back to the days of his father and his grandmother. Then royal menus were treasured souvenirs. Queen Victoria would never have tolerated a plain card. Edward VII had indulged in the rococo. The war had interrupted such Palace customs. What better chance than this to revive the menu memorable?

The Duchess looked at an extravaganza in red and gold. Round the cypher of the King and Queen were the rose, the thistle and the shamrock gay in gold ribbon. At the bottom were the crests of the bride and groom in crimson and gold. The decoration on the card for Princess Elizabeth consisted of 'G.R.E.' under the Crown and the letters 'E' and 'P' at the bottom.

The menu had taken weeks to prepare and was finalized a fortnight before the wedding. The result was enough to impress any bride. She read: *Consommé à la Windsor—Suprêmes de Saumon, Reine*

Mary—Côtelettes d'agneau, Prince Albert—Chapons à la Strathmore,[1] *Jambon et langues découpés à l'aspic, salade royale*—asparagus with *Crème mousseuse* sauce—*Duchess Elizabeth* strawberries—*pâtisserie* (in sugar baskets which the guests could take away)—and fruit.

The nine feet high wedding cake dwarfed the Duchess. She was provided with a special knife with which to attack it. The handle was formed in the shape of a Strathmore 'Lyon'. The task of cutting the massive structure looked entirely beyond her strength. But beneath the sugar icing a wide wedge of cake had already been cut, and thus it was only the icing that had to be severed. The Duchess pulled a broad satin ribbon, and away came the wedge. Seven pure gold charms lay hidden in this wedge. As it was cut up into small pieces and distributed, quite a lot of high-born dignity was lost out of the Palace windows as the struggle for the possession of the charms continued.

On her marriage Lady Elizabeth Bowes-Lyon had become Her Royal Highness the Duchess of York and the King had bestowed upon her the dignity of a Princess. As the King saw the couple off on their honeymoon he gave the bride formal recognition of her place in the Royal Family. This gave the Duke and Duchess joint precedence, and conferred upon her separate precedence as the fourth lady of the land, ranking next to Princess Mary.

As the couple said their goodbyes and the landau left for Waterloo Station, there was an absolute orgy of royal confetti throwing. The King threw it in the Great Hall. The Queen and Princess Mary pelted them from the balcony. The Prince of Wales, Prince Henry and Prince George went, bare-headed, to the exit arch and opened up a bombardment from there, shouts of triumph proclaiming direct hits. The underlying reason for the high jubilation and expending of energy was the real and heart-felt relief that 'Bertie' had found such

---

[1] In his memoirs, *Royal Chef*, Gabriel Tschumi gave the recipe for the dish named in honour of the bride's mother: '*Chapons à la Strathmore* is served cold with a vegetable salad in mayonnaise. To make it, you need a boiling chicken which is well cooked, cut in neat joints, and chaudfroided in a white chicken sauce. It is served on a flat dish covered with clear chicken jelly, and when this has set it is garnished with truffles and tips of tongue either cut into tiny squares or circles. The truffle and tongue garnishing takes a long time to prepare artistically, but it can give a very pleasant colour scheme if arranged well.'

a suitable, sweet and sensible wife. As the Prince of Wales, when Duke of Windsor, wrote: 'She brought into the family a lively and refreshing spirit.'

At the wedding party Princess Marie Louise was talking to the Countess of Strathmore. She said: 'How lovely Elizabeth is.' Lady Strathmore answered: 'Yes, lovely in every way. I have never heard an ugly word pass that child's lips.'

Four grey horses drew the open carriages to Waterloo. The postillions were in blue, the outriders in scarlet. For their first stage of the honeymoon the Duke and Duchess were bound for Polesden Lacy, the beautiful home of the Hon. Mrs. Ronald Greville on the Surrey Downs. It was at one time the home of Richard Brinsley Sheridan and from its windows spread out a grand view of the Dorking Valley. Mrs. Greville, a famous hostess of King Edward's days, whose husband, a brother of Lord Greville, had died in 1908, had long been a close friend of the Royal Family. The Duke had frequently been her guest. He was popular with the villagers for the gusto that he had injected into a garden fête for church funds.

The departure platform was bedecked with rhododendrons, hydrangeas and palms. The Royal saloon was decorated in grey and matched the bride's going away outfit. There was the usual reception committee. The newly-weds were beginning to feel the strain. But there was one more scene to face before the curtain fell.

Great Bookham was a replica in miniature of London. The station and the approach were bedecked. The Chief Constable was there, the Southern Railway in force, and a young lady with flowers from a factory. There was an arch of flags and bunting supported by primrose-draped poles. There were serried ranks of Boy Scouts, Girl Guides and schoolchildren holding sprays of hawthorn blossom. And of course the Parish Council, with more flowers and an Illuminated Address. The car stopped, for the last time. The Duke said how thrilled he and his bride were at the wonderful reception, but as they were tired after their long day they would prefer that the address were not read then.

At the lodge gate there were a few estate hands. The car passed through into the avenue. The gate closed.

At Glamis the local children were ending a picnic staged for them in the cricket pavilion. As the darkness fell everyone went up to the great bonfire that stood on Hunter's Hill. As the flames swept up, so did the spirits soar of Lady Elizabeth's people. On the land of her ancestors, amid the weird shadows, to the roar of the fire and the call of pipes, toasts to her health and happiness were drunk. For many an hour the songs and the dances and toasts went on. And the light of the blaze for her could be seen all over the Strathmore valley from Perth to Montrose.

8   Honeymoon and Home

THE Duke and Duchess spent their short stay at Polesden Lacy playing golf, walking in the countryside beautiful with spring, and in writing letters. On the day after his wedding the Duke wrote to his mother, saying that he hoped that she would not miss him too much, 'though I believe you will'. A letter arrived from his father, again stressing how lucky he was to have found such a charming and delightful wife. 'I am quite certain that Elizabeth will be a splendid partner in your work and share with you and help you in all you have to do.' The King stressed that his second son had always been easy to get on with, ready to listen and agree with his father's opinions, adding, in contrast . . . 'very different to dear David'. The Duke did not yet know how wide his liberation was to be.

They returned to London, called in at Bruton Street to see Lord and Lady Strathmore, and then went on to Glamis, plus two large dogs. At the station the Duchess's own Girl Guides were lined up to greet her. And here, on her own ground, with so many people to call on with her husband, a bitter blow fell upon her. She developed whooping cough. 'So unromantic,' commented her husband. They returned from Scotland to spend the last fortnight of their honeymoon at Frogmore, Windsor. This was the Duchess's introduction to the ghost of Queen Victoria, that Grandmama of whom her husband had been so frightened that he was liable to cry when she spoke to him. All around were the footprints of her, of Prince Albert, of the Duchess of Kent. There was much of royal heritage that the bride had yet to learn.

In the middle of June the Duke and Duchess entered their new home, White Lodge, Richmond Park. Here Queen Mary had been putting her expert touch, and with particular interest as it was in this house, when she was Duchess of York, that her eldest son had been born. About it hung three centuries of royal history.

For the Stuarts, Shene Chase had been a favourite hunting ground. The eight square miles of what then was known as 'New Park' were enclosed by Charles I, an act which caused much bitterness and was a contributory reason for the Civil War. In the Commonwealth the Park passed into the hands of the Corporation of London, who in turn handed it back to Charles II. George I built a hunting lodge there, so that he could refresh himself after the chase. But it was Caroline, Queen of George II, who was so delighted with the beauties of Richmond Park that she decided to make her home at the lodge. She built the existing central block with its classical pillars and lived at White Lodge, as she named it, for the nine years before her death in 1737. Her constant companion was the amiable Lady Suffolk and to her drawing-rooms came all the wits of the period, including Horace Walpole and Pope. It was here that Jeanie Deans, in Sir Walter Scott's *Heart of Midlothian*, pleaded with Queen Caroline for the life of her sister. Of the Park Jeanie said to the Duke of Argyll, 'It's braw rich feeding for the cows.'

Thereafter Princess Amelia lived at White Lodge, as Ranger of the Park. She tried to exclude the public from the Park, but the right of the people to free access was determined legally, and continued. It was Princess Amelia who decided to enlarge the house by the addition of two pavilions, a task completed by her successor, Lord Bute. In 1802 White Lodge was granted to Henry Addington, afterwards Lord Sidmouth, in return for his patriotic gesture in taking office under Pitt. There the reconciliation between the two men took place. And it was on the dining-room table that Nelson, shortly before the battle of Trafalgar, sketched, with his finger dipped in wine, his intended plan of attack.

The next tenant was Mary, Duchess of Gloucester, last surviving child of George III. Then it was assigned to the young Prince of Wales, as an independent establishment under tutorial guard, but he was glad when he could escape to Sandringham. So the invincible Duchess of Teck wheedled it out of Queen Victoria, and thus it became the childhood home of Queen Mary. Of great benefit to the property during this period were the energetic gardening activities of her father. The poor man had nothing else to do.

Internally the rooms were small for a royal residence, only the drawing room on the ground floor being of any size. Much space was taken up by the long corridors leading to the wings built by Princess Amelia, one of which was reserved for the children. But the stairs and chimney-pieces were fine, and the whole lent great possibilities to the interior decorator.

With the impending arrival of the Duke and Duchess of York the Office of Works began the installation of modern improvements. Kitchens and bathrooms had to be brought up to date, electricity installed, and the stables altered to the needs of cars and chauffeurs.

After only a fortnight at Richmond the Duchess had to face the ordeal that comes to all young brides—the entertaining of her parents-in-law to a meal. Warning went to the Palace that the cook was not very expert and the fare would be plain. But that lunch was a roaring success and Queen Mary was most impressed with the way the Duchess had arranged her wedding presents.

But the young couple were to find that there was very little time to turn White Lodge into a home bearing their own intimate imprint. Their honeymoon was well and truly over. Every post brought its shoal of requests, that the Duchess should visit this hospital, be patroness of that society, lay a foundation stone, open a ward, help a children's home, further a needlework scheme, open a fête or bazaar. The line on the graph of public engagements at Buckingham Palace shot up. Every request had to be examined. Following in the footsteps of Queen Mary, the Duchess was most conscientious on such matters and, because it was all new to her, the procedure took a great deal of her time. One of her baptismal engagements was the annual outing of the Fresh Air Fund in Epping Forest, when a thousand poor children were given a day of fun in the open. The Duchess got busy at the coconut shy, and knocked down a 'milky one'. Her success was immediate and very real. More and more requests poured in.

Then there were the official engagements on which she had to accompany her husband. Such a one was the Royal Air Force Pageant at Hendon at the end of June. Some engagements entailed much preparation. The Duke and Duchess accompanied the King and Queen to Edinburgh, staying at Holyrood, where a State Reception was held. So much activity was the lot of a couple who primarily wanted to be alone together, to get to know not only one another but the other's family and friends. They carried the mantle of the completeness of being just together out into the public world that it was their lot to tread.

Duff Cooper[1] was with them at a dinner party, and then they all went on to a theatre. He wrote to Lady Diana: 'The Duke and Duchess of York were there. They are such a sweet little couple and so fond of one another. They reminded me of us, sitting together in the box having private jokes, and in the interval when we were all sitting in the room behind the box they slipped out, and I found them standing together in a dark corner of the passage talking happily as we might. She affects no shadow of airs and graces.'[2]

What then really happened to the second son of the King when this young woman of twenty-two, five feet and two inches of laughter and soft colours, boundless energy and wells of fun, came to share his life in a new home? His official biographer, Sir John Wheeler-Bennett, summed it up when he wrote that from the first days of his marriage his home life was his refuge and safeguard against the world, and on the love and companionship of his wife was based his lifelong contentment.

The Duke had been overshadowed since his nursery days. He had even been bullied. A natural shyness had been exaggerated by his halting speech and the lack of the advantage of being able to make words tell. The lack of imagination of his parents towards their sons held him back. The King wanted them to agree with him, and certainly not to contradict. If he was crossed he would launch a strongly critical attack. Criticism and heavy advice were the last things to advance the cause of 'Bertie'. He was very accomplished in many ways. He needed some praise and overt love and lightness in life. So far he had found it only in Queen Alexandra. The result of his early life led to the growth of a deep inferiority complex within him, and not even the love of his wife ever really eliminated it.

[1] Lord Norwich.
[2] 'The Light of Common Day.'

The Duke now found himself in the position, strange indeed for him, of being in the company of someone who put him first above all. His ambitions, his well being, his future became omnipotent. Someone believed in him. The seeds were being sown for a complete transfiguration of his attitude to life. This in no way led towards him becoming the dominating character in his household. He would not have wished that, for he was not that kind of man. In the event the reverse was the case. When he became King a royal friend remarked: 'The Queen rules the roost, make no mistake about that.' Rather he had gained a loyal partner with a backbone of steel and a determination and a pride that were invincible.

The bond, the co-operation, between the two was soon noticed as the Duchess sat beside her husband when he was speaking in public. She would mouth the words he had to say, as if by the hypnotism of love she was calling the sounds from his throat. And sometimes her hand would steal out and touch his. For the conquering of the impediment was the real challenge that they faced together.

The Duke and Duchess began married life with a degree of intimacy and understanding that had taken Queen Victoria and Prince Albert five years to achieve. Here was no clash of ego, no divided loyalties, no necessity for an outraged husband to lock himself in his room until a penitent wife knocked and asked for forgiveness. Queen Victoria was an only child. Elizabeth was the youngest but one of nine and, being at the tail end, had learned much about the art of living in peace.

The Duke and Duchess shared a sitting-room. When he was away on State business, she wrote to him every day. On free evenings she liked supper on a tray. She strove to keep the private hours divorced from the public, and to make them serene.

The only shadow of difference that arose between the newly-married couple was over the question of time. The Queen Mother has never been a strictly punctual person. The discipline of the school bell had never rung in her childish ears. On carefully-timed programmes human interest is apt to take priority over the position of the hands on the clock. Even when leaving for an engagement on time, she is apt to think of something that she has forgotten to do at the last moment.

75

The Duke, on the other hand, had had punctuality drummed into him from the time he could walk. It was now a fetish with him. His father was the same. When the breakfast gong rang the Royal Family emerged from their bedrooms with a precision which indicated that they had been marking time behind the doors. There was nothing that the Duke disliked more than being kept waiting. He had to learn toleration in the case of his wife, but extended it to nobody else.

Yet it was not a new problem in the Royal Family. King Edward VII had suffered from the same failing, and to a far greater extent, in Queen Alexandra. On his Coronation day he had to knock on her door and inform her that if she did not hurry up he would go to Westminster without her. All the clocks at Sandringham were kept half an hour fast in an attempt to fool her.

The Duchess had an antidote to her lateness—charm. She and the Duke were to have dinner with the King and Queen. They arrived a full two minutes late. The thoughts in the Duke's mind are a secret which can be so easily imagined. His wife apologized for their tardiness. Astonishingly the King replied: 'You are not late, my dear, I think we must have sat down two minutes early.'

Among the many blessings that Lady Elizabeth Bowes-Lyon brought with her to the Duke of York was the forging of a new link of understanding with the King and Queen. From the first moment that he had seen her King George had liked her. He admired her courage, basked in her wit, approved the way she dressed and thought her most attractive. Queen Mary felt the same. Now her letters were full of the doings of 'Bertie & E.' She also had been impressed by the first meeting. In fact she had put the Earl of Strathmore's youngest daughter on the 'short list' for the Prince of Wales!

The Duchess had no difficulty in getting on well with the King. She early realized that his bark was worse than his bite and she became deeply fond of him. She wrote to Lord Dawson of Penn, the royal physician, after the King's death in 1936: 'I miss him dreadfully. Unlike his own children I was never afraid of him, and in all the twelve years of having me as daughter-in-law he never spoke one unkind or abrupt word to me, and was always ready to listen and give advice on one's own silly little affairs. He was so kind, and *dependable*! And when he was in the mood, he could be deliciously funny too!...'[1]

The more the two saw of one another the greater friends they became. The Duke and Duchess spent August at Glamis, as she had done every summer of her life, and thereafter went on to join the royal party at Balmoral. Here she was completely at home and everyone on Deeside fell in love with her. After they had left the King wrote to his son telling him that the more he saw of 'your dear little wife' the more charming he found her.

In October came their first real adventure together—a journey to the Balkans. A son had been born to King Alexander and Queen Marie, and the Serbian Royal Family had asked the Duke to be godfather. Fifteen months before he had made the same journey, on that occasion to be chief sponsor at the wedding.

For the Duchess, not only was this the furthest distance that she had yet travelled from home, but she was to see at first hand the inside of one of those Royal Houses which, one by one, were coming to an end in Europe. The horrors of the night of 11th June 1903 were still fresh in the memory. Then King Alexander and Queen Draga had been murdered in the royal palace at Belgrade under conditions so vile that the whole of Europe was revolted.

Now another King Alexander reigned over the Serbs, the Croats and the Slovenes, and his wife was a great-grandchild of Queen Victoria. She was a daughter of Queen Marie of Rumania, the 'Missy' for whom George V had harboured warm feelings when he was a young man. For three days the Duke and Duchess trundled over the railways of Europe, not only to act as *Koom* and *Koomitsa*, but also to be present at the wedding of Prince Paul and Princess Olga of Greece and to take part in house-warming celebrations, for the Serbian Royal Family had just moved into a new palace, built on the site of their old home which had been destroyed by Austrian gun-fire during the war.

There were many duties for godparents at a Serbian christening. The Duke carried the infant heir to the Throne into the chapel and cradled him in his arms for the first part of the service. Then he

[1] *Dawson of Penn* by Francis Watson.

77

handed his burden to the grandmother, who unswathed the baby. Queen Marie of Rumania passed the naked child to the Patriarch, who totally immersed him in the font. Unfortunately the old priest lost his grip of the tiny body, which disappeared under the water. The Duke was quick to the rescue. After the anointing, the Duke carried the child three times round the altar. Then a ceremonial lock was cut from the hair. The Duke's duties did not end with the ceremony. Not only was he responsible for the supervising of his godson's education, but in due season he had to be consulted on the choice of a bride. The present from the Duke was a gold coin, the other side presenting him with an embroidered vest and underpants. They got back to London in time for another gay ceremony, the wedding of Princess Maud, daughter of the Princess Royal, to Lord Carnegie.

Meantime all was not going as well as had been hoped with White Lodge. Progress was slow on improvements that were judged essential, and boilers and pipes littered the place.

In many ways the Yorks were finding White Lodge unsuitable as a home. It was too rambling, too expensive to run, and staff was a problem. Each time they had an engagement in the centre of London an extra hour had to be allowed for travelling. On one occasion they had been lost in the fog. Perhaps most telling was the lack of privacy, for the royal newlyweds were looked upon as a peep show by many who roamed the Park.

So the Duke, ever keen on his hunting, took a house at Guilsborough, Northamptonshire, for a few months. He and his wife would often motor to London and back to keep an engagement. It was a long day, but they were young, and the Duke was happy. Returning to White Lodge, with duties becoming more and more onerous as the summer approached, the disadvantages of commuting from Richmond became obvious. It was then that Princess Mary and Lord Lascelles offered to lend them their London home, Chesterfield House. With relief the Duke and Duchess moved in.

The early summer of 1924 was one mad rush for royalties. In May the King and Queen of Rumania arrived in London and two thousand guests were at the State Ball, the Duchess lovely in her full dress. The King and Queen of Italy followed, and then Ras

Tafari, Prince Regent of Ethiopia, later Emperor Haile Selassie, whom the Duke greeted at Victoria. Then there was the opening of the Wembley Exhibition. The Duke and Duchess paid a return visit with the Prince of Wales. They headed for the amusement park. The Prince and his sister-in-law sat together in the front seat of car No. 2 of the Giant Switchback. Wind-blown, thrilled, gripping the bar before them, the picture taken at the moment of start is one of the most pleasing in existence of the couple together.

She brought a touch of the light fantastic to engagements that had meant heavy going through the plough to the Duke before he met her. The Press dubbed her 'The Smiling Duchess'. Reporters described her as all 'sunshine and blue eyes'. She was a riot when she had tea with local children at the opening of the Dockland Settlement Club in Canning Town. The Duke was buoyed up by the new spirit of her when he attended the Boy Scouts' Jamboree at Wembley with Lord Baden-Powell and when he drove a tram through the crowded streets of Glasgow.

In July they were together in Northern Ireland. It was the first visit by members of the Royal Family since the King had opened the first Parliament three years earlier. They travelled from Belfast to Londonderry. When it was over the Duke wrote to his father: 'Elizabeth has been marvellous as usual & all the people simply love her already. I am very lucky to have her to help me as she knows exactly what to do & say to all the people we meet. . . .'

It was the lightness in her, and her sense of humour, that were acting as an antidote to the feeling of inferiority deep inside of him. He was finding it strange that engagements that once had proved such an effort to him could be dealt with as an ordinary way of life.

They were driving through crowded Manchester streets to a hospital. A young constable was on duty. He got the fleeting impression that the royal lady had something suckable in her mouth. Fascinated, he took a longer look. The Duchess saw him. She opened the window and threw something towards him. He caught it. It was a caramel.

9 Duchess on Safari

IN the autumn of 1924 the Duke and Duchess of York lived in a world of rifles and ciné cameras, maps and guide books, tropical shirts and drill suits, inoculations and medicines, for they were to escape the English winter on an East African journey, part official, more holiday. They left London on 1st December, bound for Paris and Marseilles. Captain Basil Brooke, Lieutenant-Commander Colin Buist and Lady Annaly went with them. This was to be something very new to both of them, and probably the greatest adventure of their lives.

On the 5th they embarked at Marseilles on the P. and O. liner *Mulbera*, as ordinary passengers, at least as ordinary as the crew and their fellow travellers would allow them to be. As far as Port Said the weather was filthy. By the 16th they had reached Aden, where they played the tourist. Then the 'first timers' crossed the Line, with all the attendant horrors for him of being shaved with a wooden razor and chucked into a tank. It was therefore galling to the Duke that when he crossed the Line the second time, he was to be blandly informed that the first experience did not count as he was only a passenger at the time. They came to Mombasa on the 22nd. They were at once tipped straight into the whirl of African life. The Duchess was dressed in cream with a neat white helmet.

There was lunch at Government House, and then a drive among the baobab trees to a wide open space where, as one description put it, 'uncouthly bedizened natives danced wildly for their delectation'. There were five thousand participants in this festival named *ngoma*. As they had been prancing for three days their movements were by now somewhat rhythmically drunk and unorthodox. Some had gilt

After the wedding. The Earl and
Countess of Strathmore, the Duke
and Duchess of York, King George
V and Queen Mary

he Prince of Wales bids goodbye
the Duchess of York at the start
the tour of New Zealand and
ustralia in 1927

Fishing in New Zealand

crowns bedecked with lighted candles on their heads. In many cases a grass skirt was the only addition to the form in which they had been made. Tom-toms beat and horns howled, and the only parallel for the Duchess from her back life was when she and her brother David, dressed as Red Indians, had raided the kitchen at Glamis. To remember the day they received a gold coin on a red ribbon and an Address thrust into the hollowed out tusk of an elephant. Then they set off in the Governor's special train for Nairobi.

Railways had always fascinated the Duke. He liked to drive engines. Now he was able to study at first hand one of the most enthralling chapters in railway history, the Uganda trunk line, built a quarter of a century before with over five million pounds of British taxpayers' money. Its gradients of one in fifty take it up to 7,600 feet. The men who built it opened up Kenya and the heart of Africa.

For 300 miles they watched, entranced, a country entirely strange to them, a land untouched by man's hands. Sixty miles away to the south the snows of Kilimanjaro reached the sky. When they came to the Athi Plain and the Government Game Preserve, they moved to a seat placed in front of the engine, so that they could watch more closely the baboons and the zebra, the ostrich and the wildebeeste.

There was an official duty to be performed in Nairobi, the opening of a new city park. The only normal thing about Christmas Day was the service in the English Church and the traditional theme of the sermon by the Bishop of Mombasa. The Duke and Duchess then went to an assembly where two thousand natives were at worship, and they received a copy of the Kiswahili prayer book. After a garden party at Government House, they watched a film.

They drove north to Embu, into the empty spaces and the private days to which they had so looked forward. They ran into a cloud burst. Five inches of rain fell on them in half an hour. It was touch and go whether they got through the fords. War dancers were waiting for them at their harbour. They spent the night in a circle of little huts. Next morning it was still raining. They set off for Meru. The water in the rivers rose and rose. It penetrated too deeply into the engine of one of the cars. It was beyond cure, and had to be abandoned. Seven people went on in one Buick.

After a rest and a dry the real safari began. They travelled lightly and lived in tents. Each morning they were up soon after five. They trudged on until the high sun told them it was time to rest. Daily they moved on until they reached their goal, Siola. There was so much for the Duchess to photograph, the vista out towards distant Mount Kenya, the glorious butterflies, the richly coloured birds. But it was the nights that were the magic. When the curtain fell the blue-black velvet of them was just beyond the tent flap. The coolness smoothed away the tiredness, the discomforts, the bruises of the day. The few lights burned and one by one went out. The silence was an experience on its own. Then a lion would roar, a hyena cry, and the zebras gallop by.

The Duchess was a good shot. Her rifle was a ·275 Rigby. She practised hard and seriously. She needed to. If she met a lion behind a bush, it was a case of who moved first, and no handicap for H.R.H.s. In fact the types of animal she had killed by the time the tour was over read like a sign post in a zoo. But when she was told that rhinos were scarce in the area, she laid her Rigby down.

Forty years ago there was not the same scarcity of wild animals as there is in Africa today nor was there the same attitude towards the shooting of them. The success of a safari was judged by the bag. Sir John Wheeler-Bennett quotes from the Duke's diary: 'We found one Oryx alone shortly afterwards & we got up to him within 200 yds by keeping a tree between us & him. I took a rest off the tree & fired & hit him. He was facing me. He went off & we followed & I hit him 3 more times when he lay down. I was going to finish him off when we saw a Rhino on the edge of a thick patch of bush. We forgot about the Oryx & went after the Rhino. We followed him into the bush & suddenly came upon not one but 2 Rhinos lying down in the thickest part of the bush 8 yds away. One got up towards us & Anderson fired & killed it. I did not fire as I could not see him properly. It was most exciting. The other one ran away. After this we went back & finished off the Oryx. It was very hot by now at 11.30 & we were glad of the mules to ride home on. Elizabeth came out with us in the afternoon after tea to look at the Rhino.'

News of the activities of the Duke and Duchess filtered back to the Press at home, and became rather garbled in the process. The experience recounted above became a narrow shave from death for the royal hunter at the end of a tusk of a charging rhino. Criticism began. Some people said that the shooting of animals was wrong in itself, and royalty should not partake in it. Some said that it was a man's sport, and not a woman's. Some were of the opinion that the wilds of Africa were no place for the King's only daughter-in-law, nearly two years wed and yet without a child. Some thought that the second eldest of the Princes should not expose himself to such obvious dangers. Among these was the King, already worried by the frequent appearances of the Prince of Wales in point-to-point races. And there were some who were most concerned by the belief that the Duke was shooting game on the Sabbath. It was in answer to this last criticism that the Duke telegraphed back that, firstly the incident complained of had not happened on a Sunday, secondly, he had not shot a rhinoceros, and thirdly, that he doubted if rhinos knew which day was Sunday. But in his letters to his father he was more circumspect, for the King was keeping as close and as critical an eye on him as had Queen Victoria when her eldest son, another 'Bertie', had visited America in 1860.

After five weeks of living rough they returned to the comforts of Nairobi. By now the Duchess was an experienced hunter. She had learned how to act when a sudden wind took the tent covering from over her. She knew how to smile when the camp was flooded, when sodden possessions had to be rescued from the chocolate mud and it was everyone for himself in the blind man's buff of the pelting rain.

They set out west towards Uganda. They found an oasis of comfort at the lovely home of Lord and Lady Francis Scott at Rongai. Lord Scott was a son of the sixth Duke of Buccleuch. Ten years later the families were to be connected by marriage, when Lady Alice, daughter of the seventh Duke, married Prince Henry, Duke of Gloucester.

On 15th February they said goodbye to Kenya, regretfully for they had come to love the country. They sailed from Kisumu on the steamer *Clement Hill* into wide Lake Victoria Nyanza, calling at Jinja to see the Ripon Falls and the supposed source of the Nile. Next day they reached Entebbe, the seat of British Government.

Now scene after scene of fascination followed for the Duchess.

83

At Kampala, the native capital set on seven hills, she saw her husband invest King Daudi, the Kabaka of Buganda, with the K.C.M.G. She sat in a splendid pavilion while warriors danced before her. She moved on into the valley of Semliki where King Solomon's men collected ivory, apes and peacocks for the Queen of Sheba. She and her husband attended a native parliament, and listened to a lengthy recitation about their thousand good qualities. They came to the shores of Lake Albert. The Duchess was tanned, tired and waging a constant war with mosquitoes. At Butiaba they boarded the *Samuel Baker*, a shallow draught steamer needing only four feet of water. They were soon to find out how she rolled. It was so hot that the party all slept on deck.

The Duke, whose eyes were firmly fixed on his sport, went off after more game. His wife excused herself and stayed put on the *Samuel Baker*. She sat by the rail and fished.

They sailed off over the wide waters to the north and, where the shore lines narrowed, joined the White Nile, which is fed by the overflow of Lake Albert. Here was a new and appealing experience. The *Samuel Baker* was more a water bus than a royal yacht. There were frequent stops at bankside villages. There was the excitement of passengers embarking and disembarking, the urgency of goods being loaded and unloaded—ivory and cotton, hides and tusks, timber and potware. On the sand the crocs and the hippos slept in the sun. On the banks the piccaninnies screamed with delight and the warriors rested on their spears. Everybody came to see the passing of the *Samuel Baker*.

Then, in those tricky waters, the rudder post was bent. All night long the crew struggled to make repairs. There was something here for the Duchess of the ordeal which Katherine Hepburn endured in the film, 'The African Queen'.

On 5th March the *Samuel Baker* reached Nimule, on the southern tip of the Sudan. Here the mode of transport was switched from river steamer to Ford cars, as now the Nile falls in fierce cascade from the plateau to the plain. It was a very bumpy hundred miles to Rejaf. But for the next thousand miles to Khartoum they travelled in the comfortable steamer, *Nasir*, luxury indeed after the experiences of recent weeks. The banks went interminably by. It was scorchingly hot. Sudd, sudd, sudd. They tied up where landings were practicable and went off after game. It was not until after the long haul to Tonga where the river turns east before the Nuba Mountains, that their first break came. They motored up into the hills to witness a march past of twelve thousand Nubian warriors. There were displays of spear throwing, dancing and wrestling. For the combats the giant antagonists wore belts hung with the tails of monkeys and Nubian what-have-yous. The Duke was delighted to see that the rules were strictly adhered to. Further on, at Kodok, the local ruler arrived with gifts—a shield for the Duchess. He excelled himself in the display which he staged. There was a 'lion' dance, the performers wearing masks and tails, and a mock battle during which a wary eye had to be kept on airborne assegais.

There was one more sight to be seen, and that of a very contrasting nature, before the royal travellers reached Khartoum. Where the waters widened at Kosti they landed and entrained for Sennar. The Makwar Irrigation Dam across the Blue Nile was nearing completion. It was to water hundreds of thousands of acres of cotton-growing country. To see the Duchess that day, in her broad-brimmed white hat and carrying a parasol, she might have been at a garden party in England instead of nearing the end of a trek from Mombasa. Khartoum came into sight on 7th April. The name of it had been written in blood across the heart of Queen Victoria. Gordon need not have died if her warnings had been heeded. There was a very different picture for her great-grandson and his wife. There were triumphal arches along Victoria Street. There was an evening reception in the beautiful gardens, and the night was full of lights.

Two days later they climbed the gangway of the liner *Maloja* at Port Sudan. The hard days were over, or so they thought. But in the Suez Canal a sand storm enveloped them and held them up twelve hours.

It was at twenty minutes past three on the afternoon of Sunday, 19th April, that the Duke and Duchess of York came back to London. The Princess Royal and Lord Lascelles were waiting to greet them. Lord Annaly was there to claim back his bronzed and toughened wife. The great adventure was over.

The width of vision and experience that the journey had bestowed on the Duchess was to prove invaluable. She was now able to talk of things she had seen and done, not only heard and read. She had learned that the initials 'H.R.H.' always apply. On occasions she had come in tired, dirty from safari and been called on, in a matter of but a few minutes, to appear at an official reception, cool, smiling, perfectly turned out. Everywhere she had travelled her courage and tenacity had been admired. She had trekked fifteen miles and more at a stretch. She had been up to her waist in mud and water. She had helped to put up her tent when it blew down and dried out her sodden clothes. She had shot for her supper. The praise, and the smile, of her echoed back from Mombasa and Nairobi, Entebbe and Khartoum.

10 'Lilibet' and Logue

THE demands on the Duke and Duchess of York in the summer of 1925 were prodigious. In her case it was the famous smile that was required to spot-light great occasions. In his, his deep knowledge of industrial matters. He was known as 'the Industrial Prince'. His brothers called him 'the Foreman'.

Their many duties centred round the British Empire Exhibition. For its second year the Duke had succeeded his elder brother as president, the opening ceremony being at Wembley on 10th May. They were there for other occasions, the Cup Final, with Mr. Ramsay MacDonald for company, the Sheep Dog Trials, with the Duchess making a very personal appearance among the competitors, and the day when ten thousand children from London County Council schools flooded the Exhibition, their roar of acclamation in the great arena nearly deafening the Royal couple.

In June they paid an official visit to Dudley in Worcestershire, staying with Lord and Lady Ednam. The Duchess's big moment was when she was turned loose in the children's section of the Guest Hospital. For the Duke it was when he was allowed to drive a miniature train at a bazaar.

The North saw much of them. On 24th June, in York Minster, the Duchess spoke these words: 'As an act of most high praise and glad thanksgiving to Almighty God for the lives and devotion of the 1,400 women of the Empire who died for their country in the War, now in the name of their sisters in all parts of the world I unveil and restore to its ancient use the Five Sisters Window.'

The danger of damage by bomb had made necessary the removal of the mediaeval glass from the series of lancet windows in the north

87

transept. It had now been returned, and restoration work completed, the cost being borne by the women of the country. The *Yorkshire Herald* commented: 'She most certainly captivated us all at York yesterday, and there is no one who is not proud to think that she bears the name of our historic and wonderful city.'

Then on to the Railway Centenary celebrations, which were drawing steam enthusiasts from all over the world to Darlington. The Duke and Duchess watched from a grandstand at Urlaynook, on the Stockton–Darlington line. Past them puffed a six miles long procession of every type of engine and carriage from the days of George Stephenson to the modern *Flying Scotsman*.

Their East African tour led to other engagements, rich in reminiscence. They dined with the African Society and, through her connection with the Women's section of the British Empire Exhibition, the Duchess attended a garden party at Lowther Lodge to meet visitors from Kenya, Uganda and other territories. At the Kodak works at Wealdstone a showing was given of the Yorks' journey from Mombasa to Khartoum. A picture of his wife in khaki shirt and shorts convulsed the Duke. Sartorially it was unique.

Glamis and Balmoral claimed them in August and September and when they returned to London it was to a new headquarters, Curzon House in Curzon Street. They planned to move into their parents' house, 17, Bruton Street, in the New Year. People were beginning to say that it was a strange state of affairs when the second son of the King had not his own house in London.

On 19th November the message came from Sandringham that Queen Alexandra had suffered a severe heart attack. The Prince of Wales and the Duke of York were asked to hurry to her bedside. There was no time to lose. The Prince was in Cardiff, the Duke in Leicestershire. The next day the Duke, leaving his wife behind, and his brother took train to Norfolk. Fog came down over East Anglia, shrouding the 'Big House' at Sandringham and blotting out the signals on the railway line. At each station the Princes asked for news. Friday afternoon wore on. A solitary policeman stood guard at the Norwich gates. An under-gardener swept away at the leaves. Headlamps made white lines through the dusk as two cars left to bring the Princes from Wolferton. At 5.25 the blinds of Sandringham came down. One by one the lights went out. Now only a lantern burned, to guide in the car which bore two future kings. They came out of the fog to the still house knowing that their grandmother was dead. They had lost their race to say goodbye.

Alexandra the Loved had gone. An age had ended. And as it ended, a new age began. It became known that H.R.H. the Duchess of York was to become a mother in the spring.

A nursery was prepared at Bruton Street. Nurse Knight, who had cared for the Duchess in her own childhood, was warned of duties ahead. In the intervening years 'Alah', as she was called, had been looking after the children of the Duchess's sister, Lady Elphinstone.

Doctors began to call at No. 17. Those to care for the Duchess were Sir H. Simson, of the Hospital for Women; Sir G. Blacker, consulting obstetric physician, University College Hospital; and Mr. W. Jagger, of the Samaritan Hospital for Women. The child was born at twenty minutes to three on the morning of Wednesday, 21st April 1926. It was a difficult birth and a Caesarean section was necessary.

There was little sleep at Windsor that night. The King had instructed that he was to be told when news came through. A little more than an hour after the birth he and the Queen were awakened by knocks and told that they had a granddaughter, and that all was well.

One of the first people to see the baby was Sir William Joynson-Hicks, the Home Secretary, who was in attendance to see that no trickery took place and that the child was the true offspring of the parents. This custom dated back to the days of James II and the 'warming-pan plot'. The Duchess was to make history, for she was to be the last mother of a Sovereign so to be pried upon. When Prince Charles was born, George VI requested that the Home Secretary should waive his historic duty.

All through the day of 21st April a crowd stood outside the grey façade of 17, Bruton Street. It was raining, but they did not seem to care. They could not have hoped to see the Duchess or her baby, but there were notable callers to watch. Momentarily, the silhouette of the Duke appeared behind the gauze curtains on the first floor, and then disappeared. A burst of cheering burst forth, and faded out. Then a neat, trim nurse looked down into the street. She knew the answer to the question that they all wanted to know. She just nodded and gave a reassuring smile before she withdrew.

The King and Queen arrived by car from Windsor. They went up to see the baby. Their comment was that she was a little darling, with a lovely complexion and pretty fair hair. Later the Duke opened his heart, or at least as much of it as was considered fit and proper in the family of George V, to his mother. He admitted that all Elizabeth and he needed to make their happiness complete was a child. And she had wanted a girl. Now he found himself with mixed feelings of wonder and strangeness, with overriding pride of the courage which his wife had shown in the past few difficult days.

There came the question of names for the baby. Both parents were set on 'Elizabeth Alexandra Mary'. 'Elizabeth of York' sounded so nice, and the other two were obvious compliments. The King gave his blessing, although the fact that Victoria was omitted did not escape him. The christening was set for 29th May in the chapel at Buckingham Palace. In the interim the Duke was kept busy with the affairs of the General Strike, a crisis which the King, in compliment to his son's close knowledge of industry, said belonged to 'the Duke of York's department'.

The silver-gilt font, eighteen inches high and adorned with cherubs, was brought from the Chapel Royal at Windsor. It had been made in 1840 for the christening of Queen Victoria's eldest child, Victoria the Princess Royal, later to become Empress Frederick of Germany and the mother of Kaiser Wilhelm. It has been used on so many occasions since then, including the christenings of the children of Queen Elizabeth II. On the day of its first use Prince Albert reported: 'The child behaved with great propriety, like a Christian. She was awake, but did not cry at all, and seemed to crow with immense satisfaction at the lights and the brilliant uniforms, for she is very intelligent and observant. The ceremony took place at 6.30 p.m., and after it there was a dinner, and then we had some instrumental music. The health of the little one was drunk with great enthusiasm.' There were to be some contrasts in the scene of 1926.

It was a Saturday and the sun was shining as the Duchess left

Bruton Street, the nurse, carrying the baby, behind her. The Princess was christened, in water from the River Jordan, by the Archbishop of York. The godparents were King George and Queen Mary, Princess Mary, the Duke of Connaught, the Earl of Strathmore and Lady Elphinstone. The christening robe was of Brussels lace. It had previously been worn by the children of Queens Victoria, Alexandra and Mary, and by Princess Mary's son. On the top of Princess Elizabeth's christening cake was a tiny silver cradle in the shape of a shell, a baby doll resting within. At the end of the day Queen Mary recorded: 'Of course poor baby cried.'

Now began the reign of Princess Lilibet. There were Lilibet hats and rompers, Lilibet cakes and dolls. Her every action was reported. Her pram excursions became royal processions. And once she could talk, the sayings attributed to her were legion. As Queen Maud had done in the case of Prince Olaf, the Duchess kept a scrap book of the things Lilibet was supposed to have said, and had not. In August the baby Princess was taken to the peace of Glamis. There her time was divided between the old nursery and the Dutch garden which Lady Strathmore had designed.

Amid the fun and interest of looking after her child, the Duchess had two pressing problems to face. The first was one of domestic convenience. The time had come when she must have a house of her own. With a nursery to cope with, moving from one borrowed house to another was an impossible situation. A London home, and a permanent one, must be found. The search eventually ended at 145, Piccadilly. Even then it was obvious that a great deal of work and decoration were necessary before it would be ready for occupation.

The second problem was connected with the impediment in the Duke's speech, and here a hiatus had been reached. It came about over the proposal that the Duke and Duchess should pay an official visit to Australia and New Zealand. The Duke had long wanted to make the trip. He had put out feelers at the Imperial Conference of 1923, but the King had considered it too early. He thought that the impediment might prove too great a handicap, and inside himself he hoped that married life would lead, if not to a complete cure, at least to a betterment. Yet the change that had been hoped for had not come to pass. Now the Australian Premier, Mr. Stanley Bruce,[1] asked the King if one of his sons would open the new Parliament House at Canberra.

The building of the new Federated Capital at Canberra was a project very close to the King's heart, for in 1901 he had opened the first session of the new Dominion's Parliament in Melbourne. Shortly afterwards it had been decided that a site for a new capital should be found, and Lord Denman laid the foundation stones of Canberra in 1913. A further foundation stone, that of the Capitol, was laid by the Prince of Wales in 1920. Now the King dearly wished one of his sons to be present at the realization of the vast plan that had been but a dream quarter of a century before. The obvious choice was the Duke of York. But the King was still uncertain as to whether the impediment in his son's speech would not be a stumbling block in the way of his success on such an important mission. And, coupled with this, was the fear that the resultant strain might bring a recurrence of past weaknesses in his health. For Mr. Bruce, who heard the Duke speak on several occasions while in Britain in 1926, the doubts were even deeper.

The Duke described his stammer as 'the curse that God has put upon me'. But there was another curse, gastric trouble, that had first showed itself during his hard apprenticeship days at Osborne. It was to blight his youth. A month after war was declared in 1914 he had to be transferred from his ship and landed at Aberdeen. There he was operated on for appendicitis. The pains continued. Early in 1915 he got to sea again, but nine months later had to consent to being put ashore once more. Alarming rumours about his health began to appear in the newspapers, but he managed to rejoin *Collingwood* in time for the battle of Jutland. Thereafter he spent dreary weeks on a hospital ship in Scapa Flow. He made one more brave attempt to continue his naval career. He joined the battleship *Malaya*. On 7th November 1917 it was officially announced that the Duke's health was such that it would not be possible for him to resume duty at sea. A relapse followed and on the 29th he was operated on for duodenal ulcer. He had fought against the trouble long and bravely, and the operation was severe. Not only was his chosen career finally over, but it was

[1] 1st Viscount Bruce of Melbourne.

realized, perhaps not seriously enough, that the Duke would for a long time, if not always, have to guard his health carefully.

His other curse, the stammer, had been with him since the schoolroom. It evinced itself in the difficulty he found in pronouncing certain initial letters, such as K and Q, G and N. That was why he spoke of his parents as 'Their Majesties' instead of King and Queen. He was embittered by experiences such as this. Soon after he arrived at Dartmouth he was asked, in front of the class, what fraction was half of a half. Although he knew the answer full well the Q of quarter simply would not come. His teacher thought he was backward and did not know the answer. He sat down to the sniggers of his class mates.

Handicaps which call for sympathy in the children of commoners are apt to be looked upon as an oddity and a subject for comment when they appear in Princes. Particularly was this the case with 'Bertie', outshone by the brilliant promise of his elder brother and the high spirits of his sister Mary. When he met people he was, as a Royal, by etiquette bound to open the conversation. He, poor boy, never knew, even if he managed to open a sentence, whether he would ever be able to finish it. He became shy, withdrew inside himself. People thought him diffident. They never knew of the hours of despair he spent by himself, wondering if he would ever make the grade demanded of the son of King George V.

The stammer showed little in the course of ordinary conversation with family or friends. It was when there was an audience before him or when he was flustered that the trouble began. That was why there were outbursts of Teck temper when programmes, carefully prepared for, were suddenly altered. It was this stammer at times of crisis that had led to the stories that he had first sent a friend round with his proposal of marriage to Lady Elizabeth Bowes-Lyon, but that she had demanded a personal appearance. Also that, when he did brace himself for the moment, words failed him and he had to fall back on a slip of paper. But then it was also said that on this memorable occasion he took an axe with him into the wood. The purpose was unexplained.

By the time of his marriage the Duke appeared to have recovered his full physical strength. His performance on the East African tour allayed any lingering doubts, and certainly did him a great deal of good. In 1926 there came proof of his fitness, and a proud moment for the Duchess. He played in the Doubles Championship at Wimbledon, with Wing-Commander Louis Greig as partner. They played veterans A. W. Gore and H. Roper Barrett, who won after an exciting match. The physical side being obviously satisfactory, there remained the stammer to conquer, and this became both a challenge and a necessity to the Duke and his wife.

The Duchess had proved of the greatest help. Her support and gay companionship had prevented him from becoming the retiring, introvert personality that is so often the fate of those plagued with an impediment. She helped him with his speeches, suggested alternatives to words with awkward initial letters, let the lighter side of life work as an antidote to nerves. When she was beside him when he spoke, she could will the words into him and the touch of her hand gave him the confidence that was so essential. But she could not play the role of mentor on every occasion and the Duke, to use his own words, continued to 'struggle through'.

A testing moment was his speech at the opening of the Wembley Exhibition in 1925. He had to stand in the centre of the arena and speak into the microphones. The day for rehearsal came. It was no less of an ordeal than if the seats had been full, but there was to be a lighter side. The Duke suddenly realized that the microphones were dead. The electricians came to the same conclusion at the same moment, and switched on. As they did so the Duke's furious voice echoed through the stadium—'The damned things aren't working!' Next day, although there were considerable pauses, he got through better than he had expected.

Every remedial measure known to the doctors had been tried in an effort to cure the stammer. Experiments had been made with the known methods of voice production and training. In all the Duke had seen nine specialists. In each case they had come to the conclusion that the root trouble was mental, the cause—nerves. The Duke accepted their findings, and with the acceptance came an increasing lack of confidence. Yet, in fact, nerves were the effect, and not the cause. His experience to date did not encourage him to search for further help and he had reached a stage when he was convinced that he must fight on as best he could. Yet, with the Australian tour looming up, his advisers were anxious to make one more effort. Word came from America of an expert in speech who was achieving brilliant results, and an equerry was about to leave to consult him when the Duke's Private Secretary met a Mr. Lionel Logue.

Mr. Logue was an expert in speech defects who had come from Australia two years before and now practiced in Harley Street. Born in Adelaide in 1880 and educated at the Prince Alfred College there, his first leanings were towards engineering. Experiences in World War One aroused his interest in the cure of speech impediments and he discovered that he had particular powers in this direction. Later his system of diaphragm breathing effected seemingly miraculous cure among children in Perth.[1]

When the proposition was first put to the Duke that he should see Mr. Logue, he was against it. His attitude was, 'Oh no, not all that over again.' He had had more than sufficiency of being told about his mental state and his nerves. It was the Duchess who won him over. She pointed out that there was much at stake and it was worth another try.

Mr. Logue began in an unorthodox way when it came to Palace procedure. He insisted that the Duke came to him. That entailed the patient making an effort of his own free will.

At three o'clock on the afternoon of 19th April 1926 H.R.H. the Duke of York entered the consulting room in Harley Street. Mr. Logue saw 'a slim, quiet man, with tired eyes, and all the outward symptoms of the man upon whom habitual speech defect had begun to set'. They were together for two hours. The Duke was told that he could be cured, but it would need a terrific effort on his part, and without that effort nothing could be done. But when he left at five o'clock it was obvious that there was hope once more in his heart. And in the Duchess's a feeling of overwhelming relief.

The Duke put himself entirely in Mr. Logue's hands. He attended the consulting room for an hour every day during the ten weeks before

---

[1] Mr. Logue was one of the original founders and Treasurer of the British Society of Speech Therapists, 1935; Founder Fellow of the College of Speech Therapists; and Speech Therapist to the Royal Masonic School, Bushey.

he was due to leave for Australia, and very often the Duchess was with him, so that she could learn the details of the cure. In addition the Duke had to find time, amid all the multifarious duties necessary before the tour, for one or two hours practice in sound and breathing exercises daily.

Mr. Logue had diagnosed that the trouble lay with the lack of co-ordination between the brain and the diaphragm. He therefore posed a practical problem to the patient, something that could be gripped upon, instead of the nebulous spectre of nerves. Mr. Logue gave out a deep seated confidence. He presented stammering as a curable complaint, and not as an oddity in a person. That his impediment could be done away with, like measles, was a new approach for the Duke. After only a month of treatment the Duchess could easily see the improvement in her husband's voice and the nightmare of the Ks and Qs, the Gs and the Ns, becoming less terrifying. But a lifetime of wrong practice was obviously going to take much putting right. Breathing had to be learned all over again. Mr. Logue was to remain at the Duke's right hand for many years to come.

Meantime the Duchess had to spend much of her time at the dressmakers. She had been able to keep her wardrobe down to more or less the bare necessities for her East African trip, but a full-blown tour of New Zealand and Australia was a very different matter. She was a 'new girl' in couture of this range and size. Fortunately it would be summer 'down under', leaving her free to indulge her love for light colourings and fabrics. But the brow at Bruton Street was not only furrowed by problems of Mr. Logue's exercises and the colour for that frock and the material for that coat. There was another headache and a heartache—the leaving behind of baby Elizabeth, but eight months old.

Mother and daughters in the doorway of the main entrance to Glamis Castle

Coronation Day, 12th May 1937. *Above*, Queen Elizabeth and her Ladies leave Westminster Abbey; *below*, on the balcony of Buckingham Palace

11 New Zealand

AT Christmas, 1926, the Royal Family gathered together at Sandringham. It was an historic occasion, on a number of counts. Firstly, King George was home again in 'the Big house', after a third of a century of cramped living in the Cottage where the lawns sweep down to the lake. Two months before Queen Mary and he had moved in on the ghost of Queen Alexandra, clearing away the mass of memories that 'Mother-dear' had piled into every corner of every room. Secondly, it was a case of 'hail and farewell', celebration mixed with the sadness of parting, for the Duke and Duchess of York, so soon to be on their way to New Zealand and Australia. And thirdly, it was very much a case of 'hail' for the newest member of the Family, for Princess Elizabeth was fittingly spending the first Christmas of her life at Sandringham.

It was a time of many memories. Twenty-six years before the King and Queen, then the Duke and Duchess of Cornwall and York, had also been preparing to leave for Australia and making arrangements for their children, the youngest the same age as 'Lilibet', to stay with their grandparents. So Queen Mary was in a particular position to be able to understand the wrench that now faced the Duchess.

Christmas had always been a gala fête in the gay days of Sandringham. In the ballroom trestle tables flanked an enormous tree and King Edward and his Queen themselves handed out the presents. But as they chattered ceaselessly in competition with one another, explaining how gadgets worked and how they could be used, and Gottlieb's band was playing at the same time, gasping recipients could hardly find an opening to say 'Thank you'. The servants each

G
97

drew two tickets as they entered. The Princesses went off to find the relevant presents, but as the Queen, wearing distorting spectacles to add to the fun, was throwing about crackers and sweets, things were apt to become mixed. Housemaids ended up with shaving brushes and footmen with make-up.

Such levity had not been inherited by the following generation and now the starlight was on the baby Princess. Her mother gave her a string of coral beads. They fascinated her, and were for long a treasured possession.

From Norfolk the Yorks travelled to St. Paul's Walden Bury, where the Princess was to spend January. There the memories flooded back to the Duchess. She said goodnight to her daughter in that same old nursery, with the faded pictures, that the gardener had framed, on the walls, with the firelight shining through the tracery of the high guard and the shadows flitting over the screen of scraps. Even Nurse Knight was there. When the final moment of parting came there was a little scene that, in the Duchess's own words, 'quite broke me up'. 'Lilibet' was playing with the buttons on her father's uniform, twisting them, fascinated by their brightness. It was as if she did not want him to go.

The King and Queen, and a great many other people, went to Victoria station to see them off. The Duke's three brothers travelled with them to Portsmouth, where lay the battle-cruiser *Renown*. On deck they said goodbye. The Duchess kissed the Prince of Wales. The Duke's standard broke at the main. The great blue and white ship of war, in which the Prince of Wales had travelled so many thousands of miles, moved almost imperceptibly away. Music came softly from the band of Marines, in their white helmets, and *Renown* headed into a path of golden sunshine leading to the south.

A cheer went up, for the little Duchess was to be seen on the promenade deck which had been contrived above the royal quarters. She was smiling radiantly and a handkerchief was in her hand. She looked very small beside her husband. There they stood, waving at the three royal brothers and the crowd, until the distance swallowed them.

The toots of the ferry boats died out, the crowds turned away from the Solent's shores, and *Renown* settled down to ocean routine.

For the Duke it was like coming home. He knew the waters and the way of life. But for the Duchess a warship was a very new experience and she learned the harder side when a snorter of a gale blew up on the second day out. She kept on walking.

First, she set about settling in with the members of the royal party. These consisted of the Earl of Cavan, as Chief of Staff, the Duke's personal secretary, Mr. P. Hodgson, Sir Harry Fagg Batterbee, political secretary, and Commander H. White, medical adviser. The Duke's Equerries were Lieutenant-Commander Colin Buist, who had been with them in East Africa, and Major T. Nugent. The Duchess's Ladies-in-Waiting were Lady Cavan and the Hon. Mrs. Little Gilmour. Then she began the exploration of *Renown*, peeping into every corner and meeting the crew. She got full marks in the engine room for turning down the offer of overalls.

Little tea parties began amid the blue chintz of her after-cabin. They were very much of her own devising, bringing with them the intimacy of the British home. The Duke was chivvied about to find room for chairs and pass cakes. Team spirit was born, and lasted. When the sun came she was an enthusiast for deck games to keep fit and she took on the unofficial role of dancing mistress.

This tour was to be for the Duchess so much more than just a State visit. She was to circle the world and all of the way, except the last leg, was new to her. If it had taken place thirty, forty years later, she would have slept, eaten, drowsed in a big jet, seen only airports that were all the same bar the temperature. As it was, the change came steadily. She moved from one little world to another little world, with a lot of water in between. And to the people in each little world their habitat was the focal point of the universe. So the Duchess moved over stepping stones of relative values, and thus was a far wiser woman when she reached her goal.

Teneriffe and 12,000 feet high Teide showed on 10th January and then the outline of the Grand Canary. That afternoon *Renown*'s salute of twenty-one guns roared out over Las Palmas, and the shore batteries answered. No greater contrast could be imagined than between Las Palmas then and now. The Duke and Duchess landed and jolted through the pot holes, amid the goats, the mantillas and the slow tram cars, to visit the Seamen's Home and to meet the

99

members of the British community. It was just a short, exciting entry in her log.

Jamaica next, and an uproarious reception in the sunshine. The Mayor of Kingston had an address of welcome ready in a casket, but he had forgotten the key. The Duke, beamingly, accepted the casket as it was. The pace of the programme was fast, including a dinner party given by the Governor, a tour of the island by car, and a dance, yet the Duke found time to visit Port Royal and furbish his facts on Nelsonia.

Then to Panama, and the twelve-hour passage through the canal, with the Duchess, fascinated, on the bridge for much of the time. She feared for the safety of the lock-keepers, perched on the edge of the gates. At Balboa she stayed at the Union Club until midnight, listening to hot American jazz. Next morning she decided to do some shopping in Panama, quietly and out of the limelight. She had underestimated her image. The Panamanian police rescued her.

Outward bound from America they came to the 'line' once more. Neptune had already sent a wireless message that he would be waiting for his special victims. The Duke argued that he had been 'done' before, but *Renown* would not accept an experience on a mere passenger ship, and he was 'done' again, this time with a distemper brush. He was invested with the copper collar of the Order of the Old Sea Dog. Honours varying from that of the Flattened Kipper to the Tainted Haddock were bestowed on other members of the party. The Duchess did not escape the attentions of the Sea King's horrid henchmen. But they treated her gently. She was anointed on the forehead with sea water and given the Order of the Golden Mermaid. Just in case, she had parasol at the ready. That night there was a cabaret show in a restaurant designed by the wardroom on the quarter-deck. The Duke and Duchess arrived in a 'taxi' which had been contrived from the two invalid-chairs that the Earl of Cavan had with him for use when his leg gave trouble.

They came to Nukahiva in the Marquesas Islands. The French administrator came aboard, the 'Marseillaise' was played and *Renown*'s guns thundered. The Duchess's introduction to a South sea island was peaceful. There were no receptions as the uniformed strength consisted of one *gendarme*. She went off on a fishing expedition with the Captain. She then arranged that the Marine band should play for the locals on shore, a performance that was highly appreciated. In return a festival of local dances was put on, in which there was much grunting and stamping, especially in the Pig Dance.

On 17th February *Renown* reached Suva, to be met by a fleet of Fijian war canoes. Here the women staged for the benefit of the Duchess the ceremony of Qalowaqa, two long lines of them garlanded with flowers drawing a war canoe across the lawn before her, an honour given only to chieftainesses of the highest rank. Then the warriors squatted on the ground and began to prepare in the battered wooden ceremonial bowl the local brew called *kava*, which it is the lot of visiting royalty to swallow. Strange-looking roots were battered to a pulp. In former times they were chewed to a slimy mass by the teeth of maidens, but the Duke was saved that. Coconut milk was added and the fluid strained through fibres. Dirges were intoned as the brewing proceeded, adding to the fear of the Duke. The taste is said to be unbelievably unpleasant. The Duke took the proffered cup, sipped, braced himself, and sunk the lot, as his father and his elder brother had before him. But he was not risking his wife, and begged that she be excused.

She felt more on her home ground next day when she went to the War Memorial Hospital and in the maternity ward played about with the brown babies. By this time her own was a guest at Buckingham Palace.

Presents were beginning to pile up in *Renown*. At Suva they received mats and bowls, water bottles and the teeth of whales, the value of each tooth being estimated locally as two wives. As they waved good-bye the airs of a Fijian song of farewell came to them across the water.

They reached New Zealand on 22nd February. There is only one way to describe their reception in Auckland—they were mobbed. It started on the water as the launch brought them in from *Renown*. On the quay the crowd broke through the police cordon. Then, as the royal Crossley, with hood down, moved towards the City Hall, swarming people brought it to a stop. It was the same story in the afternoon, when the Duke and Duchess tried to walk in Ellerslie

Gardens. In the throng the police caught occasional glimpses of her blue, close-fitting hat, well below the surface. It was even tougher for them at the drill display put on by fifteen thousand children. At the close they broke ranks and swamped the royal car. The Duchess's clothes were so fingered that some doubted if her wardrobe would stand up to the demands of the lengthy tour. When the visit was over they rejoined *Renown* and went to the Bay of Islands for some quiet fishing.

It took only a day to establish the popularity of the Duchess in New Zealand, and the fame of her spread quickly. Her smile, and the sparkle of her, made all types of people take her straight to their hearts. She was the perfect partner for the retiring, industrious and down-to-earth Duke. She won for herself a crown in North Island. Sir John Wheeler-Bennett tells a story, that came back via the Governor-General to King George V. Mr. Joseph Coates, Prime Minister of New Zealand, was talking to a well-known Communist agitator on the second day of the Auckland visit. He told Mr. Coates, 'I've done with this —— Communism.' On being asked the reason, he replied: 'Why, they're human! Yesterday I was in the crowd with the wife, and one of the children waved his hand, and I'm blessed if the Duchess didn't wave back and smile right into my face, not two yards away. I'll never say a word against them again. I've done with it for good and all.'

The Duchess had one advantage in New Zealand. The men who had been at Glamis in the war years had, by their tales, made ready the way before her. In her journey through North Island, she met many ex-servicemen. Among them was Sergeant Bennett, of the Black Watch, who had been with Captain Fergus Bowes-Lyon when he was killed at the Hohenzollern Redoubt. Some of the old boys of Glamis notified her of their whereabouts before she arrived at a stopping place, and she greeted them all with delight. But one was too shy. He just travelled hundreds of miles to be in the front rank of a crowd when she passed by. She spotted him and called him over. Then there was the scene that might have been—'Hullo, Charlie. Do you remember the rat hunt in the crypt?'

The Duke, too, had his moments of fun. As their train pulled slowly into a wayside station, he jumped off some way from the royal carriage and ran along with the crowd, completely unrecognized and cheering away loudly for the smiling Duchess who stood at her window. Whenever he was missing he was usually to be found with the driver on the engine.

From the Bay of Islands the Duke and Duchess travelled to the Rotorua district, the land of geysers and hot springs, the land of the Maoris. Here the forces of nature lie close below the surface. Prod a walking stick into the ground beside the path, and a hiss of steam is the answer. So quickly does the temperature change that it is possible to catch a trout in one pool and cook it in the next. They saw the geysers spout with clock-like precision, the mud springs gurgle, and the clouds of steam float down the valley. The human interest lay with the Maoris, for this was their chosen haunt. For the Duke and Duchess they performed their warrior dance, the *Haka*. They brought presents, including white feathers from the tail of the sacred huia bird, which bestowed upon the visitors the rank of chief and chieftainess of the Maoris. This was the speech of welcome for the Duchess. 'Daughter of an honoured House, Welcome! Welcome! Thus did that first Royal Duke appear before the eyes of our fathers, with his Lady! Welcome! The Second Duchess! Ha!'

On they went, the train taking them from Napier to Wellington, making new friends and meeting old ones, all the way. At Palmerston North an erstwhile shepherd from Sandringham was waiting to greet them. In three weeks they received over fifty addresses of welcome, met as many troops of Boy Scouts and Girl Guides. At Wellington the crowd at the Town Hall was so vociferous that the Duke needed all Mr. Logue's training to make himself heard.

It was when they reached South Island that the party noticed that the Duchess was not her usual smiling, talkative self. The road was hard and dusty. Arriving at Nelson she retired to her room for a rest. At midnight the doctor decided that, as far as she was concerned, the tour of South Island was off. She had a severe attack of tonsilitis and a high temperature. At first the Duke was inclined towards cancelling his programme and returning to Wellington with his wife. Being the kind of man he was, and having seen what he had seen, he thought that it was only the Duchess that the people wanted to see. But he was happily persuaded otherwise, and off he went to

Murchison and Greymouth, Ashburton and Dunedin, leaving his wife well cared for in her hotel.

Well cared for she certainly was. Fruit and flowers poured in from the townsfolk. There were as many enquiries as if a new baby had been born in Buckingham Palace. Each morning the Mayor called and afterwards issued a bulletin. The local paper came out with special editions covering the progress of the royal invalid. Police outside the hotel kept traffic moving and notices read, 'Proceed quietly. Sound no horns.' By her bed a telephone was installed, and each night, however an outlandish spot he was in, the Duke made his enquiries and reported his doings of the day.

Feeling better, the Duchess returned to Wellington and boarded *Renown* for the trip to Invercargill in the far south. Here the Duke was performing his last New Zealand duty, a march past of seven thousand children. It teemed with rain. The ground became a quagmire, soon to be spotted with lost little shoes and socks, though their owners did not seem to mind. They presented the Duke with a cot and a doll for Princess Elizabeth. Before he made his speech of thanks, he carefully placed the doll in the cot and tucked it up.

On 22nd March, when the Duke was due to board *Renown*, a gale ripped through the Foveaux Strait. The seas ran high and an attempt to find easier water was made at Bluff. The idea of taking him out in a New Zealand cruiser was scrapped, and a tug was substituted. From *Renown* the Duchess watched it bucketing through the waves, grateful indeed that her husband was a naval man. The problem then became the transference of H.R.H. from harbour tug to H.M.S. *Renown*. It was eventually achieved by him standing on the bridge and, with manpower behind him, being projected through the air towards the quarter-deck, where able-seamen dragged him to safety.

The Duchess commented that, for her, the experience was most unpleasant, but that her husband did not seem to mind much.

12 *Australia*

THE 26th of March 1927 was to be one of the most awe-inspiring days in the twenty-seven years of the Duchess of York. Ahead lay a great city, a vast land, and a great many people of marked and individual character. The population of the environs of Sidney alone totalled that of New Zealand. There were solemn ceremonies of remembrance and political importance to be performed. There were many speeches for the Duke to make, for which he needed guidance and support. There was even a speech that she had to make herself. There were thousands of miles to travel, and the danger to watch that tiredness did not bring a return of tonsilitis.

Two flying-boats droned above *Renown*. An escort of destroyers of the Royal Australian Navy took station. There was silence over one of the finest harbours in the world as the battle-cruiser took up her moorings dead on time. The Marine band played the National Anthem. And then the pent up boiler of sound broke loose. Sirens, bells, guns, whistles and the cheers of vast crowds strove with one another to take pride of place in the cacophony that swept over Sydney.

The roar went on all through their triumphant drive through the city. A famous Australian general was spotted at the top of a lamp post, so that he could get a view of the Duchess.

It was very different to New Zealand—more massive. At a dance given in their honour the guests ignored the music and just sat and stared at the royal visitors. When they were persuaded to dance, there looked like being a rush for the Duchess's lovely dress, and she and her partner had to perform in a ring of stewards linked hand in hand. There was also a new form of personal inspection to which they had to become accustomed. This was known as 'Public Reception'. The Duke and Duchess stood on a dais and the public filed past them, four abreast. Forty thousand was the figure estimated for one such queue. The Duchess was convulsed when the 'tail-end Charlie' of a particularly long movement of humanity turned out to be a father proudly pushing his baby twins in a pram.

The Duchess disposed of her one speech of the tour when visiting Sydney University. There she was entertained by the women's organizations of the State. It was short and sweet, and made a very good impression.

They headed north. At Newcastle it was teeming with rain, but the crowds were out in their thousands. The roof of the royal car was up. The Duke and Duchess looked at one another and whispered. The hood came down, with obvious results for the pretty hat of the Duchess. Australia remembered that.

Those hats of the Duchess had a startling effect on Australian fashions. Within a few days of her arrival creations of the relevant colours, with turned up brims and feathers at the side, were to be seen everywhere.

The first leg of their trip took them to Queensland and back. They visited the Blue Mountains and the Jenolan Caves. They had a 'billy can' picnic and danced at a Viceregal Ball in a two-acre wool shed. The Duke tried his hand at 'cutting out' bullocks from a herd. They met many interesting people, including Mr. Hendriksen, an old settler from Denmark who had been in the guard of honour when Princess Alexandra left Copenhagen in 1863 to marry the Prince of Wales.

Their next stopping place was Tasmania, 'the Garden State', and here on their arrival they drove under a triumphal arch made entirely of red apples. And then to Melbourne, to take part in the ceremonies for Anzac Day, 25th April. Past the Duke marched twenty-five thousand ex-Servicemen, among them twenty-nine holders of the Victoria Cross. The Duchess was dressed in black.

It was at Melbourne that the Duchess met an old friend. During the war a Tasmanian engineer officer had been invited to spend his leave at Glamis. He became friends with Lady Elizabeth and, when other leaves came round, he journeyed to Scotland. He recalled Lady Strathmore and her daughter getting up early to make his breakfast before he caught the train south towards the Channel. Now, after some hesitation, as he was not sure how to address her in her new role, he wrote to her. In all the grandeur and turbulence of the royal visit, he did not expect an answer. But a telephone call summoned him to Government House and there, in her private sitting-room, he found the same Lady Elizabeth whom he had last seen waving good-bye to him as he left Glamis.

The ball at Government House was a decorous affair. No need here for a ring of stewards to guard the Duchess. She moved among the guests, so small she seemed, with a dignity all her own. She danced first with the Governor-General. That was fitting. Her next partner was the Prime Minister, true to code. People were wondering who would be next. An A.D.C. moved across the floor. He returned to the dais with a young man adorned simply with medals of the First World War. She said to him: 'I want you to meet my husband.' Then, as the eyes turned, she took the floor with him. And, when the music stopped, she sat out with him as well.

At Ballarat, the gold town on the road to South Australia, the Duchess met 'the Lucas Girls', a body of five hundred women who had determined to build an Avenue of Honour to the memory of the fighting men and nurses who had gone to the War from the area. They set about collecting the money. The result was an avenue fourteen miles long, made up of three thousand trees, each bearing a name upon it.

In Adelaide the Duchess changed into the familiar dark blue of the Girl Guides' uniform and, after a march past, presented medals, just as in the old days she had done at Glamis.

The train journey that took the Duke and Duchess from South Australia to Canberra for the highlight of their tour lasted from Friday afternoon to Sunday morning. When they reached the new capital the sun was shining brightly, with a nip of frost in the air, and fifty thousand people had arrived from all over the Dominion by car and special train.

The doors of the great Parliament House were closed. The Duke and Duchess drove up in a carriage and four, escorted by outriders and postillions. A scene from Westminster was played out exactly that 9th May on the wide plain with the blue mountains as a backdrop. He was in naval uniform and she in a flowing cloak of silver-grey chiffon trimmed with fur. The greatness of the occasion had had its effect on him, and he had slept badly. It was good that she was with him.

Sixty-six-year-old Dame Nellie Melba, Australia's immortal singer, sang the first verse of the National Anthem. Then the crowds joined in and a flurry of pigeons rose into the sky. The Duke opened the door with a golden key. Once inside, he unveiled a statue of his father, who, on that same day twenty-six years before, had opened the first Federal Parliament of Australia.

They took their places in the throne-chairs on the dais. The Duke rose, and spoke. He did not hesitate once. In more senses than one, it was a great day for both of them.

The Duchess's particular piece in the Canberra celebrations was the planting of two trees. One was a willow from the Royal Botanical Gardens at Kew. Then they returned to Melbourne. There were one or two unscheduled halts on the way. At Seymour the crowd threatened to jam the signals if the royal train did not stop. It did.

Renown took six days to cover the journey from Melbourne to Freemantle. There was no peace and rest for the Duchess in the Great Australian Bight. For the 1,300 miles from Port Lincoln to King George's Sound the battle-cruiser took the full force of a gale howling its way from the icefields of the Antarctic. To the north lay the shore known to old time sailors as 'the coast of hell'. Along its barren cliffs and through its gulleys, where no river ran for over 700 miles, John Edward Eyre had made his trail-blazing, nightmare trek in 1841.

Now came the last days of Australian acclaim. They visited the Fairbridge farm school at Pinjarra, where poor children from England were being given a new start in life. The Duchess asked one small chap if he liked Western Australia better than Lambeth, and the answer came pat, 'Too right.' At a Perth theatre they met three thousand returned nurses and servicemen, being greeted with 'We love a lassie' and 'Who's your lady friend?' Sir Tom Bridges, Governor of South Australia, summed the whole thing up when he wrote to King George V: 'The Duchess leaves us with the responsibility of having a continent in love with her.'

On 23rd May the engines of *Renown* began turning for the long haul to Mauritius. Three days later they stopped. It was two o'clock on a stiflingly hot afternoon. There had been an overflow of oil, and a serious fire had broken out in a boiler-room. Four badly-burned seamen were carried away and a fire-fighting squad went into action. The danger lay in the inferno reaching the main oil supply, in which case there would be no alternative to abandoning ship, an unpleasant prospect with land three days away one way and four the other. In addition some of the boats had been damaged during the bashing in the Great Bight. But plans for flooding the ammunition chamber and for abandoning continued. Nearer and nearer the flames grew to the main oil tanks. They were within a few feet when the perspiring fire-party at last got them under control. It was ten o'clock before the Duchess was certain that she would not spend the night in a life-boat on the vast and very empty ocean.

There was a pleasant interlude at Mauritius, a cordial reception with a touch of the East meeting the West. As the Mauritians had not seen Royalty since 1901, it was a very special occasion, despite the misprint in the local newspaper that T.R.H. had announced that they could not *stand* more than two days in Mauritius. In their two days' *stay* they received one of the most outstanding presents of their tour, a map of the island in silver, four inches to the mile, with rubies marking the lighthouses, a sapphire Port Louis, and fifty diamonds the sugar factories.

North to the Red Sea, picking up the old trail at Port Sudan. Oil to be taken on, mail at Port Said. Lazy days to Malta. There receptions and ceremony again, and a Maltese scarf as a present for the Duchess. A military reception at Gibraltar and a tour of the Rock, from which rioting soldiers had planned to throw the Duke's great-great-grandfather because he closed the wine shops. One of the culprits was sent to Australia where he helped to found the great city of Melbourne. Perhaps somebody still remembered, for as *Renown* moved away the music that came to the ears of the Duke and Duchess was that of the hymn, 'Now thank we all our God'. That wagged the tail of the tour.

Renown returned to Portsmouth on 27th June, after being away for nearly six months. The royal passengers had covered thirty-four thousand miles. The three brothers were waiting in the same position as they had been on 7th January, so long, it seemed, ago. The King and Queen were again at Victoria. But, for the Duke at least, the thrill, the fun, the sense of sole achievement, had gone. He was third fiddle once again. For the Duchess, one thought soared above the others, blotting out the rest—the moments when she had her baby to herself again. Yet to her husband, a man of thirty-one who had circled the world to a song of acclamation and achieved a success beyond understanding, there came detailed notes from the King of how he was to dress on arrival, and how he was to behave. 'When you kiss Mama take your hat off.'

It had been planned that the parents should be reunited with Princess Elizabeth at their new home, 145, Piccadilly. But Queen Mary had thought up a surprise and brought the grandchild, whom she referred to as 'the bambino', to Buckingham Palace for the family reunion. Yet the Duke and Duchess did not think themselves really home until they reached 145. There they came out on the balcony, the Duchess holding the baby, and the crowd acclaimed them. It was the baptism of a new royal residence.

It was a comfortable home, a handy home, and the Duchess came to love it, and there were pangs of regret when the time came for her to leave it. Yet it was only a number. No sentry paced before its door, and its two bells, 'Visitors' and 'House', were free for all to ring. Two green pillars lent some air of stateliness to the hall. The colours were soft and warm, the nursery modern, and the domestic quarters, ruled over by a housekeeper, had been brought up to date and were easy to run. The Duchess soon had her stamp about the place. The morning room, the hub of the house, was a rendezvous and a head-quarters both for relaxing and the routine jobs of the days. On the chimney-piece were china figures of Scottish soldiers. There were a few photographs of special folk and dogs. Books and sewing lay about, and there were a gramophone and a radio. After four years the Duke and Duchess had found a home.

Yet there was to be something missing in the next decade. Their first four years together had been crammed with splendour, triumph and achievement. There had been the wedding at Westminster, almost unrivalled as a royal spectacle. Then the journey to Belgrade, to play lead parts in the pomp and age-old tradition of Serbian ceremonies. There had followed the safari from Mombasa to Khartoum, with its attendant excitement, adventure and boundless goodwill. In its train came the Presidency of the Wembley Exhibition. Next, the birth of a baby, third in line of succession to the Throne, had exalted the status of their dual role. Finally, their circumference of the globe, with the trail of triumph from Auckland to Freemantle, had given their names a wider meaning to the Commonwealth and the world.

The State visit to New Zealand and Australia was the last imperial mission of the Duke and Duchess of York, under that title. It is difficult to comprehend why. True, certain Members of the House of Commons had condemned it as a 'pleasure trip' and expressed the opinion that such an expense should not have been incurred at a time of industrial hardship. But that was a minority view, and easily disposed of. Not only was the strengthening of bonds with distant kinsmen of prime necessity, but the point of industrial depression rebounded upon itself. The cure lay in the export of British goods, motor cars, railways engines, machinery. And Britain's best emissaries to achieve this were undoubtedly the Prince of Wales and the Duke and Duchess of York.

It has been said that after 1927 Imperial and foreign missions were left in the capable hands of the Prince of Wales. In the event these consisted of journeys through Africa in 1928 and 1930 and South America in 1931. For the following four years his itineraries were only similar to those of a holidaymaker on the Continent. So, in this vital decade, vast areas under British influence were left without royal visits.

The success of the Duke and Duchess during their long journey was beyond doubt or argument. Proof was to be found in the tributes from leaders everywhere. The Prime Minister of Australia telegraphed: 'The personalities of yourself and the Duchess have brought vividly before us how human is the tie that binds us to our kinsmen overseas. As an Ambassador of Empire you have brought the Mother Country closer to Australia.' The Governor-General of

New Zealand to the King: 'It is quite unnecessary to say that they both made themselves adored by everyone. This I know sounds like a newspaper expression but it is no more than the truth.' The Governor of South Australia to the King: 'The visit has done untold good and has certainly put back the clock of disunion and disloyalty twenty-five years as far as this State is concerned.'

Yet throughout the tour, however many thousands of miles separated them, the Duke had felt the eagle, critical eye of his father upon him. There was a rap over the knuckles if an equerry was photographed out of place. It had been the same in East Africa. The Duke had been offered a farm in Kenya as a gift. The King had vetoed it. He was worried what would happen if the place did not pay! The Duke was being robbed of a confidence that was rightly his.

The surveillance and the criticism did not extend to the Duchess. Firstly, she knew how to handle her father-in-law and bring out the best in him. Secondly, she did not query the jobs that she had to do: she simply saw that they were done well. Thirdly, she may have benefited from the still fresh memory of the little Duchess of Albany, whose answer to any criticism was to beard her regal mother-in-law and have it out face to face.

King George had spent half of his life under the mantle of Queen Victoria and was versed in her ways. He was not of the rebel breed, like his father or his eldest son. Now, in his treatment of his second son, there was an echo back to the days when the Prince of Wales returned to England after his triumphal visit to Canada and America in 1860. A triumph it had been, in some places almost a riot. Letters in praise of him poured into Windsor. Yet there was to be no crown of laurel leaves. In irony the Prince Consort wrote to Baron Stockmar: 'Bertie is generally pronounced the most perfect product of nature.' He sternly told his son that the success in the New World was due entirely to his being the representative of the Sovereign. He then packed him off to solitude at Oxford and ordered him not to smoke.

With the confidence that his duties in New Zealand and Australia had given him, the Duke naturally wished to know what went on at the heart of Government. If he was considered important enough to take the leading role at ceremonies such as had taken place at Canberra, then obviously a statesmen would consider him important enough to consult on major policies. But as he had not been allowed to see confidential papers, he was in no position to give answers. He therefore asked for that permission. The King's advisers were of the opinion that he should be allowed to do so, but the King himself was not. He saw no reason why his sons should be present when he had audiences with Ministers, let alone peer into the secrets of the despatch boxes. It was his grandmother all over again. In the days before she died those same boxes had piled up outside her door as she was the only person who could deal with them. At last the Duke was allowed to look at certain lower grade telegrams, but his father even objected to that. There were to be no more Canberra moments for the Duke of York.

In the event, though she could not have known it, the block in the way of her husband learning the way of Kings was to have dire effects for the Duchess.

Instead she saw a gay young man ready to take his father's place. He was sure to marry and have children—the strain of Coburg always did. She had a child to love and train. She had manifold minor duties. There might well be other children. And there were dreams of a house in the country, with gardens round it.

Still, she might have stepped more easily into Queenship when she left *Renown* in 1927 than she did when called, with a cold in her nose, to move from 145, Piccadilly to Buckingham Palace ten years later.

13 Piccadilly Days

'MY chief claim to fame,' said the Duke of York, 'seems to be that I am the father of Princess Elizabeth.'

The interest in the baby was certainly phenomenal. It became a drill, on the tops of buses going along Piccadilly, for heads to turn left or right in the hope that a glimpse could be caught through the nursery window. The arrival of visitors, such as the young sons of Princess Mary, was eagerly noted. Visitors took station on the pavement outside No. 145 and a glimpse of the Princess became a land mark in their stay and a feather in their cap when they got home.

Nurse Knight's initial sorties with the perambulator into Green Park and Hyde Park had to cease. Without mechanical power she could make no progress through the crowds. Thereafter exercise was taken in the sanctuary of the gardens of Buckingham Palace.

The Duchess had already become accustomed to this baby worship. She had had ample experience of it in New Zealand and Australia, and it had surprised her. She had commented, in letters home, that there was always an extra cheer for her daughter. She had been inundated with letters from children asking for photographs of 'Princess Betty'. It was because she was the mother that other mothers fought to get near her with their babies. 'Down under' it seems to have been sensed that one day the baby Princess would be Queen.

Renown returned loaded with presents for her. Apart from parrots and canaries, there was a huge doll from Auckland, a doll and a cot from Invercargill, a teddy bear from Brisbane, a set of doll's bedroom furniture from Tasmania, two threepenny bits from two little girls of Adelaide, and an anonymous ten shillings for her money-box.

Princess Elizabeth was very lucky in her parents. They both aimed at the goal of happiness for her, but they aimed from opposite wings. To the Duchess childhood meant days when the sun was always shining, fairies at the bottom of the garden, chocolates and Woodbines in the 'Flea House', pictures in the nursery fire and grown-ups downstairs to play with. The Duke had other memories. His sadistic nurse had fed him at any odd moment that suited her, giving his infant stomach disorders that may well have led to his future troubles. His great-grandmama frankly terrified him. Inside herself, his mother had found it hard to countenance the more intimate details of childbirth and babyhood. His father trained his children as a keeper does his gun-dogs. Affection was there, but he would not tolerate disobedience or answering back. So, while the Duchess had now merely to reconstruct the happy procedure at St. Paul's, the Duke was filled with determination that what had happened to him should not take place in the case of his daughter. Sometimes the Duchess, accustomed to a large family, wondered if her husband was not giving too much importance to one little person.

Every morning early 'Lilibet' went to her parents' bedroom, a ritual of affection that put the day into perspective. Every evening there was a visit to the nursery, with its bookcase full of toys on the red carpet, and then the ceremony of the bath. Both appointments grew rowdier as the months passed.

In her peculiar position there was obvious danger of her becoming slightly spoilt. She soon learned to watch for the salute from the sentries at Buckingham Palace and to gracefully raise her hand in acknowledgment. When she was taken to Glamis she loudly demanded why her sentries were not there. When she saw a crowd of people she wanted to know if they had come to see her. It was mother who put matters into perspective.

Strangely enough the biggest danger of spoiling came from the direction of her paternal grandparents. The King called her 'sweet little Lilibet' and recorded all her comings and sayings in his diary. The Archbishop of Canterbury called at the Palace. He came upon the King and Princess playing horses and grooms. The King was on all fours on the carpet and she was leading him round by the beard. When she was at Sandringham he would sit beside her at breakfast and engage her in most serious conversation. In the main he received few answers, but that suited him. Unfortunately she was unfaithful to him for a boy she knew who had a wooden gun.

Her childhood days were in one direction a contrast with those of her mother. The Duchess had received her dolls and tops ninth hand, and twenty years of jammy fingers had put a patina on the nursery furniture. The secrets of the bees and the trees were patronizingly passed on by those who passed that stage before. To the Princess everything was new and had to be discovered. The rosebuds were fresh on her white bedstead. Her china, bearing two magpies and the words 'Two for Joy', was fresh from the shop window. And new, and specially loved, was the chair from Switzerland that played a tune when she sat on it.

The Duchess kept her public engagements to a minimum in the summer of 1927, but there was one event of particular importance. On 15th July she went with her husband to the Guildhall for luncheon. The City was to congratulate them on the success of their Australian tour. The Duchess sparkled as she sat by the side of the Lord Mayor. For the Duke there was the ordeal of a speech, but since his return he had resumed his attendances at the consulting room of Mr. Logue, and he acquitted himself well.

Autumn was spent in Scotland. At Balmoral the Duchess helped the Queen to run a stall at a bazaar in aid of Crathie Kirk. Princess Elizabeth was kept out of the way behind the stall. But when she was wheeled round the attractions by her nurse, the riot began. She was rescued by the King in person. Peace came when the pram was lifted completely with passenger and carried up the terrace steps.

The year until November 1928 passed peacefully by. The Duke worked hard for his many interests, his summer camps for boys, the Industrial Welfare Society, the Fresh Air Fund, the National Playing Fields Association, Dr. Barnado's Homes, the Gordon Boy's Home, there were so many of them. The Duchess concentrated on hospitals, child welfare and needlework, such as the Mothercraft Training Society at Cromwell House, the St. Marylebone Housing Association and the Royal School of Art Needlework. They were at many engagements together, at Glasgow for the Housing and Health Exhibition, to Woolwich for the opening of the new Woolwich and District Hospital, to St. Andrews for the jubilee of St. Leonard's School, and to Finsbury Town Hall for the Costermongers' Ball.

There were other kinds of days. At Blackdown the Duchess, escorted by General Deedes, inspected the King's Own Yorkshire Light Infantry, of which she was Colonel-in-Chief. She was at Epsom for the Oaks, and to see a memorable race. In the One Thousand Guineas Joe Childs on Scuttle had given the King his only Classic victory to date. There was hope that the filly would add the Oaks. But the gathering of royal spectators saw Lord Derby's Toboggan first past the post.

The Duchess was now to be seen more and more often with the King. She was with him at the Royal Horse Show at Richmond and with him when he drove from Balmoral to the Highland Gathering at Braemar. It was a perfect day and there was comment as to how well the King looked, an imposing figure with his kilt and walking stick. But the happy state was not long to continue. On Armistice Day at the Cenotaph he caught a chill, neglected it, and by the 21st he was a victim of septicaemia. The Duchess called her husband back from the Midlands where he was hunting. The Duke was the only one of the royal brothers in the country, and he only just back from Denmark where he had attended the funeral of the Dowager Empress Marie of Russia.

The anxiety grew. Crowds stood outside the Palace in the bitter cold, waiting for the bulletins. On 4th December six Counsellors of State were appointed to continue the transaction of a monarch's duties. Among them was the Duke of York. Another, the Prince of Wales, was racing back from East Africa in a destroyer. The Duke informed him by mail of the rumour in London that the reason behind the hurry was the fear that brother York might pinch the Throne! The Prince arrived back on the 11th, having covered, in some miraculous way, six thousand miles in nine days.

A worry for the Duke and Duchess, beyond the illness of the King, was the outward calm of Queen Mary. It was quite obvious how she felt, but she kept those feelings strictly to herself, not even unburdening herself to her family. She could have shared her emotional strain with the Yorks, or with Princess Mary who had come up from Goldsborough. But she kept herself bottled up, and the fear grew at 145 that if the King continued long in his crucial state, or if he died, then the Queen would have a breakdown.

But Queen Mary was not that kind of a woman. As yet neither her family nor the country appreciated the depth of the well of courage inside of her. It was her training, her example and her bravery that were the vital elements in the regal training of Elizabeth, Duchess of York, a training that was to stand her in good stead when the tests came.

Her mother-in-law bubbled over with interest in the little things in life. She loved to find a bargain in an antique shop, to eliminate ivy from a garden, to work at her tapestry. It was only the great moments that brought out the magnificence of her. The Delhi Durbar. The ball that the Kaiser gave for the wedding of his daughter in Berlin in 1913, when the British Queen, in a dress of cloth of gold, stole the scene. The days in Madrid after the wedding of King Alfonso and Queen Ena, when the assassin still walked the streets and Queen Mary insisted on driving about in full regalia when others wanted to hide up until the danger was over.

It was her constant tact and lack of emotional feeling that had troubled the Duke in his bachelor days at the Palace. It was always to be the same. To the Prime Minister, she referred to the Abdication crisis as 'a pretty kettle of fish' and then drove out to see the ruins of the burned Crystal Palace. When the news came through from Sandringham on 6th February that George VI was dead and, distraught, Princess Mary, then Princess Royal, ran into her mother's room, it has been reported that Queen Mary said to her, 'Please do your hair properly when you come before the Queen.'

The other Queen that the Duchess had known as an example, though but for a short time, was Alexandra. Between those two Queens there was a world of contrast. It never showed more clearly than when dread telegrams came to cottages on the Sandringham estate during the war. Queen Mary would tap at the door and say: 'Rotten luck. What lot was he in? Oh, jolly good lot.' Queen Alexandra would sweep in whispering, 'Oh, my dear, my dear,' and take the sorrowing widow or mother in her arms.

It was King George's will to live that carried him through. Fortunate indeed was it that in this direction he took after Queen Victoria rather than Prince Albert. By Christmas he was out of immediate danger. In February he was taken to Craigwell House, Bognor. It was after he had been there some weeks that the Duchess was able to make a really useful contribution towards his recovery. She sent Princess Elizabeth and her nurse to stay with him. The two took little walks together, she guiding him by the hand and prattling away. One afternoon they made sand castles in the garden. The Archbishop of Canterbury saw them and was of the opinion that they were some of the most epic sand pies ever turned out and that they should be wired in and preserved. Yet many months were to pass before the King regained his strength.

Meantime there were happenings, gay and sad, in the Duchess's own family. In February 1928 her brother Michael married Miss Elizabeth Cator, who had been a bridesmaid at Westminster five years before. There were so many women and girls outside St. George's, Hanover Square that the Duke and Duchess had great difficulty in getting into the church, let alone escaping afterwards. The following year her brother David married Rachel Pauline, younger daughter of Lieutenant-Colonel H. H. Spender-Clay. Now all the Duchess's surviving brothers and sisters were married. But in 1930 came sadness. The Hon. John Herbert Bowes-Lyon, Lord Strathmore's second son, died in February and was buried at St. Paul's Walden Bury. The Duke and Duchess attended the simple service at the little country church.

In March 1929 the Duchess enjoyed a unique experience. She and her husband became the first royal personages to visit Germany since the war. They made a diversion to Berlin on their way to Oslo for the wedding of Crown Prince Olaf of Norway, and took the opportunity while there of leaving a card on President Hindenburg.

Prince Olaf was marrying Princess Martha, niece of the King of Sweden and second daughter of Prince Charles of Sweden, and it was the signal for great rejoicings in the Royal Houses of Norway, Sweden and Britain. Prince Olaf's mother, Queen Maud, was the daughter of Edward VII, and therefore he was the Duke's cousin. He had been born at Appleton House, Sandringham, and brought up with the children at York Cottage. A gay and daring young man, he sometimes worried his mother. He saw her watching him as he prepared to descend a ski jump. He commented: 'I'll bet the old girl is shaking in her bloomers.'

Now the Duke and Duchess were at Oslo to represent the King, and the Duke was best man. The reception they received in the streets of the Norwegian capital took them back to their days in Auckland. It was a far happier affair than the wedding of the Crown Prince of Italy in Rome the following year. The Duchess was due there too, but developed bronchitis and had to stay at home. The Duke, himself with a heavy cold, went alone. The royal precedences were muddled up and at one point in the service those officiating seemed doubtful who was the bridegroom. Without the softening effect of his wife to calm him, the Duke relieved himself with some outspoken comments about the arrangements in general.

In the quiet years before the Jubilee, Scottish sojourns and Scottish events played an important part in the life of the Duchess. In addition to the August days at Glamis, there were now autumn holidays at Birkhall, lent by the King. It was the beginning of a long association. When the Duchess became Queen she moved to Balmoral and, in due course, Princess Elizabeth took over Birkhall. On the death of George VI mother and daughter changed residences. It is today the Aberdeenshire home of the Queen Mother.

When Princess Elizabeth was the only child in the family, Birkhall was the one place in the countryside where the Yorks could be alone. They loved the Jacobite stronghold that the House of Hanover had purchased but a century after the battle of Culloden. The original portion of the house was built by the Gordons in 1715, the year that the Earl of Mar raised the Standard of the Jacobites at Braemar. One wing was added in the nineteenth century, and two in the twentieth. Prince Albert had originally intended that it should be the residence in Scotland of the Prince of Wales, but he preferred Abergeldie. So Birkhall became Balmoral's 'dower house'. Many interesting royal guests have stayed there, outstanding among them being Florence Nightingale. She walked the gardens with Queen Victoria, the two 'plotting and planning' for the start of an Army medical service. Thus was the Royal Army Medical Corps born.

Hidden away from the eyes of tourists, the Duke and Duchess roamed the Balmoral lands with dog and gun, rod and baby, and found the real peace that was so essential to both of them. Their link with Deeside grew stronger and stronger, while that of the Prince of Wales weakened.

In 1929 in Scotland the Duke and Duchess shared a duty that was to be one of the most important undertaken up to the time of the Abdication.

The Duke was appointed Lord High Commissioner to the General Assembly of the Church of Scotland, the first royal holder of the office since 1679. Furthermore, it was the year of union between the Established Church of Scotland and the Union Free Church of Scotland. Eighty-six years of disruption were to end. It was in 1843 that disagreements over the right of the local presbytery to reject the minister whom the lay patron presented to the benefice led to the schism in the Scottish Establishment and the beginning of the Free Church. Queen Victoria was in full sympathy with the governmental declaration against 'interference with the patron's ancient and hitherto unrestricted rights'. At long last agreement between the two sides had been reached. The last independent Assemblies were to be held in May and the first united Assembly in October. It was hoped that the King would be present at the latter, but there were doubts whether his health would allow of it.

On 20th May the Duke and Duchess arrived at Holyroodhouse, the Palace in the heart of Edinburgh which many in Scotland consider should be more frequently used as a royal residence. Prior to a State Dinner, the Lord Provost presented the Key of the City. Edinburgh made fête days indeed of the occasions when the Duke and Duchess drove to St. Giles Cathedral and the two General Assemblies. It was not only the pageantry, splendid as it was, nor the fact that the King's son was Lord High Commissioner, that called the people into the streets. It was also that in the landau, with its escort of Scots Greys, sat the former Elizabeth Bowes-Lyon, of Glamis.

Their visit coincided with the celebration of the six-hundredth anniversary of King Robert the Bruce's first Charter to the City. At the gateway to the Castle the Duke unveiled statues of Robert the

Bruce and Sir William Wallace, Scotland's warrior kings who had fought for liberty.

The Duchess was in her element at a garden party for children given at Holyrood. Everybody wanted to know about the progress and latest doings of Princess Elizabeth, who had been left behind in London. The Duchess wrote to her mother-in-law: 'It almost frightens me that the people should love her so much.'

In October they were back at Holyroodhouse, having driven from Deeside. The great day of Union had come, and ten thousand people crowded into the Assembly Hall to see it come to pass. Among the many that the Duchess met that day was Mrs. Douglas Bannerman, who was over ninety. She had been present at the Disruption and now had lived to see all the bitterness end.

Deeply moved by the religious ceremony in which they had played a part, stirred by the general sympathy for the King in his illness, the Duke and Duchess returned to the autumnal peace of Birkhall. They were to need the contentment that grew with the rambles round Balmoral's hills and burns, for in the year ahead lay important events as yet unseen. At Melton Mowbray the Prince of Wales was to meet a charming American lady. And, for their own part, a child was to be born.

14   Add a Princess and a Garden

TO the Duchess of York August meant Glamis, and 1930 was no exception although her second baby was due that month. Not since the boy who was to be Charles I saw the light at Dunfermline had an heir in direct line to the English Throne been born in Scotland. The only other royal birth to take place north of the Border in over three hundred years was that of Queen Victoria's thirty-sixth grandchild, Princess Ena of Battenburg,[1] on 24th October 1887, an event which took place at Balmoral. It was at her christening that Dr. Cameron Lees, of St. Giles Cathedral, Edinburgh, made his classic mistake. He misread the mother's writing and named the child Ena instead of the intended old Gaelic name of Eua.

Mr. J. R. Clynes, Home Secretary, was notified that he would be required at Glamis early the following month. On the 5th the Labour statesman donned a suit of tweed and set off for Scotland. On arrival he was informed that, as things looked at present, he was at least a fortnight too early. The Dowager Countess of Airlie came to the rescue and he became a guest at her castle eight miles away. She took him to local flower shows and the like, but the wait was long.

The call came on the evening of Thursday, 21st August. The sky was black with thunder clouds and a curtain of rain swept across the valley and blotted out the hills. Lightning lit the battlements and the ensuing claps were as if nature was firing a royal salute.

The baby was born at twenty-two minutes past nine, and once again it was a Caesarian birth. Her weight was six pounds and eleven ounces. Mr. Clynes, looking down at her with a smile on his

[1] H.M. Queen Victoria Eugenia of Spain.

123

face, pronounced, 'I have never seen a finer baby.' Then he left the cradle in the Tapestry Room and telegraphed the news to the Lord Mayor of London and the Governors-General of the Dominions and the Crown Colonies.

The bells rang out, now clear, now lost in the avalanche of the thunder. On the top of Hunter's Hill a giant bonfire spread the news. It was lit by four local girls, with the same torches that had set off the fire on the wedding night of Lady Elizabeth. This was a day that Glamis folk were always to remember and there was wild celebration in honour of the child that they knew as 'the lassie's bairn'.

In London, the bells of St. Paul's pealed and a salute of forty-one guns was fired from the Tower. Then it came the duty of the Duke to walk down to the village and register the birth of his daughter at the shop which combined the offices of grocer, post office and registrar.

But he did not hurry to the shop. The reason for his tardiness was that the Duchess had discovered that the next space in the registration book was numbered thirteen! This was a number that definitely was not wanted. The solution was the arrival of another baby, and one, in fact came, a son named George to Mrs. Gevina Brown, of that parish, three days after the birth of Princess Margaret. In an interview in the *Sunday Express* in 1964 Mrs. Brown described what took place. 'Shortly after George was born I got a postcard from the registrar at Glamis asking me to come along and register the birth of my boy. I couldn't understand at the time why I had been sent a postcard, because I was fully aware of the registration procedure. Later I went along to Glamis post office to see Mr. Charles Buchanan, who was the sub-postmaster and also the village registrar. He told me that the Duchess had been holding off registering Princess Margaret until I registered George because she did not want No. 13. ... I was a little unhappy at registering George under No. 13, although I am not really a superstitious person. However, I knew that if I delayed the Duchess would do the same thing, so I decided to sign the book there and then. ... But I have no regrets. The Duchess, as she was then, is a charming person and spoke to us often as we cut through the castle grounds on the way to church on Sundays. ...'

The King's illness, the fact that the Duke and Duchess were more in the public eye after their world tour, the novelty of a royal birth in Scotland, the strange setting of an age-old castle in a thunderstorm, even the belief that 'Thursday's child has far to go', all these combined to produce a phenomenal interest in the arrival of the new Princess. There was much speculation as to what the future held for her. There were many forecasts, some full of accuracy as events were to prove. Mr. R. H. Naylor, in the *Sunday Express*, considered the planets. From Uranus, he said, would come her original mind and her unconventional nature; from Saturn, a sense of duty and service; from Venus, the love endowing her with vivid emotions. He ended: 'This royal child will be essentially a woman of the New Age. Events of tremendous importance to the Royal Family and to the nation will come about near her seventh year and these events will indirectly affect her own fortunes.'

Foulsham's Almanac forecast these traits in her character— 'unbounded energy, wilfulness, independence, great interest in everything around her, unconventional manner in public'. On matrimony: 'Marriage, if it is to take place at all, will do so when she is twenty-eight The union can only end in sorrow.' And then this: 'Jupiter and the moon in the ruling sign of Scotland indicate that the Princess will always be dear to the hearts of the Scots, and some day she will find a haven of peace and rest in the midst of her loyal country folk.'

The Duchess had made no firm, pre-natal plans for the name of her baby. Perhaps, and with good reason, she reckoned on it being a boy. Male children preponderated in the Coburg strain. Prince Albert, the Consort, was one of two boys. Among the children, grandchildren and great-grandchildren of Queen Victoria and the Prince there were one hundred and ten boys to sixty girls. King George V and Queen Mary had five sons to one daughter, and their first two grandchildren had both been boys. In the event the preponderance was to continue to an amazing extent.

Looking back for girls' names among those that had been used in their direct lines in the previous two centuries, the Duke and Duchess had the following selection to choose from: on the Strathmore side—Nina, Cecilia, Caroline, Frances, Ann, Henrietta, Charlotte, Mary, Hyacinthe and Dorothy; on the Windsor side—

Mary, Alexandra, Victoria, Louise, Claudine, Augusta, Dorothy, Henrietta, Agnes, Charlotte, Sophia and Caroline.

As a first name the Duchess now plumbed for one from her own background—Ann. For the second, she looked back to Stuart days and chose Margaret. A few days after the birth she wrote to Queen Mary, telling her of the decision. Ann of York, she thought, sounded so nice, and Elizabeth and Ann went well together. There was another consideration which she did not mention. The names would commemorate, hand in hand, England's two great Queens.

Meantime the King and Queen had moved from Sandringham to Balmoral and on the 30th they drove over to Glamis to see their new grandchild. They were delighted with her and relieved to see the Duchess looking so well. And yet a shadow crossed the scene. The King did not like the name of Ann. Wherein lay his prejudice? He should certainly have had no quarrel with the Queen who passed on the baton of Britain to Hanover, though he may have been thinking of her maternal disappointments. A reminiscence of the lady of Cleves may have brought before his eyes an unsuitable portrait of ugliness. Or he may have been recalling Anne Horton, whom George III disliked and whose marriage to the Duke of Cumberland brought into being the Royal Marriage Act. Certain it was that since the days of the 'good Queen' her name had been avoided at royal christenings. And George V was not a man who liked novelties. He got his way. 'Ann' was put into cold storage for use in the following generation.

Not being able to name her child in the way that she had chosen, must have been a bitter pill for the Duchess to swallow, but 'Bertie' had been taught not to cross the will of his father, and there it was. But when it came to her second choice, the Duchess did not ask for an opinion. She simply wrote and said that 'Bertie' and she had decided that it should be Rose. It was the name of the Duchess's sister, Lady Leveson-Gower, and Rose of York not only sounded nice, it was very fitting.

Again the font was brought from Windsor to Buckingham Palace, again a white cake was made, on top a silver cradle containing a baby doll, and on 30th October Princess Margaret Rose was christened by the Archbishop of Canterbury. The godparents were the Prince of

Wales, Princess Victoria,[1] Princess Ingrid of Sweden,[2] Lady Rose Leveson-Gower and the Hon. David Bowes-Lyon. Princess Elizabeth now referred to her sister as 'Bud'.

With two children, and the attendant nursing and domestic staff, coupled with the desire that they should have a peaceful life and fresh air, the Duke and Duchess decided that they must find a rural retreat handy to London. But before they could take this plan further, a point had to be settled. The Duke's name had been put forward for the Governor-Generalship of Canada. It was generally agreed that he would fill the post admirably, and that the Duchess would be a great acquisition to him. The Duchess was pondering on the problems facing her children in the Dominion when she heard that the Labour Government had cast doubts on the advisability of the appointment. It was thought that the Canadians were too close to America and the democratic life there to appreciate Royalty in their midst, a sentiment which made the King furious. He looked back at the great successes of the Marquess of Lorne and Princess Louise, and of the Duke and Duchess of Connaught. Unfortunately he could not know that, a quarter of a century later, the suggestion would emanate from Canada that his son's wife should occupy that very same appointment. As it was, the Government had its way, and the Duke and Duchess turned once again to house hunting.

On a September day in 1931 they found themselves, at the suggestion of the King, in the south-east corner of Windsor Great Park, by Norfolk Farm and Cumberland Lodge. They picked their way through weeds and, by way of a greenhouse, entered a dilapidated building. There were signs that once there had been grandeur here, but now partitions crossed a fine hall and all around was the air of disuse and crumpling decorations. This was the Royal Lodge and exactly a century had passed since it had been the favoured home of royalty.

Originally a hunting lodge, and known as Lower Lodge, it had been renovated by the Duke of Cumberland when he became Ranger of the Park after Culloden. Sixty years later the Prince of Wales, by this time Prince Regent, decided that he wanted a house at Windsor

[1] Second daughter of King Edward VII.
[2] Granddaughter of the Duke of Connaught and now H.M. Queen of Denmark.

where he could be away from his mad father and carping family. He decided on Cumberland Lodge, but while repairs were being carried out, he moved into Lower Lodge. He liked it, and there spent much of his time until the end of his life. He carried out his usual extravaganza of rebuilding and decoration, thus inciting criticism from Parliament and the people, but he did not let this deter him. He rechristened it the Royal Lodge, although it was generally known as his Gothic Cottage.

After his wife's death, and with his unpopularity increasing, he spent more and more of his days here, shut up with the Conynghams. He shunned the publicity of Windsor Castle and Buckingham Palace, despite the vast sums that he had spent on both. By the closing stages of the 1820s he was blind in one eye and almost blind in the other, terrified of going mad, and often with as many as seventeen leeches on one knee at a time. Thus was described his life at the Royal Lodge: 'He leads a most extraordinary life—never gets up till six in the afternoon. . . . He breakfasts in bed, does whatever business he can be brought to transact in bed too, he reads every newspaper quite through, dozes three to four hours, gets up in time for dinner, and goes to bed between ten and eleven. He sleeps very ill, and rings the bell forty times in the night; if he wants to know the hour, though a watch hangs close to him, he will have his valet . . . down rather than turn his head to look at it. The same thing if he wants a glass of water; he won't stretch out his hand to get it. . . .'[1]

When he died William IV had most of his brother's hide-out demolished, leaving little more than the unfinished banqueting hall, the work of Wyatville. From the discarded materials Queen Adelaide had a tea house built, calling it Adelaide Cottage. Here, of a summer's afternoon, she would come with as many as twenty of her ladies. A Windsor gardener recalled how they amused themselves, 'some in reading, some in working samplers and things, some in walking and talking, and as they takes no notice of we, we takes no notice o' they.'

Through the Victorian era the Royal Lodge slept. It was patched up to make a grace-and-favour dwelling, a variety of minor tenants made alterations to suit their requirements, but, as a great name, it had gone.

[1] *Queen Adelaide*, by Mary Hopkirk.

The terrifying ghost of Butcher Cumberland and the revolting spectre of dying King George IV had apparently departed by the time the Duke and Duchess of York peered and poked around. They saw instead the imprint of master architects and the possibility of great vistas from the windows and the paradise of a garden of their own. The Duke, in the unchanging language that he used to his father, said that the place would suit them admirably.

The transformation of the Royal Lodge was the Duchess's greatest adventure in home-making. Here no prying eyes disturbed her peace and she could pace and plan and measure and dream in a world that was all her own. Partitions came down and the grandiose Georgian hall became a drawing-room. Two wings took shape, one on either flank, linked by the nineteenth-century building. The work was done slowly and carefully, and when the whole was diffused with pink-wash of the Suffolk shade, there emerged a royal residence of delight and charm.

When Princess Elizabeth was six a further addition came to the Royal Lodge. As a birthday present the people of Wales gave her a model house. Fifteen feet high, and in the style of the traditional Welsh cottage, it was thatched and had a chimney. In all it boasted six rooms, complete with bathroom and running hot and cold water. 'Y Bwthyn Bach', Welsh for 'The Little House', was inscribed over the door. To add the lived-in touch the Welsh Terrier Association presented a puppy, named Ianto, to go with it. For several months the cottage remained on exhibition in Cardiff, during which time it raised a large sum for charity. Then it was taken to Windsor and erected in the garden of the Royal Lodge. A formal garden, with a pedestal in the middle, was made before the cottage door. Princess Elizabeth had been handy with a brush and dustpan ever since she could walk, and now she was in a little girl's paradise. She swept and ironed, dusted and cooked, worked in her garden and cut her own flowers, with 'Bud' crawling behind, demanding to be allowed to play her part.

To the Duchess and her husband the greatest thrill about the Royal Lodge was that at least they had a garden of their own. In 1931 it consisted of about fifteen acres, with an acre and a half of it down to fruit and vegetables. By the time of the death of George VI it had swollen to ninety acres. On taking over they found some azalea beds and some borders of shrubs, and that was about all, except for a wilderness at the bottom of the wide lawn. It was in the clearing of this wilderness that their first efforts were directed.

If the Duchess had found anything lacking in her married years, it was the lack of a garden. She had been brought up in a household where the names and habits of flowers and shrubs were an integral part of the conversation. She had absorbed horticulture naturally, as she had French. Lady Strathmore was an acknowledged expert on gardening matters, as was Mrs. Scott, her grandmother, whose skill was long remembered in Italy. Little Lady Elizabeth's first plot was in the Dutch Garden at Glamis, and she plied her guiles and smiles to get just what she wanted out of the head gardener, Mr. McInnes. Her first love was for the flowers of spring, a many-coloured quilt of polyanthus, the vivid blue of the hyacinth, and the nodding heads of the daffodils. In the war years, when gardens were so great a relief, she progressed to red rambling roses, thyme and lilies of the valley. In contrast, she loved the vistas and the glades and the pools of St. Paul's, a place which had made a deep impression on her husband.

The Duke's first real interest in a garden was when he moved into the Royal Lodge and at last had one of his own. As a boy he had had some experience in regimenting cabbages and lining up carrots, in the manner that the Prince Consort had drilled into his children at the Swiss Cottage at Osborne. His interest lay dormant until his marriage. Then, with his wife's expert comments and appreciation of the beautiful, it began to stir. When he visited famous gardens, he took notice. He was quick to absorb and for a novice his knowledge was wide when he began planning at the Royal Lodge. Being mature, he tended to specialize. His forte was in landscape, and on rhododendrons he became undefeatable.

Yet September 1931 was an unfortunate moment for the Yorks to begin a fresh home, with the unavoidable additional expenses. The country was in a state of financial crisis, the Labour Government had resigned and a National one formed. On the 5th the Keeper of the Privy Purse wrote to the Prime Minister, Mr. Ramsay MacDonald: 'I am commanded by the King to inform you that in the grave financial situation with which the country is confronted his Majesty desires personally to participate in the movement for the reduction of national expenditure. The King has decided that his Majesty's Civil List should be reduced by £50,000 while the emergency lasts. ... I am to add that the Queen and the other members of the Royal Family who are in receipt of Parliamentary Grants are all desirous that reductions of these Grants should be made during this time of national crisis.'

The Yorks suffered with the rest. They looked sadly at their depleted income and increasing expenses, and knew that a sacrifice would have to be made. The Duke, examining the cut in his £25,000 a year, knew what it must be. He sold his six beloved hunters and gave up hunting with the Pytchley. But when the horses were sold they fetched little more than one hundred and fifty guineas apiece.

Meantime the Duchess, fully recovered after the birth of Princess Margaret, had been busy on the royal roundabout. She had been in the sun at Ascot, in a truly Ascot hat, and driven down the course in the royal parade. In July she had opened the Princess Beatrice Social Centre in Fulham, and a thousand tenants of the Metropolitan Housing Corporation gave her and Mr. George Lansbury a rousing reception. Then off across the Channel with her husband to inaugurate a British Week at the Colonial Exhibition in Paris. Though a great lover of sweets, it was gingerly, and with suspicion, that she nibbled a native concoction in the Moroccan Building.

Then to family affairs. On 10th August, at Glamis, the Earl and Countess of Strathmore celebrated their golden wedding. There were thirty-four in the family photograph, ranging from Lord Strathmore at seventy-six to Margaret Rose toddling up to her first birthday.

In October came a wedding that was a milestone in the Duchess's role as mother, for Princess Elizabeth was to try her hand at being a bridesmaid for the first time. On the 24th, Lady May Cambridge, daughter of the Earl of Athlone and Princess Alice, was married to Captain Henry Abel Smith at the parish church at Balcombe, in Sussex. Queen Mary was there, with her four sons and one daughter-in-law. The Prince of Wales arrived in an extraordinary car of airship design, but it was the little Princess who stole the limelight. She came in a white fur wrap, and looked entrancing. Her feet danced to the Wedding March, and she was presented with a white lily from the church as a prize for good behaviour. Other points of interest were that Lady May was the first British royal bride to omit the word 'obey', and that one of the bridesmaids was the lovely Lady Alice Douglas Scott, soon to join the Duchess as a daughter-in-law of the King.

15 The Duchess and the Heir

A
T the time when Lady Elizabeth Bowes-Lyon was con-
sidering on the problem of whether to marry the Duke of
York, she was talking one day to the Prince of Wales. He
said to her: 'You had better take him and go on in the end to Buck
House.'

The words were of interest on two counts. Firstly, it had been
Queen Mary's original idea that the Lady Elizabeth should marry
her eldest son and thus begin the sure road towards the Palace.
Secondly, some indication was given that the Prince had early con-
sidered the possibility that he might not reach the Throne or that
some event might cause him to withdraw from the right of succession.
In the event the seeds of abdication were sown long before the
Prince met Mrs. Wallis Simpson at Craven Lodge.

In 1918 King George and Queen Mary faced a problem over their
eldest son which in many ways resembled that which had confronted
Queen Victoria and Prince Albert in 1861. Then 'Bertie', Prince of
Wales, was showing signs of a tendency towards fast living. He liked
the ladies, and had already been involved. Prince Albert was convinced that unless his son was quickly settled in a home of his own,
with the steadying influence of a wife, he would never become fit to
take over the reins of sovereignty. When the same time came in the
life of David, Prince of Wales, it arrived later than it had done for
his grandfather owing to the interruption of the war years, and
furthermore he had been seasoned by his experience in the trenches.
Neither were King George and Queen Mary to be compared in
emotional awareness, ambition and control with Queen Victoria and
her husband.

Although the King was determined that his sons should hold him in fear, the guiding force behind this was tradition. He had been frightened of his father, and his father had been frightened of his parents. Therefore, *ipso facto*, the principle continued. The treatment had begun early for David. Soon after Edward VII came to the Throne, Lady Oxford was asked to tea at Windsor. She sat next to the boy and found him shy and charming, but she noted how his father and grandfather chaffed him all the time. That night she asked her husband if he thought such teasing was good for a small boy. Lord Oxford replied: 'From the days of Peter the Great to the reign of Queen Victoria this has been a custom with Kings. It is not my idea of family fun.'

There was a wide divergence in approach to emotional matters in the relevant mothers. Queen Mary could not bring herself to talk of affairs of the heart with her children. When her eldest son, as King Edward VIII, returned from his much talked of cruise on the *Nahlin*, Mrs. Simpson being his guest, the Queen confined her queries on the holiday to the state of the weather in the Adriatic. Queen Victoria took a very different line. After 'Bertie's' aberration with a young lady of Cambridge in the autumn of 1861, she insisted on knowing the full details, despite 'Bertie's' plea to his father that she should not be told. It was the same when her second son, Prince Alfred, strayed at Malta.

Queen Victoria and Prince Albert had achieved the married state of their Prince of Wales by *force majeure*, brushing aside his fears of the nuptial bed. But in 1918 it was obviously impractical to ensnare David, Prince of Wales, with the simple ruse of letting him encounter, as if by accident, a penniless Princess in a cathedral. As European Princesses were rare, and in any case unpopular with the British public, the bait would have to be the daughter of a senior member of the peerage, and such young ladies are not prone to matters of arrangement. The suspicion that such a line was being followed had, in fact, flashed through the mind of Lady Elizabeth Bowes-Lyon.

Yet there had been hopes that the matter would solve itself. It was widely reported that the Prince of Wales was in love with the Duke of Sutherland's daughter, Lady Rosemary Leveson-Gower, and many people thought that he would like to marry her. In this case the problem of the King and Queen would have been solved. But in 1919 Lady Rosemary married Lord Ednam, and in the years ahead no signs of an alliance of such a nature showed.

In the inherited traits of the Royal Family certain emotional likenesses have showed clearly from generation to generation. The cause may lie in the distant background of health and also in the union of families closely interrelated. Such obvious tendencies were ignored in royal schoolrooms, where an effort was made to produce offspring to a standard plan, sometimes with dangerous results. The one side leaned towards the highly volatile, the other to the lymphatic. In the family of George III the contrast was to be seen in George IV and the Duke of Cambridge; in that of Queen Victoria, Princess Louise and Princess Beatrice; in that of Edward VII, King George V and the Duke of Clarence. There has seldom been little doubt as to which side of the line a Prince or Princess stood. In the family of King George and Queen Mary the contrast could be seen in the two eldest sons. And it is a contrast that has often led to volcanic eruptions in affairs of the heart.

The Prince Consort knew of this trait, and set about the elimination of it in his family with the same discipline that he had exercised upon himself when young. He distrusted women as a whole, and none but Empress Eugenie of the French could put a twinkle in his eye or receive more than the touch of a cold hand. Yet his distrust would have been even greater if he had lived in the 1920s instead of the 1850s. Now a generation of young womanhood, released into emancipation in the space of four years, who had been called upon to do men's work and had done it well, who had known tragedy and seen life at its worst, had flung aside their bonds and tasted freedom. Starved of pleasure, they were now pleasure-bound, without restriction.

It was into this cauldron that the Prince of Wales, unsettled in his heart by great experiences that had come to him so young, was thrown. To use his own words about the 1920s, he worked hard and he played hard. Work hard he certainly did, both at home and abroad. He became Britain's greatest ambassador. He achieved a degree of popularity that has probably never been rivalled by a royal personage. He was the world's most sought-after bachelor. And on his pinnacle he came to rebel against the Victorian order of life and to yearn for many changes.

Seeking for a satisfaction, partly of relaxation, partly of achievement, he found it best in the hunting fields of the Midlands, and on the point-to-point courses. Being on one of six horses to rise simultaneously for a fence, or finding himself in the lead at the last under the crowded hill at Epperstone. He met a motley assortment of people while out with the packs of Northamptonshire, Nottinghamshire and Leicestershire. He thus describes them in his memoirs: 'Intermixed with the local landed gentry, who form the sure base of any hunting community, was a lively sampling of dashing figures; noblemen and their ladies; wealthy people who had discovered that the stable door was a quick if expensive short-cut into society; a strong injection of Americans from the famous eastern hunts; ladies whose pursuit of the fox was only a phase of an even more intense pursuit of romance; retired admirals and generals; cavalrymen and Guardsmen; good riders on bad horses; bad riders on good horses. . . .'

He paints the picture well. There were many, with new found wealth, for whom the quarry was the Prince of Wales, and his patronage, and not the fox. Temptation is a matter of degree, and no man had it greater than he. 'And so,' he says, 'the 1920s spun for me their bright magic.' Yet some of the fairies who handled the wands were not approved of in the cold cloisters of the Church and behind the castle walls of the Establishment.

To the Duchess of York, in her early married years, the sports and pastimes of her eldest brother-in-law, the rebellion within him, his aims and concepts of change, the social revolution in which he dabbled, touched her life but lightly. She was not to know that the moving finger would, within a few short years, reshape her destiny. They mingled together gracefully on the royal stage, but, when the curtain came down, they left from opposite wings. The gulf between them was that while she, after due consideration, had entered the royal circle prepared to accept it as it was and serve it accordingly, he, born into it and rebellious against its bonds, was bound for change and revaluation.

The day that the Duchess went to Westminster Abbey heralded a complete transformation both in routine and thought. Thereafter every waking hour was occupied with the problems immediately to hand, the finding of a suitable home, her manifold royal duties, her overseas tours, the impediment in her husband's speech, the arrival and upbringing of children. She has never criticized the actions of others. Given a job of work to do she has always done it with all her power. She was to tell her daughters—'Your work is the rent you pay for the room you occupy on earth.'

The Prince of Wales was delighted when his brother married Lady Elizabeth Bowes-Lyon. He made that delight very clear on the wedding day. He later wrote that she 'had brought into the family a lively and refreshing spirit.' But in their private life the Yorks saw little of the Prince. One reason for this was the continuing round of tours undertaken on both sides. Another was that they had very different ideas on how to spend the hours of relaxation.

The Prince and the Duke were fond of one another, and the bond of brotherhood tied them together. They shared certain interests, in particular hunting. But 'Bertie' was too like his father for real intimacy. The elder brother summed up: 'Strongly rooted each in his own existence, they tended to be withdrawn from the hurly-burly of life that I relished.' In addition each had wives for whom they called as soon as they reached the front door.

Of an evening the Duke and Duchess liked to slip out quietly and go to a film. To attend a theatre without fuss or dine quietly in the soft lights. If the Duke was out late there was likely to be a telephone call enquiring as to his estimated time of return.

Then the Duke and Duchess gave the Prince of Wales something that he could find nowhere else—the love and interest of nieces. Thereafter he became a more frequent visitor at 145, Piccadilly. He would join in the evening session of nursery games. He became versed in accomplishments very strange to him, like animal grab and snap. Liking the hurly-burly, he found it here in a very novel form. There was an original and favourite game called Winnie-the-Pooh. In hushed silence, before the fire, the Duchess would read from a story book. When she had finished, it was the part of her daughters and brother-in-law to mime the characters of which she had told. One evening, as he left, the Prince turned to his hostess and said: 'You make family life so much fun.'

As soon as she could talk Princess Margaret Rose gravitated towards the Prince of Wales as a moth turns to a flame. There was so much in the make-up of the two that was in tune. He soon became her favourite uncle. It was to be hardest of all, when the time came, for her to understand.

Meantime, in 1932, there began buzzes among the people who like to buzz and are the first to do so, of the relationship between the Heir to the Throne and Mrs. Wallis Warfield Simpson, a married American lady of charm and wit and intellect. But buzzes had been heard before in 145, Piccadilly and this was not as yet allowed to disturb the tranquillity of that peaceful home.

In the early 1930s the tide of royal popularity ran high. The King had fought his way back from the gates of death and gained esteem by his financial sacrifice in the national economic crisis. Princess Mary, the Forces' sweetheart of the First World War, had become Princess Royal. Three Princes were likely to marry and there was expectation for the resultant gilt and gingerbread. Two little Princesses danced through the headlines and drove in their carriage through Regent's Park. And 'The Smiling Duchess' kept on smiling and grew in stature every year.

In the three years before the death of King George V the Duchess's programme was arduous and never ceasing. In 1932 she completed a task with which she had been entrusted in Australia. Then the women of Victoria had asked her to carry to London the banner of the Australian Section of the Toc H League. She had taken it to All Hallows' Church, Barking-by-the-Tower. Now she was present at the Dedication Service there, and later at the ceremony at Church House Westminster, organized by the Toc H League of Women Helpers.

Among the most important tours that she undertook was that of South Wales. The Duke knew Cardiff well and was a Freeman of the City, and this was not the Duchess's first visit to the Principality.[1] The Welsh turned out for her in their thousands and immediately took her to their hearts.

[1] In August 1926 the Duke and Duchess were initiated as Bards at the Welsh Eisteddfod at Swansea.

Scotland saw much of her. In 1932 she was at Arbroath to name the new lifeboat. The following year she went over the sea to Skye, and to Dunvegan Castle, the stronghold of the Clan Macleod. This was the first official visit of royalty to the misty isle for four hundred years. In November they were in Edinburgh for the Armistice Day ceremonies.

Thousand upon thousand the total of their miles piled up. They made their first official visit to Plymouth; at Bath five thousand Boy Scouts greeted them in the Royal Victoria Park; at Middlesborough they opened the new, half-million-pound bridge over the River Tees; in Sheffield they opened the new Central Library and the Graves Art Gallery and toured steelworks; at Lincoln they attended the thanksgiving service for the restoration of the Cathedral.

Yet the temple that the Duchess was building to house the treasure of a people's love was laid on the sure foundation of many little pebbles laid in hard cement. There was nothing of sensation or public acclaim in the organizing work that she did on behalf of, or the many visits she paid to, hospitals, missions, homes for children, schools and welfare societies. Their name is legion—Dr. Barnado's, Middlesex Hospital, Moorfields Eye Hospital, West Ham Central Mission, National Society for Maternity and Child Welfare, Croydon General Hospital, to mention but a few. Then there was St. Mary's Hospital, Paddington, of course, a special favourite. When it was remarked to her during the Second World War that the fact that St. Mary's had escaped bomb damage was in the nature of a miracle, she replied: 'A miracle? That may be so. You know, I include St. Mary's in my prayers every night.'

To the young and to the old, to the ill and to the disabled, the visits of the Duchess were marked in red on the calendar of their days. Each person being an equal fraction of the nation, there was behind her, when she became Queen, an army of friends whose voices were seldom heard but who had implicit faith in her.

It was pleasing, at this period, to see the Duchess taking Princess Elizabeth with her on public occasions. The Princess's baptism of crowds came at scenes which children love, the Aldershot Tattoo, the Richmond Horse Show, the Highland Games and the Circus at Olympia. These led to a more formal engagement. In April 1935 she went with her mother to Westminster Abbey for the distribution of the Royal Maundy. As the King was seventy, as many old people received a pound each, plus as many pennies as the King had years, in specially minted coins.

The Duchess, with her husband and her two daughters, had been to the Abbey on 29th November of the previous year, one of the gayest and most brilliant days of the 1930s. Prince George, newly created Duke of Kent, was married to beautiful Princess Marina of Greece, and it was the first royal wedding to be broadcast. The Duke of York walked with his brother, Princess Elizabeth was a bridesmaid, and the Duchess sat on the red and white chair in the chancel, Princess Margaret Rose, a mite in a silvery dress, on a footstool beside her. Later the Royal Family came out on the balcony at Buckingham Palace, the King himself ensuring that his grand-daughters got a good view of the rolling tide of humanity below.

The King's health was holding up better than many people had forecast, yet he was a very tired man. Still he held fast to the reins of kingship, though owing to the dangers of fatigue, he allowed the Prince of Wales to represent him on increasingly frequent occasions, and the Duke of York to assist in the administration of Sandringham and Balmoral. At seventy his bite was less fierce, but he barked more often. He became impatient, more liable to carp and find fault. He would sit in his window at Windsor, watching his people strolling below in the sun. Raising his eyes to Heaven, and probably Queen Victoria, he would ejaculate: 'Good God, look at those short skirts. Look at that bobbed hair!' It was Queen Mary who bore the burden. His only loves, apart from his wife who was part of him, were the Empire, Sandringham, shooting, and the ladies at 145, Piccadilly.

He found out that from the window of his study, and with the aid of field glasses, he could pick out a part of 145. Each morning after breakfast, when he had put a cigarette in his holder and inspected the weather, he would train those glasses upon Piccadilly. From a certain window there could be seen a wave. Princess Elizabeth was saying 'Good morning'.

There came the summer of the King's content. He and his Queen had been twenty-five years upon the Throne. On Jubilee Day, 6th May 1935, they drove to St. Paul's for Thanksgiving. Before them, with a Captain's escort of Royal Horse Guards, through that in-numerable crowd, went the Duke and Duchess of York, she in powder blue, the two Princesses dressed to the colour of a pink rose and with bonnets to match. It was upon this carriage that so many eyes were focused. For each passing year the elder of the little girls grew nearer to the Throne.

To the Duke and Duchess came the honour of representing the King and Queen in Scotland, and four days later they were at the Jubilee celebrations in Edinburgh, staying with Lord and Lady Elphinstone at Carberry Tower.

That summer the royal roundabout revolved unceasingly, churning out its gay tunes and tooting to herald the end of an age linked to Queen Victoria. To the Duchess there came a new experience. She became airborne for the first time. In July she flew with her husband to Brussels for the 'British Week' of the International Exhibition there. The new mode of travel did not suit her and she was air-sick. Her heartfelt comment was: 'It is lucky that this is not a procession.'

At the great ball which marked the completion of the ceremonies, she danced with King Leopold, descendant of the 'Uncle Leopold' who had played so great a part in the early days of Queen Victoria. Upon this old Etonian Monarch the 'Curse of the Coburgs', placed upon the House by the Kohary monk, had already struck. In 1934 his father had been killed by a climbing accident in the mountains. It was to strike again and again. Two months after the Yorks returned to London, the Duke travelled back to Belgium, this time to represent the King at the funeral of Queen Astrid,[1] who had been killed in a motor crash.

There were two Scottish days of that year that were of particular appeal to the Duchess. At Glamis the Black Watch, the regiment of her home county and the regiment of her brothers, marched past and received new colours. And in Paris, in November, the Duke and Duchess were guests of honour at the dinner of the Caledonian Society of France.

It was in this month that the Duchess gained another sister-in-law, and a daughter of Scotland at that. In August the engagement had been announced of Prince Henry, Duke of Gloucester, to Lady

[1] Princess Astrid of Sweden, married in 1926.

Alice Montagu-Douglas-Scott, third daughter of the Duke of Buccleuch, who had been a friend of the King since boyhood. But in October the Duke died, and the wedding on 6th November took place in the Chapel at Buckingham Palace instead of Westminster Abbey. Princesses Elizabeth and Margaret were bridesmaids, 'too sweet', Queen Mary said. That evening the King wrote in his diary: 'Now, all the children are married but David.'

That was the problem. That was the dark cloud that edged across the sunset of his life. For eighteen months and more the name of Mrs. Wallis Warfield Simpson had been a dagger in the body of his peace. He had been shown cuttings from the American press. Britons resident abroad had been sending home angry letters. Old friends had whispered to him that he should talk to his Heir. His answer was: 'There's nothing I can do with the fellow.'

There was, of course, much that he could do while he remained alive. If a union was proposed, or feasible, he held the trump card of the Royal Marriage Act. But so far apart had the King and Queen drawn from their eldest son in matters affecting his private life, that now they could not talk to him. Yet no one was more versed in the vagaries of royal hearts than the King. Free of them himself, except for one false and libellous allegation, he had watched his father step, light-heartedly at least, from love to love. There had been crises for his brother and those sisters of his, 'the whispering Wales girls'. There had been problems among his uncles and aunts. They were problems played out behind the curtain that hid them from the public in the pit and stalls. The Palace hush was as impenetrable as the London fog.

Now the Palace kept its hush, and the Press was silent. Although she had curtseyed before him, the King cast Mrs. Simpson out of every part of his life except his innermost thoughts. When his biographies came to be written, her name was not upon the pages.

In natural course the rumours, and the evidence, reached 145, Piccadilly. Certainly the Duke and Duchess of Kent knew how matters were. Yet to the house of York it remained a problem that would sort itself. 'Bertie' had always played second fiddle to David. He expected him to lead, and queried little how he did it. 'Bertie' was the faithful brother, always ready to help out, even if this entailed such a chore as clearing the brushwood away from Fort Belvedere. The point had, however, now become increasingly clear that, as the Prince of Wales was forty-one and his affections clearly focused on a married woman, Princess Elizabeth would one day be called to take her place at the head of the nation. The Duchess was therefore in a most unenviable position. There was nothing for her to do but keep on smiling and watch the drama unfold.

Then, in December, the Duchess retired to bed at the Royal Lodge with influenza. It developed into pneumonia. For her husband this new anxiety was added to another. The King was ailing. A series of sadnesses, the deaths of the Duke of Buccleuch, Queen Astrid, Lord Jellicoe and, mostly, that of his favourite sister, Princess Victoria, seemed to have broken his spirit. Christmas was to him the greatest day of the year. He loved to have his family around him. That he should be gay this particular 25th December was vital. But the Duchess was too ill to leave home. So it was, on the 21st, that Princesses Elizabeth and Margaret travelled down to Norfolk with their grandparents, to put the warm of sunlight into the icy, snowbound fens.

For the Duchess, ill as she was, it was a sacrifice not to be able to see her children peep round the bedroom door on Christmas Day, see their delight at presents, hear their gay laughter as they played in the garden. Instead, in the cold afternoon, she heard the voice of a weak old man sending out from Sandringham his last message to the Empire.

In the 'Big House' in Norfolk the other members of the family were doing their utmost to keep up the spirits of the King. The Prince of Wales was there, the Duke and Duchess of Kent with their little son,[1] the Duke of Gloucester and his bride, and the Princesses Elizabeth and Margaret to give the tonic that was needed. It was for them that the presents that came from the twenty-foot tree on Christmas Eve gave the biggest thrill. Yet in the party there was one who felt strangely ill at ease. It was the Heir to the Throne. He saw grandparents engrossed with their grandchildren, husbands with their wives, a mother with her baby. For him there was no such comfort. There was a sense of loneliness for he who had romped

[1] Prince Edward, now the Duke of Kent, born 9th October 1935.

in this house, at this special season, in the days of Edward and Alexandra.

The King went out for a ride on Jock, his pony. Beyond the gates he saw a line of motor cars and that a crowd had gathered. He asked a lodge-keeper what they wanted. When it was explained to him that they were people, many from a distance, who did not know that the grounds were closed when the King was in residence, he ordered them to be let in at once.

A small house party had been arranged for the second weekend of January, but as the guests arrived on the 15th the King retired to the bedroom which he was not to leave again. That evening the Queen asked the Duke of York to help her out with the entertaining. There was a conference by the bedside in the Royal Lodge. The Duchess was recovering well from the attack of pneumonia, and both agreed that the call should be answered. The Duke arrived at Sandringham next day, and on the 17th the Prince of Wales was summoned. On the 18th the guests left, the Princesses travelling with them to rejoin their mother. In the morning they had built a snowman on the lawn. The picture of them snowballing one another, Princess Margaret laughing on the ground as she waited her sister's throw, went round the world, and was the last happy royal picture of the reign of George V. Then they went to say good-bye to their grandfather, and were gone.

In his red-carpeted room the King lay peacefully, listening to his wife reading to him and watching the log fire flickering away the time. At five minutes to midnight on 20th January 1936 Sandringham's very good squire went out on the evening tide.

The Royal Family, 1939

In America, June 1939. The King and Queen with President Roosevelt and Mrs. Franklin Roosevelt

Buckingham Palace, 11th September 1940

16　*The Short Story of a King*

NEXT morning these words appeared in capital letters on the front page of the *Daily Express*: 'NINE-YEAR-OLD PRINCESS ELIZABETH, ELDER DAUGHTER OF THE DUKE AND DUCHESS OF YORK, IS NOW SECOND IN THE LINE OF SUCCESSION TO THE THRONE. ONE DAY SHE MAY BE QUEEN ELIZABETH OF ENGLAND.'

The Duke was at Sandringham. The Duchess was alone with her children at the Royal Lodge. She had to tell them that the grandfather who had recited to them would recite no more:

> 'Up the airy mountain,
> Down the rushy glen,
> We daren't go a-hunting
> For fear of little men.
> Wee folk, good folk,
> Trooping all together.
> Green jacket, red cap,
> And white owl's feather.'[1]

She knew now that there was only one life between 'Lilibet' and Queenship, and that life her husband's. And 'Lilibet' was only nine. And as she pondered on many things, the Duke flew back to London with King Edward VIII, the first British Monarch to fly.[2]

There then had to be settled the question of whether the Duchess should go to Sandringham to return with the body of the King.

---

[1] William Allingham's rhyme was a favourite of King George V, and he had taught it to his own children.

[2] Although much comment was made about this, Queen Maria Christina of Spain had flown in a balloon as long before as 1889.

That open sweep of north Norfolk is a treacherous part in winter, and the Duchess was but shortly recovered from pneumonia. Yet for her there was only one answer, and on the 22nd she travelled there with her husband. Queen Mary was in need of support, to have around her people whom she knew well. It was now fifteen years since she had met the Duchess, and there had grown a strong bond of trust and friendship between them. The Duchess of Kent had only been her daughter-in-law for fifteen months, and the Duchess of Gloucester but three. Thus it was that when the gun-carriage moved slowly along the avenues towards Wolferton station, with the Queen in her carriage were the Princess Royal and the Duchess of York.

The Duchess was to see much of great courage in the days to come. Even at the death-bed of her husband it had been the Queen, in a wonder of self-control, who had comforted her sons. That self-control continued through the emotional climax of the pageantry of a nation's mourning. The Duchess was beside the royal widow all through the funeral day, and there were moments then to touch a young mother's heart. As the cortège wound from Westminster to Paddington the pressure of the crowds brought it to a halt. There was sun in Piccadilly, storm clouds to the north and a glimpse of a rainbow in the sky. On the mauve-draped balcony of No. 145 stood Princess Margaret, a sad little five-year-old dressed in grey. She curtseyed as the gun-carriage lumbered by.

Princess Elizabeth was waiting at Paddington station, and as the coaches arrived she anxiously peered through the dark veils to find her mother. From Windsor station to the Castle she travelled with Queen Mary, Queen Maud of Norway, the Princess Royal and the Duchess. The Princess sat in the Garter stalls. When the service was over she stood for a few seconds, a trembling figure, looking down into the cavern that had swallowed her grandfather. It was an ordeal for the child, and an ordeal for the mother too.

They had been such friends. Once, after a slight difference of opinion with her, the King had left the room. She had called him back. Thinking that he had won, delighted he returned, only to be solemnly reminded that he had omitted to close the door.

A new reign meant more work for the Duke and Duchess, despite

146

the quietude of six months of full Court mourning. So busy was King Edward that he found it impossible to keep up with his many presidencies, such as those of hospitals, and in certain cases these were taken over by the Duke, who was quick to visit them and learn their problems. There was promotion too. Now that he had become Heir Presumptive his Service ranks rose from Rear-Admiral to Vice-Admiral, from Air Vice-Marshal to Air Marshal, and from Major-General to Lieutenant-General. Parliament, realizing the Duke's new duties, increased his Civil List from £25,000 to £50,000.

In 1935 the honours and appointments officially quoted after the Duchess's name were 'G.B.E., Hon. LL.D. Belfast, St. Andrews and Glasgow, Hon. D.C.L. Oxford; Dame Grand Cross of the Order of St. John of Jerusalem, and Commandant-in-Chief of the Nursing Divisions of the St. John Ambulance Brigade, a Freeman of Stirling, Colonel-in-Chief of the King's Own Yorkshire Light Infantry.' There was much to be added in the years that lay ahead.

One of the first jobs allotted to the Duke was to make a survey of the Sandringham estate, with a view to making economies. He spent a fortnight there with Lord Radnor.

Immediately on the death of his father the new King had ordered the clocks to be put back to Greenwich time. From the years when his grandfather had reigned there as Prince of Wales, clocks had always been kept half an hour fast, partly so that the Prince could get an extra thirty minutes of shooting and partly to ensure that his wife was not late for meals. The staff took this as a sign that life around the 'Big House' was to change, and they were right.

The Duke's report was clear, concise, and full of commonsense and, although some of the recommended changes were against the promptings of his heart, in the event most of them were carried out when he became Squire. But the King regarded Sandringham as 'a voracious white elephant', with its trunk in the Privy Purse sucking up the gold, and alterations began at once. There were cuts in staff. There were changes in the kennels and the stables. Rumours ran around that the estate was to be sold. The King has said that he was only opening windows to let in a little fresh air. But open windows cause draughts in corridors, and then people catch colds. Rumbles of discontent came from Norfolk.

In the meantime a visitor called to see the Duchess at 145, Piccadilly, Mr. Norman Hartnell, to discuss the provision of black outfits to be worn during the mourning period. The Duchess had met Mr. Hartnell three months earlier, when he made the dresses for Princess Elizabeth and Margaret for their role as bridesmaids to the Duchess of Gloucester.

There came, at this time, signs of a subtle change in the demeanour of the Duchess. Her smile was less ebullient, more restrained, more regal. She had perfected the measured tread which locomotes royal ladies. There was a new chic about her. She appeared more dress conscious. She once said, 'Some clothes like me and some don't.' She was certainly wearing the ones that liked her now. And, if she looked slimmer, it had to be remembered that she had just recovered from pneumonia and passed through a time of great strain and sorrow. In fact she had lost two stones.

There were a number of reasons for the change. She was now not only 'The Smiling Duchess', but also the mother of one who might one day be Queen, and the cameras had an insatiable appetite for Princess Elizabeth. Then the King had no wife to play the female lead. And two young sisters-in-law were setting a high standard in fashion and beauty.

Early in March the Yorks went to Compton Place, near Eastbourne, the house where King George had stayed the year before. Here the Duchess completed the last stage of her convalescence. On the occasions when she was seen, such as attending at Eastbourne Parish Church, the change in her was noted.

The winter of mourning for a King turned peacefully to spring and then to summer. It was peaceful, at least in the confines that hold the sanctity of Windsor. Princess Elizabeth began swimming lessons. The Duke and Duchess planted and plucked in the oasis of their garden, which grew in beauty every year. The Duke, researching on the history of the Royal Lodge, was often to be seen on his way to the Castle Library. But in Europe the kettle of power that the Dictators had placed on the fire of their ambitions was already beginning to jig and whistle. And in the American magazines the name of Mrs. Wallis Simpson was often at a story's head.

While the more sensational publications of the United States were not to be numbered among the British organs of news and views, the seedsmen's catalogues and the faded archives on the tables of the Royal Lodge, the Court Circular was readily available. On two occasions had Mrs. Simpson's name appeared among the King's dinner guests at York House, mixing with the Baldwins, the Churchills, the Lindberghs. It was also known that, at nearby Fort Belvedere, for those gatherings known to King George as simply 'week-ends' (the tone of his voice made an adjective superfluous), Mrs. Simpson was often in attendance, with an aunt as chaperone. To the Royal Family hers was just a name that would slip away into the night of time as other names had slipped before her. So the Duke and Duchess minded their own business. Yet the matter was fast becoming, not only their business, but the business of the nation.

On 16th July the Duchess underwent a most unpleasant shock. On that day the King, accompanied by the Duke of York, had presented new colours to battalions of the Brigade of Guards in Hyde Park. He began the ride back to Buckingham Palace, the Duke beside him.

In the crowds on Constitution Hill stood a man later to give his name as George Andrew McMahon, a man with a grievance. In the pocket of his jacket was a loaded revolver. His obvious agitation drew the attention of Special Constable Dick, and he moved in closer. As the King and the Duke came from Hyde Park Corner and under the Arch, McMahon pushed his way forward, the revolver in his upstretched hand. Then Dick threw himself upon the armed attacker. The revolver spun across the roadway, striking the hind leg of the King's horse. Neither the King nor the Duke knew what the flying object was. But no explosion came. They rode on. Soon they turned towards one another and grinned.

It was fortunate for the Duchess that she learned that her husband was safe before she read the first accounts in the evening newspapers.

The Court now moved from full to half mourning. The full programme for the Duchess began again. On the first day of the release she opened Coram's Fields and the Harmsworth Memorial Playground, the result of great efforts to save the old Foundling Hospital site. The busy days continued until it was time to turn to Scotland once again. Meantime the King was cruising down the Dalmatian coast on the yacht *Nahlin*, amongst those on board being Mrs. Wallis Simpson. The shore line was thick with reporters.

Queen Mary busied herself through the days with matters domestic and personal. She had much to do. There were the multiple possessions of her husband to sort out, and also many of his sister, Princess Victoria, who had died only a few weeks before him. She had to arrange her move from Buckingham Palace to Marlborough House, and to settle the necessary alterations and redecoration of her future home. There were affairs to be settled at Windsor, Sandringham and Balmoral. But she was glad of the work, for it kept her mind off other things, chief among them being the friendship of the King with Mrs. Simpson.

The words of a husband in the last months of his life ring clear thereafter in a widow's ears. Queen Mary was hearing them now, words spoken in the summer of 1935, some of them in the presence of Cosmo Lang, Archbishop of Canterbury. King George had said that this affair was not as the others had been. That this was enduring, and it was that which worried him. Again, in his last December, he had burst out with, 'I pray to God that my eldest son will never marry and have children, and that nothing will come between Bertie and Lilibet and the Throne.'[1]

She saw Mrs. Simpson's name in the Court Circular, but still she held her tongue. She told her closest friends that she did not believe in interfering in the personal matters of children. But there was another reason. She knew that, of those children, the eldest was the most obstinate and difficult to sway. In fact she feared that interference might drive him further in the other direction.

Then the Press cuttings about the *Nahlin* began to come in. She read them all through and put them aside without comment. She filled her diary with records of the weather and her daily perambulations between Buckingham Palace and Marlborough House. Her deep fear was that she would be asked to receive Mrs. Simpson. This she had promised her husband before he died that she would not do. True, they had met briefly in the gay moments of the wedding of the

[1] *Thatched with Gold.*

Duke and Duchess of Kent, but Queen Mary was determined that it should not happen again.

At Birkhall the Yorks lazed away the early autumn of the Highlands. Picnics and ponies, dogs and guns. There were expeditions to Altnagiubhsaich by the clear water of Loch Muick and clambers up Creagan Lurachain. The Princesses ran in the footsteps of the children of George V, Edward VII and Victoria. Here, and here alone, was the record of the line of Queen Victoria and Prince Albert complete, with over eighty years of traditional visits at set times. Balmoral and its wide lands breathed peace and tranquillity. Loves had blossomed here, but there had been no deaths. To the elders of the Royal Family Deeside was sacrosanct.

In the middle of September the sanctity of Prince Albert's *schloss* was broken by the chink of cocktail glasses and a tinkling piano in the plaid apartments. The King had arrived with a party of guests, among them the Duke and Duchess of Kent, Mr. and Mrs. Herman Rogers and Mrs. Wallis Simpson. Of them, only the Duke of Kent had been imbued with the Balmoral tradition. There was, naturally, strong contrast to be noted here between the quiet visits of King George with his retinue of Ministers and intimates, and even more with the days of Queen Victoria, when guests who wanted to smoke a pipe had to do so out of the window and often meals would pass without a word being spoken except those of the Queen to her dog.

The Balmoral party was content in itself, and there was little communication with the Yorks at Birkhall or the Gloucesters, who were at Abergeldie. The Duke was with the King at the inspection of the King's Guard of the Gordon Highlanders, but he did not manage to get a word alone with his brother. The Duchess contented herself with her children at Birkhall. But when the Princesses had gone to bed there was much that her husband wished to discuss with her. Changes in management and staff were being carried out at the Castle. The King had arranged them in direct talks with the Crown authorities and the Duke was not consulted. In fact he did not know of them until they were *fait accompli*.

The real worries of the Yorks now began. It seemed that, not only were they drifting apart from the King on the current of affairs, but also that the rope that held brother to brother was becoming frayed.

The Duke had been consulted about Sandringham. Why, then, not about Balmoral? Was he considered to have one foot too firmly planted in the nineteenth century? The Duke considered himself part of Balmoral, and the people of it knew and liked him well. As for the Duchess, they had known her now for fifteen years. She was one of their own when she came as a bride, and she fitted there as snugly as a kilt does to a Lyon. She was, in fact, better known about Deeside than the majority of the Royal Family.

The King's party left the Castle at the end of September, the Yorks moved to Glamis. It was from there that the Duke wrote to his mother, saying how sad he was about the changes that had come to Balmoral and that he had known nothing about them. The family, which had been so reticent amongst itself, was beginning to come together.

Back in London in October the royal march took on its usual tread with little sign of anyone being out of step. Off went the Duchess, with the two Princesses, on her annual visit to the Lord Roberts' Memorial Workshops for Disabled ex-Servicemen. The King moved into Buckingham Palace, Queen Mary into Marlborough House, and Mrs. Simpson into a small house that she had rented at Felixstowe by the Suffolk sea. At Ipswich, on the 27th, her petition for divorce from Mr. Ernest Simpson was due to be heard.

Then a letter arrived at 145, Piccadilly that penetrated into the last alcoves of peace left to the Yorks. It was from the King's Private Secretary. It told how the Prime Minister had asked the King to persuade Mrs. Simpson to withdraw her petition and had been told that there could be no interference with the affairs of an individual. The Duke and Duchess turned to the American newspapers. There it was being confidently said that, once the divorce was through, the King would marry Mrs. Simpson.

On 27th October that divorce was granted. It would become absolute in April 1937. The Coronation of King Edward VIII had been fixed for 12th May.

The Duke and Duchess had resolutely refused to accept the possibility, let alone the probability, that the King would finally allow his love to override his duty to the extent of marrying a twice-divorced woman. Both knew that, if he were to do so, he could not remain as

Sovereign. Now they hung to the hope of a miraculous solution. But a pall of gloom hung over the Piccadilly home. The Duke's feelings regarding his brother were thus summed up by Sir John Wheeler-Bennett: 'As young men they had been friends and comrades, and, after the Duke's marriage, the gaiety and companionship of the Duchess had been an added link in their friendship. Now he felt shut off from his brother, neglected, ignored, unwanted. The situation at Balmoral, during the King's brief visit, had been like a nightmare, not only because of the decisions reached without his knowledge, but because of the hopelessly complicated personal element. He felt that he had lost a friend and was rapidly losing a brother.'

The rift was very clear to the Duchess. One afternoon the King and a Buick-load of his friends, Mrs. Simpson among them, arrived at her home. There was gay chatter over the tea cups, a breeze of scintillation, and the interlude was over. The perfect hostess had played her role. She was not to play it again. The Duchess had met Mrs. Simpson for the first, and only, time. 'Who is she?' asked Princess Elizabeth as the royal car passed out of sight.

With all the seething anxieties within her, publicly she carried on as if there was not a cloud in the sky. Her smile was just as warm. She became Patroness of the Coronation Planting Committee. At a meeting in November she addressed members of local councils gathered from all over the country. She told them that the object of the Committee was to encourage a national effort to make both countryside and town more beautiful. She said: 'I have travelled about a good deal in this beautiful country of ours during the last twelve years. Whether in the big manufacturing towns, mining villages or quiet countryside, one felt that ugliness was creeping in everywhere. . . . Now is the opportunity for our generation to add to the beauty of towns, villages and countryside.'

Few there guessed that it was to be upon her head that a crown would be placed in Westminster Abbey on that day in May.

It was on the 16th that the King told his mother and sister that he intended to marry Mrs. Simpson. The deed was to be done after dinner at Marlborough House, but, to his surprise, he found his young sister-in-law, the Duchess of Gloucester, there. The account of this meal, given in his memoirs, is clear indication of the ordeal through which royal in-laws were passing at this time. As course followed course the Duchess never uttered a word. At the conclusion she blurted out that she was tired, curtseyed and almost fled from the room.

The Duke of York heard the news next day. He was too non-plussed, at first, to speak, and his innermost feelings remained unsaid. When he got back to No. 145 he did not make his entrance with the customary decorum associated with royal returnings. He flung open the Humber door and, bent double, leaped across the steps, as a scrum half dives for the goal line.

The Duchess dreaded the thought of her husband's accession as much as he did, and there now followed much conversation between Marlborough House and No. 145. The Duke saw Mr. Baldwin. Both Queen Mary and he saw the King again, but there were no signs of a change of heart. Then, on the 29th, the Duke and Duchess went to Edinburgh to fulfil long-standing engagements. Arrangements were made for them to be kept in constant touch with developments.

It was a dismal Sunday evening when they left and all through the night the thud of the wheels below their sleeper reminded them that they were being carried further and further away from a crisis that they felt they should not have left. The Duke was installed as Grand Master Mason of Scotland in the place of the King. The Duchess attended a reception given by the Lord Provost of the City for the wives of Masonic officers. The Deaconess Hospital was reopened. In the crowded Usher Hall the Duchess received the Freedom of Edinburgh. They attended a variety performance at the Empire Theatre. It was in the box there, holding a splendid bouquet, that she made her last public appearance as 'The Smiling Duchess'.

On the evening of 2nd December they were back in the sleeper, southward bound. Full of foreboding as to what news was waiting for them at No. 145, they did not have to wait until they reached their home. As the train ran into Euston, as the thousands poured to work, the newspaper placards flashed their message to the returning travellers. 'The King to Marry'—'The Marriage of the King'. Dr. Blunt, Bishop of Bradford, had spoken to his flock. The Press silence was over.

That evening the Duke and Duchess dined with Queen Mary. She had asked the King to come and see her. Tired out, he arrived from Fort Belvedere. The King told his mother, in the presence of the Duke and the Princess Royal, but not the Duchess, that he could not live alone and must marry Mrs. Simpson. In his notes that the Duke made on the Abdication period he used a line instead of the name Simpson, a somewhat telling abbreviation.

Before he left Marlborough House the King asked his brother to come and see him at the Fort next day, Friday, the 4th. The Duke and Duchess went to the Royal Lodge. The meeting was put off until Saturday. On Saturday it was put off until Sunday. No word came then, so in the evening the Duke rang up. He was told that the King was in conference and would ring back. The Yorks sat by the telephone, but no call came. It was not until seven o'clock on Monday that the Duke at last saw his brother, to learn of his irrevocable decision to abdicate. He went back to his Duchess for dinner.

There was almost relief for them, now the terrible suspense was over. But being the kind of man and brother he was, and she the kind of wife, the Duke went back to the Fort after dinner, simply because he felt that his presence might help in the hour of need. The Duchess packed up and waited. Then, when he returned, the two drove together to London. If ever a man wanted the touch of a wife's hand, the Duke of York did that night. They were together, close together, behind the white path of the headlights, driving into uncertainties beyond the ken of human mind.

Then, as if events were not already heavy enough for her to bear, the Duchess developed influenza. Fretting, she lay in her bed at 145, Piccadilly, knowing that these were the moments when the Duke was most in need of her reassuring presence by his side.

There were crowds outside the house now, all day and far into the night, clinging to the railings, trying to get a peep through the windows, watching the callers come and go. Mostly curious sight-seers these, cheering, gossiping, but there were other sounds coming to the Duchess's bedroom, from the road below and from the murk towards the Palace. People were shouting, singly and in unison, 'We want Edward, We want Edward, We want the King, God save the King.'

On the morning of the 10th King Edward VIII calmly signed the six copies of his instrument of abdication and the copies of his message to the Dominion Parliaments. King George VI succeeded to the Throne. In the afternoon Queen Mary called on the Queen Consort and Empress of India. She was sitting up in bed, still thick with cold. She handed the Queen Mother an anti-germ impregnated handkerchief.

There was a vast crowd, cheering wildly, when the Duke got home. His daughters curtseyed to him. Princess Elizabeth wrote, slowly and in capital letters, at the top of her evening prep, 'ABDICATION DAY'.

His Royal Highness Prince Edward of Windsor made his farewell broadcast speech to the shaken, uncertain millions, and at two o'clock on the morning of 12th December boarded *Fury* at Portsmouth for Boulogne. From France he telegraphed to say that he had had a good crossing and was glad to hear that the Accession Council had gone off well. He ended: 'Hope Elizabeth better. Best love and best of luck to you both. David.'

17 A Crown of Thorns

THE newspapers of 12th December 1936 were collectors' pieces. Their circulation was enormous, and in the evening a great number of them were carefully folded and stowed away in bottom drawers as fragments of history. Many of them are still there. Certainly to the new Queen Elizabeth there was much of import in their pages.

> 'Humpty Dumpty sat on the wall.
> Humpty Dumpty had a great fall.
> All the King's horses and all the King's men
> Could not put Humpty back again.'

So quoted Mr. Maxton[1] in the House of Commons, in moving an amendment to the Abdication Bill. The report of his speech continued: 'This crack-up of the monarchy is not merely a matter of the failures of a man or the passions or affections of a man. It is something deeper and more fundamental than that—the whole breaking up of social conceptions, the whole break-up of past ideas of a Royal Family that was clear of the ordinary taints and weaknesses of ordinary men. . . .'

Mr. Campbell Stephen[2] had said words which made a direct hit on the Queen: 'I know that the new Monarch is a married man, but so was Mr. Simpson. As it has happened with others so it may happen here.'

Wide coverage was given to the retiring King's broadcast message

[1] ILP, Glasgow, Bridgeton.
[2] ILP, Camlachie.

157

of farewell. Never before had there been such a vast radio audience, fifty millions listening in the United States alone. In the reports one sentence was picked out in black type. It contained the words of Prince Edward on his brother, the new King.

'He has one matchless blessing enjoyed by so many of you and not bestowed on me—a happy home with his wife and children.'

The Prince's voice had lingered on 'a happy home' and sunk to a softer key for the last three words.

Then there was the message of commendation for her second son from Queen Mary. 'With him I commend my dear daughter-in-law who will be his Queen. May she receive the same unfailing affection and trust which you have given to me for six and twenty years. I know that you have already taken her children to your hearts.'

Despite her restrained message, Queen Mary was hopping with anger. She was too outraged for tears. She had no sympathy to spare for her eldest son. All of it she gave to 'Bertie' and Elizabeth, for it was they who were making the sacrifice. Tighter and tighter drew the knot that bound her to them. It was not until the Duke of Windsor married that she thawed a little. Then, recalling the words of the ill King George V, she said: 'It is no ordinary love that he has for her.' This was later to be corroborated by Sir Winston Churchill: 'The Duke's love for her is one of the great loves of history. . . . Make no mistake, he cannot live without her.' That love was to be confirmed beyond doubt by the passing of the years.

In the dark winter of 1936 the Monarchy was saved, primarily, by the good sense of the British people everywhere, and, secondly, by Queen Mary and the Duchess of York who became Queen Elizabeth. Long before Queen Victoria had forecast that the Monarchy in Britain would not last beyond the 1930s. She had had her experience of Republican aims. She was looking, then, at the Duke of Clarence as the Heir, but later she was able to buttress the continuity by marrying May of Teck to Prince George. What she could not envisage was the introduction into the Family of the daughter of an historic House, little taller than herself, with all of her courage, all of her loyalty and strength and, in addition, armed with a quiver full of charm.

Pages of history as yet unturned will pay full tribute to the part played by Her Majesty Queen Elizabeth the Queen Mother at this crucial time. Yet glimpses are on the pages now. In the *Sunday Express* of 25th March 1962 Mr. John Gordon, replying to criticism of his pungent comments on Royalty, wrote: 'As for the Queen Mother, after the abdication of King Edward VIII she gave guidance, support and tactful leadership to her husband at a most critical time, which may well have saved the Monarchy when it was rocking. No praise can be too high for that service.'

Throughout the crisis Queen Mary and her daughter-in-law had made perfect partners and played their parts well. The older woman was a world figure, and she personified the rock-like solidarity of the Throne and the mother sorting out the problems of her sons. She showed herself in the streets, twice driving over the river to see the ruins of the burned Crystal Palace. She busied herself with Christmas shopping. Her understatements—such as that to Mr. Baldwin, 'This is a pretty kettle of fish'—helped to restrain exaggeration. Her explosion, 'Really! This might be Rumania!' helped to keep matters in perspective.

The Duchess kept herself completely clear of the whirlpool of events in which her future lay. In this she showed great wisdom. She concentrated on supporting and caring for her husband.

The abdication led to a division of loyalties, not only in Britain but throughout the Empire. Edward VIII had travelled widely and was a loved figure in Canada, where he owned the 'E.P.' Ranch, in South Africa, in Australia and in New Zealand. In these countries there was a strong feeling that some solution to the problem of his marriage should be found and that he should stay as King. In Britain those who felt his passing most were the people in the distressed areas, in the Forces, ex-Servicemen, the Midlanders, and a great portion of the younger folk who looked to him as the prophet of modernity. There were many among his supporters who had loud voices and clever pens.

On the opposing side there were those who adhered, simply and unquestioningly, to Queen Mary. The new King had his band of devotees, mostly from the boys' clubs, but, as Duke of York, he had been completely outshone by his brother. But there was another element in the country, particularly strong north of the Border. It was composed of the disciples of 'The Smiling Duchess'. They were quiet people, with soft voices, and no sharp points to their pens.

Now the many pebbles that she had laid in the hard foundation of a nation's love stood firm against the test. For fourteen full years she had been touring the country. She had brought rays of sunshine into the days of the lonely old and the unfortunate young. She had stopped, and smiled, by so many thousands of hospital beds. She was a corner-stone of many women's organizations. A silent army was strong behind her. She stood for everything that they found right in life.

In the long rows of drab Victorian houses outside the towns, behind the privet hedges in the villages, in the lodges by the big gates, in the farmsteads on the hills and down the green lanes, there dwelt, behind the lace curtains, many folk who had spent half of their life in the reign of Queen Victoria. A great number of the women had had experience of domestic service, in the days when Burke's Peerage was in every servants' hall. With George V, they had fought a rearguard action against the twentieth century. They had come to maturity in an age without electricity, sewerage, radio, aeroplanes, cars—even safety bicycles. Their link with the outside world had been the weekly paper from the nearby town, 'The Leisure Hour', 'The Quiver' and 'Family Herald'. They had gossiped over the newest ensemble in the wardrobe of Princess Beatrice and gloried in the good works of Princess Christian.

To these people, who opened their front doors but a crack to strangers, cocktails were a new fangled sin and divorce utterly abhorrent. They bowed their heads to the Chapel or the Archbishop of Canterbury, and they followed the light of good works and a happy family life. They associated Americans with Al Capone, jazz, black singers, and millionaires with horn-rimmed spectacles. Queen Victoria, they knew, had always found them rather odd.

In silent resolution they fell in behind the new Queen, with her solid, home-loving husband and her two dear little Princesses.

A few days after the abdication the Queen wrote to the Archbishop of Canterbury: 'The curious thing is that we are not afraid. . . .' Clear in her mind were the pictures painted in her fourteen years of service as Duchess. She knew that the people who

With Field-Marshal Smuts in South Africa

Prince Charles learns the secrets of grandmother's handbag

The Dashing White Sergeant

had welcomed her then would back her now. They did. They still do.

Yet she had need for courage. First, she had to withstand the shafts of bitterness that emanated from the devotees of Edward VIII, who had seen their idol wrenched suddenly, finally, from the Throne that they considered part of him. Malicious rumours began. Although no scandalous accusations were aimed at the King and Queen themselves, the rumours included other members of the Royal Family. Strange stories were told about the last hours of the abdication. It was said that the royal relatives were divided against each other—and that at a time when unity was an essential for the survival of the Monarchy.

Secondly, the Queen had to support a husband who was angry, tired out, astonished, bewildered and, to a certain extent, bitter. The turbulence of the Tecks seethed in him. The impediment in his speech, which in recent years had so much improved, clearly showed again. Criticism from certain quarters riled him. It was being said that he was unfit and would not be strong enough to stand the Coronation. His illnesses in the Navy during the First World War were recalled. He was labelled 'the rubber-stamp' King, who would sign just what he was told. It was hinted that King Edward had really gone because he had stood up to the politicians, criticized their handling of the depressed areas. Now the politicians had bought themselves a cypher.

Those who were in Court circles in those grim days were never to forget the way in which the Queen completely submerged her own fears and stood four-square beside her husband, soothing, calmly letting a ray of sunshine through the dark clouds which hung over Piccadilly.

The King knew very well how much he was dependent upon her. When he broadcast to the nation on his Accession day there was an unfathomed depth of sincerity and feeling as, hesitantly, came the words: 'With my wife and helpmeet by my side, I take up the heavy task which lies before me.'

He proved his gratitude on his birthday, 14th December, that date about which so many royal events have circled since the Prince Consort died at Windsor in 1861. His gift to his wife was the Order of the Garter. It was a touching expression of his gratitude. She wrote to Queen Mary: 'He had discovered that papa gave it to you, on his, papa's birthday, and the coincidence was so charming that he has now followed suit and given it to me on his own birthday.'

The Queen had another task, to tell her children of what had happened and what lay ahead. After a conference with their governess, she told the Princesses quietly of the changes that had come and of how they would all be going to live in Buckingham Palace. Princess Elizabeth screwed up her face and asked, 'You mean for *ever*?' She suggested that an underground passage be dug to the Palace so that they could come back to their old home to sleep.

Fortunate indeed was it that it was Christmas time, with people occupied with buying presents, going to parties, arranging holidays and, most important, when religious thoughts were to the fore. Santa Claus soothed the abdication fever from heated brows. But there had been no like monarchial crisis since George IV engaged in his unseemly fracas with Queen Caroline. Or since 1867 when a notice 'TO LET' was hung on the gates of Buckingham Palace, when the Prime Minister warned Queen Victoria that if her ghillie, John Brown, attended her at a military review in Hyde Park the mob was likely to tear him from the box, when the Commander-in-Chief said that he did not wish to be present if Brown was there, and the Prince of Wales raced down to Windsor to try to make his mother see reason and put aside her favourite. Britain in 1936 would have done well to ponder more deeply on the case of John Brown. Queen Victoria had shown that Monarchs of the Line cling resolutely to those without whom they feel they cannot continue to work in the lonely room at the top. But Queen Victoria was a better tactician and a more fearsome character than her great-grandson, who may have thought that, as she had done, so he could do. Yet Queen Victoria may have offended the Church and the Establishment, but she did not cross their ethics.

The Queen's public life as Consort began when, recovered from influenza, she left by car for the Christmas holiday at Sandringham. Beside her were Princess Margaret, waving gaily at the cameras, and her husband, showing obvious signs of strain. On the occasional seat before them Princess Elizabeth was glowing with anticipation for the pleasures of Norfolk. And she herself, with the smile undimmed beneath the chic black hat, and the fingers of her right hand prettily raised, looked, as she has always done, every inch a Queen. It was just the picture that the nation wanted to see that Christmas-tide.

So Queen Elizabeth stayed in a Sovereign's residence for the first time as first lady in the land. Her mother-in-law journeyed down with them, and it was her staff that ran the impromptu Christmas visit to the 'Big House'. But by this time Queen Mary had endured even more than she could stand. In one year she had seen her husband weaken and die, experienced a mourning week of un-surpassed national sorrow, moved her home, broken with associations that had lasted for quarter of a century, and throughout been harried and torn by a crisis which had ended in the abdication of her eldest son. Now she retired to her room. She sat and pondered on the things that had been, and might have been. Yet, as if in recompense for some of them, she received a Christmas present of all surpassing beauty. On 25th December Princess Alexandra of Kent was born. And with the glad tidings came the news that one of her names was to be Elizabeth, in compliment to her aunt.

On 4th February the King and Queen were at the christening at the private chapel at Buckingham Palace, the baby being given the names of Alexandra Helen Elizabeth Olga Christabel, the last be-cause she was born on Christmas Day.

The months that followed were to be the busiest in the life of Queen Elizabeth. There was the move from 145, Piccadilly to Buckingham Palace to be arranged. Clothes for the Coronation had to be ordered, and the procedure of the ceremony learned. She had a heavy programme of pre-Coronation engagements to fulfil, for public appearances were an essential part of the cure for abdication jitters. And, perhaps most important of all, she had to ensure that her husband kept in good health and that the little time that he could spare for home life was quiet and undisturbed.

Poor King George was now paying the price, and a high one, for his father's omission to train him in the routine duties of a monarch. He found himself bewildered and astonished at the amount of work that poured from the dispatch boxes. Whilst his elder brother had had a far wider experience of public life, and was in any case far quicker in decision, George VI had a detailed mind and wanted to know all about the contents of the papers that he signed. He had inherited the gift of clear and concise thinking from his great-grandfather, Prince Albert. But just as Queen Victoria's husband had risen early to write by the light of his green lamp, and had eventually worked himself to death, so now the same tendencies showed in the new King. He worried about his capabilities and was never, throughout his reign, to realize how good a King he was.

And, regardless of how much work he had to do, he still had to find time to spare for Mr. Lionel Logue, for he knew the importance of unhesitating speech when the time came for his crowning.

The Queen's Coronation dress was made by Handley Seymour, those of her Maids of Honour by Norman Hartnell. At a long table at the Royal School of Needlework in Kensington ten women sat embroidering the Queen's Coronation robe, entwining upon it the emblems of all parts of the British Empire.

The King and Queen made their first state drive on 13th February, visiting the People's Palace in Mile End Road. The rousing reception in the east end of London left them with no doubts about the feeling for them. Their first appearance at a big sporting event was when they travelled to Liverpool for the Grand National. Their presence, coupled with the victory of Royal Mail, made it a red letter day for Aintree. Then the Service contingents from overseas began to arrive, the Australians first, then the New Zealanders, followed by the Royal Canadian Mounted Police and picked men from the regiments of India and Burma. Great electric chandeliers were hoisted into position in the Abbey and wide carpets arrived for the nave. Kings and Chiefs, Presidents and Premiers, reached London daily. Decorative lions and crowns were gilded, and the poles went up.

Early on Sunday mornings the troops began their rehearsals through the streets for the processional march. Even at half past six the crowds were five deep on the pavements. 21st April was Princess Elizabeth's eleventh birthday and the Queen gave a tea party for her. The banners hung proud in the wide streets and the Union Jacks and the bunting made patchwork quilts of the alleys. Sunderland beat Preston North End at Wembley and the victorious captain took the Cup from the Queen. The Dominion Premiers dined at Buckingham Palace, and the lights went on. The Queen went to the Abbey to tread and kneel her part in practice. The Home Fleet came up the River.

On the evening of Sunday, 9th May, the Queen knelt in Buckingham Palace, her husband beside her, and the Archbishop put his blessing upon them.

Early on Tuesday morning people began picking their places along the Coronation route, the first of the five million. By the time the shops and offices closed there were groups all along the way. By eight o'clock there was not a space left on the base of Nelson's Column. Picnic stoves were lit and the smell of frying sausages and bacon drifted through the Park. Children put their heads on pillows and fell asleep on the hard ground, four, five, six of them in line under a tarpaulin or an old carpet. The last trains from the suburbs brought in another tide, more thousands now searching for a few inches of gutter in which to rest their feet. The restaurants and the clubs turned out their revellers. In dancing groups, on the top of cars and taxis, they passed through the multitude, singing, throwing streamers. There was no silence in the night. As the revellers made for home or sunk asleep, those who were to care for Coronation day began their preparations.

The lights in the rooms of the King and Queen went out early that evening. Yet there were to be many, stretched out in the damp under the cloudy sky, who were to sleep more soundly than the King and Queen in their regal beds in Buckingham Palace.

18   A Crown of Glory

THE Queen stirred in her sleep. Through the mists of
drowsiness, it seemed as if someone was talking in her room.
The blue eyes opened. Her husband was already awake.
It was just after three. The voice spoke again. It belonged to an
electrician. He was testing the loud speakers on Constitution Hill,
ignorant of the privacies into which he was intruding.

Deep in the pillows the search for rest began again. Tramp,
tramp, tramp came the sound of marching feet from Knightsbridge
way. The troops were taking up their positions along the processional route.

At five o'clock all pretence that the dawn was for sleeping ended
abruptly. The music of the Royal Marines Band, from just outside
the Palace windows, brought Princess Elizabeth from her bed. She
drew the curtains and, with an eiderdown around her, peered out
into the mist. She saw a trickle of people making their way into the
stands, and soldiers marching by. Then she lay down until it was
time for early breakfast. There was to be none for the King. He had
the same sinking feeling inside of him that he had experienced ten
years earlier, before he opened the first Parliament in Canberra.

Just after half past ten the State Coach, built for George III in
1762 and besplendoured with the decorations of Cipriani, left
Buckingham Palace. It was drawn by eight Windsor Greys and
flanked by Yeomen of the Guard. To the fore, and to the rear, were
divisions of a Sovereign's Escort of Life Guards.

There were more people out there to greet King George VI and
Queen Elizabeth than the total population of the nation in the time
of Queen Elizabeth I.

166

Twenty minutes earlier they had cheered themselves hoarse at the sight of a very splendid lady in a glass coach making her way to the Abbey. Queen Mary was breaking with tradition. Never before had a Queen Dowager attended the crowning of her husband's successor. A stickler for the exact continuity of history, she had overcome her prejudices and asked her son if she could attend the ceremony so that she might show to the crowds the real solidarity of the Royal Family. It was not only solidity that she radiated, but also strength and composure to the two so wholly concerned.

Both strength and composure were to be needed on several occasions before the ceremony was over. The Queen's procession started on its way up the Nave first, the clergy ahead, bishops to either side of her and six trainbearers behind. Then a Presbyterian chaplain fainted. It took those about him by surprise, and for an interval no one knew what to do. There was hardly room left to stand up in the Abbey, let alone find place for a prostrate pastor. But he was spirited away to a place unknown and the stately tread went on, the woman whom no emergency can shake looking as if nothing had happened.

The King, too, had his troubles. His Bishops Assistant were those of Durham, and Bath and Wells. They supported him on either side and held the form of Service. But when it came to the taking of the Coronation Oath, neither Bishop could find the relevant words. The Archbishop held down his copy so that the King could see. Unfortunately, he had his thumb over the passage required.

At the Introduction the Dean of Westminster offered the surplice that the King must don, inside out.

The seven-pound St. Edward's Crown of England had, before the ceremony, been marked with a piece of red cotton to show which was the front. Some tidy-minded soul had taken it away. The Archbishop turned the Crown this way and that in search of the cotton. The King, watching him, remained uncertain as to which point of the compass his symbol of ultimate authority was facing.

It was the duty of the Lord Chamberlain to dress the King. But his hands were shaking. After the hilt of the sword had registered a near miss to the King's chin, His Majesty took on the job himself.

His worst moment came as he was leaving the Coronation Chair.

He was turning, and off balance, when he was brought to a dead halt by pressure in the neighbourhood of his neck. Almost down, he saw that a hefty Bishop was standing on his robe. Happily, naval officers have the knack of moving people with a few well chosen words. His Grace quickly got off.

The Queen was more fortunate and passed with regality and demureness through this, her Coronation.

It was at twenty minutes to three that the crowned Queen came from the Abbey. The two little Princesses, holding hands and their heads bowed, moved under the guardian eye of Queen Mary. There had been a Family fear that the long ceremony might prove too much for six-year-old Margaret and that she might fall asleep, which, commented her sister, would be a disgrace to them all. But, except for several short occasions when she used the Royal Gallery as a pillow for her head, she had survived well, playing with her books and whispering confidences to 'Lilibet'.

Under a cloudy sky the stately procession, like a sash of tapestry, began to weave its long way back, by the Embankment, Trafalgar Square, St. James's, Piccadilly, Regent Street, Oxford Street, Marble Arch and Constitution Hill. It took forty-five minutes to pass any one point. For many of the five million it was their first sight of the Queen. For them it changed her from a picture to a living emblem. It was Queen Marie of Rumania who said of her at this Coronation time: 'She has an inborn sweetness and is in reality much more attractive than on the pictures taken of her. She has a most lovely complexion and her eyes are like blue lights. . . .'[1]

She came out on to the balcony of the Palace, looking out over the acres of human enthusiasm which rain could not damp, as serene and self-controlled as if she was opening a garden fête at Sandringham. She was thirty-six, a child of the twentieth century. Yet that day she had a living link back to the time when Queen Victoria was the same age as she was now. Homage was paid to her by three of Victoria's children—the Duke of Connaught, to whom the great Duke of Wellington had been godfather, Princess Louise, Duchess of Argyll, who was nearing ninety years of age, and Princess Beatrice, one-time Princess Henry of Battenburg.

[1] *A Biographer's Notebook*, by Hector Bolitho.

168

The day that had begun at three o'clock allowed of no relaxing. The photographers claimed a hard hour. Then, at eight o'clock, the King made his broadcast speech to the nation. It was as much of an ordeal for her as it was for him. Mr. Logue was there. 'Now take it quietly, Sir,' he whispered. The words came well.

'The Queen and I will always keep in our hearts the inspiration of this day. May we ever be worthy of the goodwill which, I am proud to think, surrounds us at the outset of my reign. . . .'

In the gay whirl of that Coronation summer clothes became an increasingly important factor in the life of the Queen. Although, in the first days of the reign, she had announced that she had no intention of trying to become a leader of fashion, it was part of her job to be a radiant picture, to hold attention, to wear a fitting outfit for each occasion, and to give her husband the support of having a lovely and a well-dressed woman by his side.

Throughout May, June and July she was changing, changing, changing. Only odd days here and there were free of engagements, and some days had three or four. On the day after the Coronation there was a drive through north-east London, and a State Banquet at Buckingham Palace. On 14th May the King and Queen received Empire troops and distributed medals, and in the evening went to a dinner at the Foreign Office, and held a Court Ball. On the 15th there was a reception for Foreign Envoys. Then followed a visit to Windsor Castle, and acclamation from the Whitsun crowds. On the 19th they drove to the Guildhall for the City of London's magnificent luncheon, and it was here that the Queen excelled herself. With her long dress caressing the ground, she had a dignity, a chic, a radiance which hypnotized the Lord Mayor and the Corporation.

In her wisdom she was playing her role to an exactitude that best ensured the success and consolidation of her husband's position. He always preferred to be on the edge of the spotlight's circle, rather than at its centre. The bright ray did not give him the elixir of inspiration that showed so strongly in Edward VIII. This was a natural reaction to being outshone in the schoolroom, his subordinate relations with his parents, his early illnesses and the impediment in his speech. He never ceased to marvel at the qualities and attributes of his womenfolk, looking at them in puzzlement as if he thought, are they really mine? The King deeply appreciated the sight of a well-dressed woman and was interested in the care that went into the making of the finished article. As a boy he would go into his mother's room as she was adding the finishing touches to herself before a reception or a ball. He would peer around her dressing-table, lisp his questions and tell her how lovely she looked. He had given advice on the dresses to be worn by the trainbearers at the Coronation. And now, as his children came to see them off from the Palace on great occasion after great occasion, he would tell them that, if they were lucky, one day they might be as beautiful as their mother.

Yet the sudden emphasis on dress did not come easily to the Queen. For that, King George V had largely been responsible. He had very pronounced views on women's clothes, and the most pronounced was that he could not abide change. Children, he insisted, should be dressed as children. Wives should stay as they were when they were married. Variation was tantamount to cheating on the men who had selected them in a certain guise. Queen Mary had, in her early days, experimented with large summer hats, but the opposition had been so continuous and disturbing that she had given up the struggle. Thus she invented a uniform that stayed with her through her long life, complete with stick for prodding and the tapping over the head of those who transgressed the code of royal courtesies.

For eleven years the Duchess of York had been the only daughter-in-law, and the only royal lady of a like age was Princess Mary, carefully watched over by her father and her husband. The King liked the Duchess as she was. The conservatism of Handley Seymour suited him well. Then, after his death came the mourning period and the abdication crisis, when there was much more to think about than dresses. But Edward VIII and his lady, and two young Duchesses, had let the light in, swept the peccadillos of George V away, and in the gaiety of the Coronation festival, fashion was in sway. Queen Elizabeth found the answer, and she was to find a better answer still.

The royal marathon continued, with Portsmouth the next port of call. On the bridge of the royal yacht *Victoria and Albert* the King and Queen and bareheaded Princess Elizabeth looked out at six miles of warships, Lord Louis Mountbatten filling in the technical details for the Princess. That evening the crowded shores saw, and heard, the Fleet lit up.

Before the month was ended the King and Queen had attended the Empire day service of Thanksgiving at St. Paul's, been entertained to dinner at 10, Downing Street by the Prime Minister, attended a reception by the London County Council at County Hall and, in contrast, Queen Mary's seventieth birthday party.

Another date that meant much to Queen Mary was 3rd June. On that day in 1865 her husband had been born right there in Marlborough House, while Lord Palmerston was still Prime Minister. Now it was to have a wider association for her, and for Queen Elizabeth. On that 3rd June, at the Château de Candé in France, H.R.H. the Duke of Windsor married Mrs. Wallis Warfield, as Mrs. Ernest Simpson had become when her divorce decree became absolute. The bride was as handsome as ever and, outwardly at least, unmarked by the grape-shot. But now, though their names were the same, the letters that preceded his could not, by Letters Patent of 28th May 1937, precede hers. The lack of those three letters, in the dining halls of the great, put them several tables apart.

Now the new King said: 'We are not a family, we are a firm.' Certainly the Queen and he needed the support of every member of the firm that summer, and they received it in full measure. Despite the functions that were purely theirs, the Courts, the garden parties, the balls, Royal Ascot, Trooping of the Colour, the review of ex-Servicemen, there were so many events that needed the royal touch. Fortunately the firm was strong in numbers, and wide in range of years of service. A sight of the children of Queen Victoria was eagerly sought. In the age layer below them came Queen Mary, Queen Maud of Norway,[1] the Earl of Athlone and Princess Alice, Princesses Helena Victoria and Marie Louise. In the group of the King and Queen came Princess Mary and the Earl of Harewood, with their children in the school age. Then the recently-married Dukes

[1] Queen Maud died in 1938.

171

of Kent and Gloucester, with the Kent babies representing the nursery. There were ninety years of royalty to peep at.

In July the King and Queen showed themselves to those living far from the capital, in Wales, Northern Ireland and Scotland. In St. Giles Cathedral, Edinburgh, the King invested his wife with the Order of the Thistle.

The King and Queen were already being more closely associated together in people's minds than any other Sovereign and Consort in history. They appeared side by side more often than even George V and Queen Mary had done, and certainly much more than Edward VII and Queen Alexandra. 'It is difficult to picture His Majesty without the gracious lady who was ever at his side, easing his path and bringing the support of her sympathy and her affection. Where she passed the sun shone, and was reflected in his eyes.'[1]

The Royal Family spent August and September at Balmoral, unwinding. There was time to talk again of the fish in the river, the birds in the heather and the flowers in the forest. There were certain Victorian knots, which had been untied in the previous Reign, to be tied once more, but the changes had been too short-lived to upset the tranquillity of Deeside. There was time, too, to take stock of the changes that four seasons had brought. Only a year before they had been together at Birkhall, on a visit that had begun as a vacation and ended as a nightmare. From the date of their departure to the date of their return, there had scarce been a day without its crisis or public engagement, and no time at all for roses and rhododendrons. But, as the Queen had said when the door of 145, Piccadilly closed behind her for the last time, 'We must take what is coming to us, and make the best of it.'

During her first days as Queen officials had been somewhat disquietened, and justifiably so, by the thought that she might make some remark or comment, or be tricked into so doing, that would cause embarrassnent to the Government or the Court. King Edward VIII's remark that something must be done about the depressed areas of Wales, harmless enough in itself, had been expanded from one of personal sympathy to that of a national issue, and the memory of it was still very clear. With only a few hectic days

[1] Sir Owen Morshead, Librarian, Windsor Castle, in a broadcast, 9th February 1952.

to prepare herself the Duchess of York had been transformed into Queen Elizabeth, and with only five months to go before her Coronation, instead of the eighteen months probation that is customary for Queens. It was asking a great deal of a woman to expect her to adjust herself to the dangers of the unique role at such short notice. Unwise words spoken as Duchess of York (though there never were any) could be hushed up, glossed over, or merely dismissed as carrying no weight. Words spoken as Queen, even asides, were front page news, and even lip readers were employed to get them. Thus it was that, to begin with, officials kept within earshot of her when possible. The words that came to them might have been those of the most tactful and experienced of diplomats. She had known exactly the task ever since she joined the royal menage. Before she became engaged to the Duke of York she had told him that she was afraid 'as royalty never, never again to be free to think or speak or act as I really feel I ought to think, or speak or act.' It was real love that took that fear away.

Back in London in October the King needed all the Queen's love and support, and all Mr. Logue's skill and patience, in preparing for his speech at the opening of Parliament. Not only had he to speak sitting down, which is more difficult for those with impediments, he also had to have the Crown on his head. So, seated and becrowned, he practised away at Buckingham Palace, his wife for audience.

In November King Leopold of the Belgians paid a State visit to London. At the banquet in his honour the Queen wore, in the words of Mr. Norman Hartnell who made the dress, 'a robe de style of gleaming silver tissue over hooped carcase of stiffened silver gauze, with a deep berthe collar of silver lace encrusted with glittering diamonds'. This was Mr. Hartnell's first important dress for a member of the Royal Family, and the germ of it had been born in the Winterhalter portraits which the King had shown him at the Palace.

The year of the crowning ended with the family party at Sandringham. On its last day Queen Mary wrote of it as 'a very wonderful and interesting year'. That she was able to so describe it was in large part due to the efforts, courage and understanding of her eldest daughter-in-law.

19   Paris—Canada—New York

ON 23rd June 1938 the Countess of Strathmore, the seventy-five-year-old mother of Queen Elizabeth, died suddenly at Glamis. The Queen was hard hit. She owed so much to that gifted woman who had instilled into her the love of home and consideration for other people. It was indeed a good beginning that Lady Strathmore had given to her large brood, founded on the democratic ways of Scotland and the recognition of human values. Her reward had been to see her daughter crowned in Westminster Abbey.

Her death came at a most unfortunate moment, for on the 28th the King and Queen were due to leave on a four-day State Visit to Paris. Europe was seething under the threats of Hitler and Mussolini, and the journey to Paris was of obvious importance. It was at first thought that the King would go alone, but in fact that was far from the Queen's conception of duty and support. President Lebrun was consulted, and he suggested a postponement until 19th July. The Queen agreed to accompany her husband on that date.

But now she was faced, in her mourning, with a problem that seemed insuperable. And so was Mr. Norman Hartnell. Since early in the year he had been working on the Queen's dresses, some thirty of them, dresses for banquets and balls, fêtes and garden parties, State drives and military occasions, the opera and the ballet, luncheons and receptions. A wealth of thought and study had gone into the selection of the colours, shades to suit both the occasion and the Queen, the uniforms around her and the Orders that she wore.

Early in June the fittings took place at the Palace. Everything was well in hand. Then the news came of Lady Strathmore's death, and all work stopped. By the time Mr. Hartnell was told of the new date of departure for France, he had but a fortnight to carry out the changes made necessary for mourning. The colours that he had so carefully chosen were now no longer possible. Black, purple and white were the limits. White was chosen, a precedent being that of the wedding of Princess Alice and Prince Louis of Hesse in 1862.

As if by magic all the colours on all the dresses had to fade out and emerge as white. And in two weeks the magic was done, with silks and satins, velvet and lace.

The populace of Paris has ever staged great fêtes for the arrival of British Queens. Queen Victoria, the first British Sovereign to enter the French capital since the infant Henry VI was taken there for his crowning in 1422, won an acclamation in 1855 that was unrivalled even by that given to Napoleon on his return from Austerlitz. In 1907 the beauty of Queen Alexandra did much to strengthen the Entente Cordiale. In 1914 the wild enthusiasm for Queen Mary surprised no one more than herself. Yet, in the case of each visit, ugly and cynical comment had come from Berlin.

It was the same now, on the occasion of perhaps the greatest triumph of Queen Elizabeth. In the streets of Paris she received a welcome of unrestrained delight that was chronicled throughout the world. Her smile, her simple dignity, her obvious pleasure at being once more among the French, the creations which framed her in the style of a century before, combined to make a picture that remained fresh and loved throughout the weary years that lay ahead. The sunshine of her blotted out the threat of dark aircraft shadows in the sky, the squat tanks in the Place de la Concorde, the endless lines of men in battle khaki. The charm of her lightened the hearts of politicians and generals and for a time, in the splendour of the Elysée Palace and the lighted gardens of the Quai d'Orsay, they forgot the threat of Adolf Hitler.

Column after column in the newspapers belonged to the Queen alone. Her every dress was described in detail. Revellers in the streets were reading the morning editions before they went to bed. Mr. Norman Hartnell, basking in the sunshine and success of those summer days, recalled the headlines: 'Today France is a Monarchy

175

again. We have taken the Queen to our hearts. She rules over two nations.'

In his memoirs, *Silver and Gold*, he described the five all-white dresses that the Queen wore for the main occasions:

'One for the evening reception at the Elysée Palace had its bodice and billowing skirt composed of hundreds of yards of narrow Valenciennes lace, sprinkled with silver. For the Gala at the Opera Her Majesty wore a spreading gown of thick white satin, the skirt draped with festoons of satin, held by clusters of white camellias. The Queen wore a dress that trailed on the green grass of the lawns at the Garden Party at Bagatelle. It was of the finest cobweb lace and tulle and with it was worn a sweeping hat delicately bordered with white osprey.

'It was while watching the ballet, performed by the lakeside on the Ile Enchanté, that the Queen opened a parasol of transparent lace and tulle and delighted all the onlookers. At a stroke, she resuscitated the art of the parasol makers of Paris and London.

'A magnificent luncheon was held in the Galeries des Glaces at the Palace of Versailles where the Queen appeared in a spreading dress, again of ground length, in white organdie, embroidered all over in openwork design of *broderie anglaise*. The white leghorn hat was softly trimmed with a ribbon of dense black velvet.'

On the way home the King and Queen stopped at Villers-Bretonneux, near Amiens, to unveil the memorial to the eleven thousand Australian soldiers who lay, graveless, in France when the First World War ended. With thoughts of the Somme fresh in their minds, they arrived back in London to find fears of another world conflict uppermost in British minds.

The Royal Family was at Balmoral when the Czechoslovakian volcano began the rumblings which indicated eruption. The Prime Minister, Mr. Neville Chamberlain, was a guest on Deeside early in September, as yet not realizing the seriousness of the situation. Then, ten days later, Hitler spat out his vilification of President Benes and on the 14th the King returned to London. The tension grew, and Mr. Chamberlain's talks with Hitler in Germany showed little hope of a solution over Sudetenland. Trenches began to slit the green sward of London's parks, volunteers digging by the light of flares far into the night. Cellars were earmarked for shelters, and gas masks were fitted. From the termini crowded trains took children and hospital cases far out into the country. Young men flocked to join the Territorial Army. All night the streets of London were full of anxious crowds.

In those days charged with the expectation of catastrophe, the Queen had an appointment to keep that was at once of the greatest importance to Scotland and a great compliment to herself. On Clyde-side, on 27th September, she launched the 83,673-ton Cunard liner that bore her name. Her speech was broadcast, and in it she included a message from her husband: 'He bids the people of this country to be of good cheer in spite of the dark clouds hanging over them and, indeed, over the whole world. He knows well that, as ever before in critical times, they will keep cool heads and brave hearts. . . .' Queen Mary, very proud of her own Cunarder, was listening at Marl-borough House and thought that Elizabeth 'made her speech admirably'.

Then Mr. Chamberlain was asked to meet Hitler once more, this time at Munich. He came back to Heston on the 30th, waving a piece of paper in his hand. 'Peace in our time.' Tired crowds, relieved beyond measure, dropped their eyes from the skies and instead focused them on the statesman of the moment as he stood on the balcony of Buckingham Palace. The Royal Family continued their autumn holiday at Balmoral.

After the strain of the past two weeks, light distraction was called for, and the Perth Repertory Company was invited to perform at the Castle. After some puzzling as to what play would be most suitable for the small stage which had been set up between the twin stair-cases, *The Fourth Wall*, by A. A. Milne was chosen. The audience numbered some three hundred and the Queen, in the front row, was so close that she almost merged into the players. David Steuart, director of the artistic side, said of her: 'I was quite spellbound by the beauty of the Queen, since now I realized that photographs did no justice to it at all. That night she was in a black crinoline dress with tiara and was a perfect picture.'[1]

The company stayed as guests of the King and Queen, their bed-

[1] *Balmoral*, by Ivor Brown.

MOTHER OF THE QUEEN

rooms being widely dotted about the upper stories of the Castle. After the royal goodnight had been wished to each and every one, there came the task, in the stillness of the night, of homing down corridors which seemed identical in tartan, antler and Landseer. It was a royal performance to remember.

In November King Carol of Rumania and Crown Prince Michael arrived in London on a State visit. Mr. Hartnell had created for the Queen a dress of pearl grey satin. But, on the morning of the banquet at which it was to be worn, full details of it appeared in a newspaper. King George, like his great-grand-mama on a previous occasion, was not amused. The dress was not worn.

'Peace in our time.' The sweetness of the message mingled with the Christmas tidings and the soft blanket of snow deadened the menace of marching feet. The bells rang out over the white park at Sandringham and the pheasants called in the wood. The Queen put on a funny hat, the Princesses made their snowmen, and there were films in the evenings. But the time was short. On 15th March Czechoslovakia went under the Nazi tide, and Mr. Chamberlain called Adolf Hitler a perjurer. In tiny fragments his piece of paper was scattered on the cold winds. Little places became household words of deep anxiety—Memel, Danzig, Albania.

As an antidote to the molestations in Eastern Europe, Londoners were treated to the gaiety and pomp of the visit of the President of the French Republic, President Lebrun, and Madame Lebrun. The sight of the King's lady and the President's lady driving together to the Palace made war seem far away.

Now, when they were alone, the chief topic of the Queen and her very worried husband centred round their projected tour of Canada and America, timed to start in May. It was a long-standing invitation. The Canadian Prime Minister, Mr. Mackenzie King, had suggested the visit when he was in Britain at the time of the Coronation. When, a year later, the outline arrangements had been agreed upon, President Roosevelt had suggested that the tour should be extended to include America. He would have liked to include the two Princesses among his guests, but the Queen, bearing in mind American receptions to former royal young people, excused them on the grounds of their age.

The King was in doubt whether, owing to the international situation, he should cross the Atlantic at this time. He was a man who liked to be at his desk at times of emergency. But his advisers convinced him that the crisis in Europe was still some months ahead, and in the meantime he could do no better service for the British cause than showing himself in North America. But he insisted on one amendment to the plans. The Cunard liner, *Empress of Australia*, should be substituted for H.M.S. *Repulse*, for he did not want Europe to think that Britain did not 'mean business'.

For the Queen the visit posed greater wardrobe problems than even she had yet faced. The programme demanded as many changes as seven per day. She had to be prepared for heat as sultry as that in Washington, and cold as intense as on the Rockies' peaks. She had to have outfits that went with Wellington boots, and frocks to wear before knots of country folk at wayside stations at four o'clock in the morning. And the whole wardrobe had to be packed so that the hats should not be creased and so that each morning, her dresser would have handy the clothes required for the particular day. There had to be new outfits for Ottawa, new outfits for Montreal. No city or town would appreciate an ensemble that had already been described further up the line.

The Queen had a particular interest in the United States, as there is American blood in her veins. H.M. Queen Elizabeth the Queen Mother is linked not only with General Robert E. Lee, the famous Confederate leader (1807–1870), but is also one of the nearest of kin now living to George Washington, being his second cousin six times removed.

The American connection originated through the marriage of a Bowes-Lyon into the house of Abel Smith, a family that was to make a second connection with the Royal House when Lady May Cambridge, daughter of Princess Alice and the Earl of Athlone, married Captain Henry Abel Smith[1] in 1931. In 1853 the thirteenth Earl of Strathmore (as he was later to become) married Frances Dora, daughter of Oswald Smith, of Blendon Hall, Kent. Frances Dora

[1] Sir Henry Abel Smith.

179

was the paternal grandmother of Queen Elizabeth the Queen Mother.[1]

It is through the mother of Frances Dora that the direct link with American ancestry can be traced. It began when an English gentleman, Augustine Warner, sailed from England across the Atlantic in 1650 to escape the rigours of Cromwell. He settled in Virginia, and prospered. He had a son, Augustine, and a daughter, Sarah. Sarah married Lawrence Townley, and they were the ancestors of General Robert E. Lee. Augustine married a Virginian, Mildred Reade, and died in 1681, leaving daughters. Mildred, the eldest, married Lawrence Washington and thus became grandmother of the first President of the United States. Mary married John Smith, of Purton. Their daughter, Mildred, married Robert Porteous, a Virginian planter, in 1700. Five years later a son was born to them and also named Robert. The Porteous family came back to England in 1720 and the son, Robert, entered the Church. In 1736, when a rector in Bedfordshire, he married Judith Cockayne. Their great-great-granddaughter became the wife of the thirteenth Earl of Strathmore.[2]

Thoughts and feelings of many kinds must have chased around the Queen's mind as she neared Southampton Water and the Cunarder, *Empress of Australia*, on the afternoon of 5th May. There was sadness at parting from her children, and anxiety over the threat of war. There was danger of icebergs in the sea lanes, and the rumoured possibility that the Nazis might send a warship to intercept the liner and attempt to hold her husband and herself. There was the excitement of seeing new countries. There was the honour of making history, for this was to be the first time that a reigning Sovereign had

---

[1] John Smith bought land in Cropwell-Boteler, Nottinghamshire, in 1623. His son, Thomas, married, secondly, Fortune, sister of Abel Collin of Nottingham. In 1713 their youngest son, Abel, married Jane Beaumont. George, their eldest son, was created a Baronet in 1757, and in the next generation the name of Bromley was assumed. Their youngest son, Abel, banker and member of Parliament, married Mary Bird, of Barton, Warwickshire. They had six sons and two daughters. The third son, Robert, was created Lord Carrington. The fifth son, George, married Frances Mary, daughter of Sir John Parker Mosley in 1792. The second son of this union, Oswald, married, in 1824, Henrietta Mildred, daughter of the Very Reverend Robert Hodgson, Dean of Carlisle and his wife, Mildred Porteous. Their third daughter, Frances Dora, was married to the thirteenth Earl of Strathmore.

[2] A detailed analysis of the Queen Mother's American ancestors, by Mr. Hector Bolitho, appeared in the issue of *Past and Future* for December 1958.

visited any of his Dominions and the first time that a British King or Queen had set foot in the United States.

Queen Mary and the two Princesses travelled with the King and Queen to see them off. Queen Mary subjected the royal cabins to close scrutiny, and gave them her approval. Then, with her grand-daughters beside her, she stood on the jetty, waving her handkerchief at the departing liner and its naval escort. Princess Margaret said that she too had a handkerchief, and began to look for it. Her elder sister commented bravely, 'To wave, not to cry.'

In the event the danger in the Atlantic came from icebergs, and not from German men-of-war, of which there was no sign. In fact for days on end there was no sign of anything, so thick was the fog. Not for many a year had the icefields drifted so far south. Day long the liner jostled its way through endless fields of loose ice. Now and then an iceberg would appear. Now and then there was a stretch of solid ice through which the liner had to force its path. They were three days behind schedule. The King took a sophisticated view. If, as apparently was the case, the only place that a King could rest was in the middle of an ice field, then he was prepared to rest there. And rest he did.

Sir John Wheeler-Bennett quotes from a letter written by the Queen to Queen Mary: 'For three and a half days we only moved a few miles. The fog was so thick, that it was like a white cloud round the ship, and the foghorn blew incessantly. Its melancholy blasts were echoed back by the icebergs like the twang of a piece of wire. Incredibly eery, and really very alarming, knowing that we were surrounded by ice, and unable to see a foot either way.

'We very nearly hit a berg the day before yesterday, and the poor Captain was nearly demented because some kind cheerful people kept on reminding him that it was about here that the Titanic was struck, and *just* about the same date . . . !'

On 17th May Queen Elizabeth stepped for the first time on to Canadian soil. There, at Quebec, she sat on her ornate Throne. For some years past there had been talk of isolationism in French-speaking Canada. Within two days such talk had faded as the snow does before the sun. Her smile, her clothes, her fluency in the French language, led the newspapers to say that she had reconquered Canada.

181

When she drove with the King through twenty-three miles of the streets of Montreal, their reception was so rapturous that critics who had come to scoff were dumbfounded. It was the same in Ottawa, where the King presided over the Canadian Parliament, and received full marks for his French accent. There they drove through the streets in a landau drawn by six horses, and with an escort of the 4th Princess Louise Dragoon Guards, taking their name from the lovely daughter of Queen Victoria married to the Marquess of Lorne, who had been Governor-General of Canada sixty years before.

The Queen was now showing, more than ever, her genius for making a royal tour a success by adding the little things of life, pinches of salt that gave taste to occasions that might otherwise have been purely impressive routine. She thought of the photographers. She would lead and encourage the King, who sometimes wondered why, to a spot where the background lent interest to a picture. She had developed a news sense for the right kind of publicity.

She was laying a foundation stone in Ottawa. It could have been just one more laying of one more foundation stone out of so many. There came to her ears the burr of the Highland tongue, and the realization that many of the masons working on the building were Scots. So, taking the King with her, off she walked to where they were standing. There were seventy thousand people watching them. The King and Queen of Canada stood in among the workmen, laughing, joking and swapping reminiscences of Scotland. That day the Queen knocked a nail into the Nazi coffin.

At the unveiling of the War Memorial the Queen thought she was altogether too far away from the ten thousand veterans of the First World War lined up for the occasion. She said, please could she go a little nearer. She was told that it would be quite in order for the King and her to go right among them, if they did not mind taking the risk of being swamped. The little Lady Elizabeth Bowes-Lyon, who for five years had cared for and cosseted, ruled and played with, the fighting men of the Dominions, had no doubts of being able to look after herself, even among ten thousand tough Canadians. Her former role was not unknown to them. The Queen was swamped. The five feet two of her disappeared. Detectives, as guardians, lost all point. Perspiration poured from them as they struggled to keep contact with charges whom they could not even see. American news-papermen raised their hands in amazement and commented that no President would risk such an experience. Yet there was only softness there, and tears in old eyes, for Flanders was far away and there were many memories.

The royal train, with its guard of Royal Canadian Mounted Police, headed on into the west. There were eight thousand miles of railway line in all. The rumble of the wheels went on through night after night and sometimes, in the early light, the Queen would go out in her 'hostess dress' to greet and wave to little knots of prairie folk who had gathered at wayside stations. Toronto. There was a special Scottish welcome waiting for the Queen at Glengarry. Lake Superior and Port Arthur and Fort William. Winnipeg, Brandon and Regina. Calgary, with the Duke of Windsor's 'E.P.' ranch lying to the south. Then up to the cold of the Rockies and down to the Pacific, by the water's edge of which the Queen posed for a particular picture. And back again. Just over three weeks after landing at Quebec they came to rest for a while by the thunder of Niagara Falls.

Although they were about to become the first British King and Queen to enter the United States, there had been a number of royal visits in the past century and a half. When the Duke of Kent, father of Queen Victoria, was Prince Edward, he lived in Canada for ten years and became known as 'Canada's Prince'. His popularity did much towards drawing Canada and the United States together and smoothing down feelings which had remained ruffled since the War of Independence.

While he was at Halifax, Nova Scotia, he received an invitation from Mrs. Washington, wife of the President, to attend her New Year reception at the White House. Although it was less than thirty years since British troops had set fire to the White House, the invita-tion was accepted in the spirit in which it had been sent, and the Prince was enthusiastically received in the United States.

The first visit of British Royalty to the White House having been paid by the father of the Queen, the next was that of a son.

In 1860 the Heir-Apparent to the Throne, the Prince of Wales, who ultimately became King Edward VII, visited Canada and the

United States. It was many years since a member of the Royal Family had toured abroad, and the reception the Prince of Wales received everywhere was terrific.

When on October 3rd he arrived at Washington he was greeted by thousands of cheering Americans who lined the route from the railway station to the White House, whither he had been invited by President James Buchanan. President Buchanan made an exceptionally urbane host, for he had been American Envoy to Great Britain in the earlier part of his career. Hostess at the White House at the time was the President's niece, Miss Lane. At the dinners and receptions given in his honour the Prince captivated all whom he met with his personality, and he thoroughly enjoyed a trip arranged by President Buchanan and the pretty Miss Lane to Mount Vernon, the former residence of George Washington. The party went down the River Potomac in a revenue cutter.

Near Washington's Tomb the Prince of Wales planted a chestnut tree in honour of the great American who was born an Englishman. This act greatly pleased the Americans, and eyewitnesses spoke of the charm of the scene in which the young Prince stood beside the sixty-nine-year-old President, bare-headed, paying silent tribute to the founder of the United States.

There was only one thing that the Prince missed while staying with the President. The housekeeping rules of the White House forbade dancing, 'even on the carpet'. But the genial old President, with true American hospitality, saw to it that in every other respect the Prince was perfectly happy during his stay. To the end of his days the Prince remembered the kindness with which he had been treated. When he departed he presented portraits of Queen Victoria and the Prince Consort to his host and hostess. These Miss Lane regarded as her personal property, but eventually President Lincoln appropriated them as the property of the State.

In February 1883 the President of the United States issued the first invitation to a Governor-General of Canada to visit Washington. The Governor-General on this occasion was the Marquess of Lorne, husband of Princess Louise. In his honour a magnificent dinner was given. Lord Lorne put it on record that the tables were decorated with models of canoes and snowshoes in sugar and white carnations in honour of Canada, but also mentioned that he had to talk solidly for five hours to the President and his other guests.

A very dramatic incident occurred when, as Duke and Duchess of York, King George V and Queen Mary arrived in the St. Lawrence River after their voyage from Cape Town in *Ophir*. As the ship dropped anchor wave after wave of cheering from the multitudes lining the river bank rose in the air. Suddenly the shouts died away, for aboard the Duke's ship the flag of the United States was being slowly hoisted. It rose until it reached half-mast. There it stayed, and by that signal the thousands of Canadians learnt that President McKinley, who had been shot by an assailant two days before, was dead. But now, as King George VI and Queen Elizabeth dined in an hotel by Niagara Falls, the memories were all of the King's grandfather who, on 15th September 1860, had also watched the greatest water spectacle in the world. How different then. The Prince's knuckles were white as he clenched them in the agony of his suspense and he turned his eyes down to the ground to avoid a sight that he could no longer bear to watch. One hundred and sixty feet above the boiling waters a tiny figure swayed on a tightrope. It was Charles Blondin. The French acrobat not only walked across the rope, he did the crossing again with a man on his back and yet again, this time on stilts. When he pretended to fall and swung under the rope, the Prince had had more than enough. When Blondin was presented to him after the display he said: 'Thank God, it is all over! Please never attempt the feat again.' Blondin then offered to carry the royal visitor across the Falls on his back, or to push him across in a wheelbarrow, whichever he preferred. The offer was politely, but firmly, refused.

No such offer was made to the King and Queen, and they crossed the boundary, securely and prosaically, in the royal train. They went first to Washington. The drive from the station to the White House, under the blanket of sweltering heat, through crowds denser than had ever before congregated in the Capital, gave them a foretaste of things to come.

President and Mrs. Roosevelt had expected to meet a nice, quiet young couple who had been foisted with a big job for which they had been inadequately trained and which they did not wish to undertake.

185

Instead the President found a restrained ruler of infinite wisdom and understanding, with many ideas that coincided with his own. His wife met a little woman possessing regal presence and unending charm. Within hours a friendship was forged that was to last until only one of them was left.

Peace and equanimity lay over the White House, in all its rooms bar one. That was the butler's pantry. There, in hurt silence, Mr. Alonzo Fields nursed, and pondered on, the pinpricks that had pierced his dignified hide. The source of the trouble lay in the servants of the Queen. He was later to comment: 'The King and Queen were two grand people, but their royal servants could have stayed in England. They required more service than the King and Queen, the lady-in-waiting or his Majesty's aides.' One of the offenders was described as 'a real browbeater', whose tongue could make the other servants run around like scared rabbits. 'She was an overwhelming snob. She criticized about everything we did with a sharp tongue.'

But no echo of the inner conflict pierced the dividing green baize door. The Washington welcome for the King and Queen was unparalleled. The Queen had received a baptism in American compliments when Ambassador Kennedy in London had told her that she was 'a cute trick', but now the father of the future President was completely outdone. Cries of 'Attaboy Queen' were hurled towards her not-distant ear. The King was told, 'My, you're a great Queen picker!' Harry Hopkins's[1] daughter told him that at last she had seen the Fairy Queen. When she put up her parasol in the blazing sunlight, the women of Washington stampeded the shops so as to be able to follow her example, and the industry boomed, as it had when she did the same thing in Paris. Congressmen either looked at her as if she was a piece of Dresden china or went the other way and confided in her all the domestic problems round their own parochial pump. Nobody remembered anything about George III.

Their progress through the heat was non-stop, unremitting, and varied. The Queen inspected Girl Scouts. They went to Mount Vernon, above the Potomac river, where the sun had set on George Washington. There was a State Dinner at the White House and a

[1] Mr. Hopkins, who died in 1946, was then Secretary of Commerce.

Congressional reception at the Capitol. Then, without a break, off in the evening to New York. The day began peacefully enough with a trip round the harbour in a U.S. destroyer, but it was when their feet were on dry land again that the tumult broke out. They experienced the ticker-tape treatment. At the World's Fair the crowds rendered 'Land of Hope and Glory' at full blast. Time, however carefully planned, came to mean nothing. The programme was several hours behind when Columbia University was reached.

Meantime, ninety miles away on the Hudson river, the President, his mother Sarah Delano Roosevelt, and his wife were waiting to greet the King and Queen with a refreshing cup of tea. The kettle boiled on, but still no sign of the royal guests. Then, in the distance, church bells sounded and car horns screamed in competition, and two tattered Royalties drove up at the end of a drive that had been crowd-lined and flower-strewn all the way. By now the tea things had been cleared and in their place was a tray of much needed cocktails.

The President had said: 'They are coming away for a quiet week-end with me. I'll put the King into an old pair of flannels and just drive him about in my old Ford.' And that was how it was. They sat before the fire and talked. The Queen put a telephone call through to her children. There was a picnic, and swimming, a favourite pastime of the President. They attended morning service at the parish church, where the procedure followed was identical with that in any village in England, including prayers for the welfare of Their British Majesties. That evening they set off again for Canada.

Some years later, in a conversation with Mr. Hector Bolitho, Mrs. Eleanor Roosevelt described their departure: 'As Queen Elizabeth was leaving, she suddenly said to me, "Oh, I forgot to thank your chauffeur for driving the King so carefully." The man was brought and the Queen thanked him. He was an old servant of ours, from Hyde Park Village. He hurried home and the news of the Queen's gesture spread. We all drove into the station, where the King and Queen were to catch the train. We found the slopes crowded with people from the village. Suddenly, as the train moved, without any-one seeming to give a signal, they all joined in singing *Auld Lang Syne*.'

187

There remained a less edifying, but more solid, memorial of their visit. This took the form of a high-grade seat for a water closet, and it hung, like a horse's collar, in lone splendour in a shop window in the village. The story behind it, recounted by John Gunther in *Roosevelt in Retrospect*, centred round the President's mother, Mrs. Sarah Delano Roosevelt. She was a woman of great strength of character and indomitable will. She sat at the head of the table in her home of Hyde Park. She was rich, but for her there was a deep divide between capital and interest. She was known for her tardiness in paying bills.

Before the King and Queen arrived Mrs. Sarah Delano inspected their quarters. She decided that certain sanitary improvements were needed in the bathroom, and also a new lavatory seat. She called in a plumber, and the work was done. When the account for the work came in, the old lady considered that she had been overcharged, and refused to pay. So the plumber went again to Hyde Park. He departed with the lavatory seat. This he hung in his shop window, with a notice below it, 'The King and Queen sat here.'

The King and Queen were reunited with their Canadian entourage and travelled to Halifax where, one hundred and fifty years before, Queen Victoria's father had lived with his French Canadian mistress, Madame Julie de St. Laurent.[1] On 15th June they sailed from there for home on the *Empress of Britain*.

The King and Queen whom London welcomed home with rapturous delight were soon found to have grown in stature and in confidence. It was also noticed that the King had left his impediment behind him on the other side of the Atlantic.

---

[1] From *A General Description of Nova Scotia*, printed at the Royal Acadian School of Halifax in 1823: 'In travelling from Halifax to Windsor the first object of attention is a country seat erected by H.R.H. the late Duke of Kent when Commander-in-Chief of British North America. It is called the Lodge and is a very handsome wooden building situated on the border of Bedford Basin (upper end of the long harbour) and commanding a view of that beautiful sheet of water and the high hills on the opposite side. In front of the Lodge is a rotunda or music room; in the rear the greenhouse, buildings and offices of different descriptions. The whole is surrounded by a wood principally of birch and beech trees laid out in very good taste.'

20 'Tell Me, Mirror on the Wall . . .'

I N July 1939 the belief that she was not photographing well was
distressing Queen Elizabeth. There was not an iota of vanity in her
perturbation. As First Lady, she considered it her duty to give
her utmost to her position, both in work and presentation. And there
was no doubt that many of the pictures of her were not compli-
mentary. It was not that she lacked composure—Sargent had
described her as the most natural sitter he had ever known. It was
not that she lacked picture sense—press photographers had noticed
how she chose the fitting background. It was simply that, when the
blue of her eyes, the pink of her cheeks, the life in her smile were
translated on the plate, somehow the personality of her became
smudged.

She was not alone in knowing this. It was so often said. A professional cameraman had given his opinion: 'That little woman has
grounds for a libel suit every time her picture is taken.' David
Steuart had commented when he first saw her beauty: 'Now I
realized that photographs did no justice to it at all.'

Cecil Beaton was summoned to the Palace. As he walked the
corridors self-confidence was mesmerized from him, in the way that
Palaces have. He thus described his first glimpse of her: 'The Queen
was in the act of moving towards a desk. All about her a blue haze
emanated from the French silk walls embroidered in bouquets of
silver. The room seemed a pointillist bower of flowers. . . .'[1]

The two began to talk. 'We discussed dresses. "You know, perhaps the embroidered one I wore—in Canada . . . ?" A slight hesitation prevented the remark from being conceited, for the Queen must

[1] *The Candid Eye of Cecil Beaton.*

189

have known I was aware of what she wore on her Canadian tour. 'The Queen made other tentative suggestions: "And I thought, perhaps, another evening dress of—tulle? And a—tiara?" All this wistfully said, with a smile, and raised eyebrows.

'The charm of manner was so infectious that, no doubt to the Queen's astonishment, I found myself subconsciously imitating her somewhat spasmodic flow of speech and using the same gentle, staccato expressions. I wrinkled my forehead in imitation of her look of inquiry as I asked if—perhaps—as much jewellery as possible could be worn?

'The Queen smiled apologetically: "The choice isn't very great you know!"'

Hitherto the time limit imposed on photographers had been twenty minutes. On that day Mr. Beaton worked for over three hours and the evening light was falling before he took his hidden treasures away. The Queen was photographed in a crinoline gown, in 'spangled tulle like a fairy doll', in a garden party dress of champagne set off by a parasol. She posed by pillar and painted panel, in doorways and by priceless desks, on sofas and tapestried chairs. Away with Mr. Beaton went one of her handkerchiefs, that she had tucked behind a cushion. It was a tiny memento of a momentous day, for it was on that afternoon that the Queen's perturbation about her photographic likeness faded away.

There came another day in that July of 1939 that the Queen was ever to remember. It was then that she met her future son-in-law. The King had decided that he wished to visit Dartmouth College, not only to see how training for the Navy was progressing, but also to revive memories, some pleasant, some painful, of his time as a cadet. There may also have been another reason. With the King and Queen ton the Royal Yacht *Victoria and Albert* went the two Princesses and Lord Louis Mountbatten. On the way to the river Dart the Reserve Fleet was inspected at Weymouth.

It was not the most suitable of dates to learn of the life at the Royal Naval College, as one portion of the cadets was down with mumps, and another with chicken-pox. Owing to the risk of infection the Princesses were not allowed to attend chapel the following morning, staying in the safety of the Captain's home. They were

left in the care of the Captain's messenger for the day. He happened
to be eighteen-year-old Prince Philip of Greece.

Strangely enough, Princess Elizabeth had not met Philip of
Greece before. In fact the Royal Family, with the exception of the
Milford Havens and Lord Louis Mountbatten, knew very little about
him, despite his being often at Kensington Palace as a boy. At a
wedding in 1935 the Marquess of Carisbrooke, erstwhile Prince
Alexander of Battenberg, had enquired who the good-looking, fair
lad was. So much had gone under the waves in so short a time,
except in the memories of the two very old daughters of Queen
Victoria who still dwelt in Kensington Palace.

The boy and the girl had the same great-great-grandmother in
Queen Victoria. But while Queen Alexandra was great-grandmother to Princess Elizabeth, she was, owing to divergence in
marriage times, great-aunt to Prince Philip. Looking up into his
family tree he could see, quite close to him, a Czar of Russia, a King
of Denmark, a King of Greece, a Queen of England, a Grand Duke
of Hesse, a King of Prussia, a Queen of Sweden. Yet, despite this
plethora of crowns, his school friends had been convulsed with
laughter when he signed himself simply 'Philip of Greece' and
invented for his benefit a series of grand sounding Ruritanian
titles.

The mists of anonymity fall quickly when a royalty leaves the
Palace door. In the case of Prince Philip's parents the tragedies and
divided loyalties of the First World War, followed by the convulsions
of Greece and a shortage of money, had moved them away from
Victoria's fold. Yet the wedding of Princess Alice of Battenberg and
Prince Andrew of Greece in 1903 had been one of the last great
get-togethers of the royal relatives of Britain, Russia, Greece,
Prussia, France, Hesse and Hanover, before war split them all
asunder. Queen Alexandra was there, and the Czar and Czarina,
the Ruler of All the Russias running, unguarded, through the
Darmstadt crowds and pelting the bride with slippers.

By the time Philip was born in 1921 things were very different.
He had known what it was to walk to school without a raincoat
because his parents were short of money. In the mode of an Algerian
pedlar, he had attempted to sell family carpets in the Paris streets

to collect enough cash to buy a bicycle. But his uncle Louis had always cared for him. And he was caring for him now.

Prince Philip's four sisters were much older than he was, and had all been married by the time that he was ten. Now he had to face up to the problem of amusing the daughters of the King and Queen. He tried a model railway, but that was not a great success. Lemonade filled an awkward gap. Then came the master stroke of croquet. This silent and vicious pastime was ideal, as much-impressed Princess Elizabeth was not saying anything anyway She was not accustomed to the undivided attention of young men of eighteen, and there is a fresh wind about all the Battenbergs. Prince Philip's grandfather had been exiled to the China Seas for letting that wind blow too fresh round the sanctity of Princess Beatrice one evening at dinner at Osborne. Of course, the fresh wind suited Princess Margaret fine.

Mother came back from chapel and took over control. They all had lunch on the royal yacht. In the afternoon Prince Philip's role was an easier one. It was that of guide, showing the girls the swimming bath, the buildings and the grounds. By the time he reappeared for dinner, Princess Elizabeth was in bed.

The Queen and the Princesses had a great time at Balmoral that August. The King had invited two hundred of his boys to camp at Abergeldie. He himself was Camp Chief and each day he headed parties out across the heather and the hills, talking of the birds and the deer, the burns and the cairns. The Queen entertained the boys to tea at the Castle and, in return, she and her daughters had supper with them in camp. Pipers played round the bonfire on the night of parting. *Auld Lang Syne* was sung, echoing for the Queen the singing of it at the station at Hyde Park only so few weeks before. It is doubtful if the King was ever as happy again as he was during the days when the camp was at Abergeldie.

On the 24th he was called back to London on the business of war.

21 Queen Among the Bombs

THE Queen took her children to Birkhall and there installed them in security and seclusion. She recalled their governess from holiday, and left them in the care of Sir Basil Brooke, the Queen's Treasurer. On the 29th August she joined the King at Buckingham Palace.

In the strange, groping world of black-out and blinds, balloons and sirens, there was a great deal of work for the Queen to do in her office next to her husband's. The whole complicated splendour of regal life had to be pared down to ration size. Arrangements had to be made for the safety of the older members of the Royal Family. There were new jobs to face—the Queen became Commandant-in-Chief of the three women's Services. The gilt of royal homes had to go under dust sheets until peace came again.

Queen Mary was the first to be moved. She was at Sandringham, in the danger zone of the East Coast, when war was declared on 3rd September. In the First World War bombs had dropped around the estate, a present to Queen Alexandra from the nephew whom she referred to as 'the very devil'. At three o'clock on the morning of the 4th an air raid alarm sent Queen Mary down to the basement of the 'Big House'. A few hours later she left for the Duke of Beaufort's home of Badminton in Gloucestershire, her entourage of over sixty in a cavalcade of motor cars behind her. That evening her niece[1] watched the procession arrive with mixed feelings of awe and trepidation.

Sandringham slipped into war gear, and became an efficient agri-

---

[1]The Duke of Beaufort had married, in 1923, Lady Mary Cambridge, daughter of Queen Mary's brother, Adolphus, 1st Marquess of Cambridge.

cultural cog in the war machine. The golf course, which Edward VII had made, was ploughed up. The 'Big House' was closed and, on their brief visits to Norfolk, the Royal Family stayed at Appleton House. Then, to save petrol, the Queen drove around in a pony trap, the King and Princesses following on bicycles.

Buckingham Palace became the mid-week office and home, Windsor the week-end interlude. The Castle was the strong point in case of emergency. Here important visitors were entertained. The Royal Lodge was for relaxation. It was only there that the King wore civilian clothes. The Queen wore 'civvies' throughout the war, the uniform of the mothers of Britain.

Mr. Herbert Morrison,[1] Home Secretary and Minister of Home Security, gave his opinion that the example of the King and Queen did more to keep up the spirits of the people than any other single factor. By constantly moving about the country they kept the image of the Monarchy alive. In the ten-coach royal train they travelled tens of thousands of miles, boosting production in factories, visiting fighting and defence units, cheering the wounded, bringing sympathy to bomb-damaged cities. The train, built in the last days of Queen Victoria, became a mobile home to them. They preferred to spend their nights in it, rather than be guests at some big house in the area where they stopped. The train was connected by telephone with Buckingham Palace, and they were able to keep in constant touch with the latest developments on the fronts. Thus it was that, on some lonely siding, the King and Queen might be seen taking their evening stroll beside the line, amid the coal bunkers and the still goods waggons.

Food rationing was strictly adhered to at the Palace. No deviation was allowed. In this George VI was like his father who, during the First World War, had accused a visitor to Sandringham of being a traitor to his country because he asked if he might have a second egg for breakfast. On a day of crisis the King and Queen were contenting themselves with a snack of sandwiches. A Minister called. The Queen offered him one. The King commented: 'I don't know what is in them. Sawdust, I expect.'

Nor was there any relaxing of the rules for royalty over clothing

[1] Lord Morrison of Lambeth.

coupons. The Queen was fortunate as she could fall back on the large wardrobes made for the visit to Paris, and to Canada and America. In time these were altered where possible and handed down to Princess Elizabeth. The King's problem was shirts. When collars and cuffs became frayed, the Queen had them replaced with pieces from the tails.

With fuel short, the vast rooms of the Palace and Windsor grew very cold in winter. Only tiny electric fires, like glowing embers, welcomed royal guests. Round the bath lines were painted five inches from the bottom so that there could be no mistake over the amount of water allowed.

Yet, when the first few days of war were over and the expected deluge of bombs from enemy aircraft had not materialized, and 'the phoney war' of autumn and winter had settled in, surprisingly few safety precautions surrounded the King and Queen. They had not even their own air raid shelter at the Palace. There was the same chance for all in the basement. The lull went on, month after month. It was deemed safe to bring the Princesses back from Scotland, and they were installed at Windsor. There the A.A. guns stood silent round the ramparts.

Then, in April, came the first rumbles of the gathering storm. Denmark and Norway were invaded. The thunder grew nearer. With the dawn of 10th May came the news that the frontiers of Holland and Belgium had been crossed, and that the Low Countries and France lay in peril. By that evening Mr. Winston Churchill was Prime Minister.

Three days later, at five o'clock in the morning, Queen Elizabeth learned at first hand of the anguish and dangers that can come with queenship. Queen Wilhelmina of the Netherlands was on the telephone begging for help for her stricken country. Then, having tried in vain to rejoin her forces, she was brought to Harwich in a British destroyer. She arrived at Buckingham Palace with only a tin hat to supplement the clothes in which she stood. The British Queen took good care of her.

There were soon two royal exiles staying as guests of the Queen, Queen Wilhelmina and King Haakon of Norway—'Old Norway' as he called himself. These two stressed to their host and hostess the dangers of Hitler's way with Monarchs. He wished, at all costs, to capture them, and then use them for the purpose of taming the activities of Resistance movements.

King Haakon was particularly worried about the safety arrangements for Buckingham Palace. What would happen, he asked the King and Queen, if German parachutists were suddenly to descend from the sky? Quietly the King pressed an alarm bell. Then the party moved out into the garden to watch the result. The scene stayed as tranquil as a Wodehouse afternoon at a stately home. Unworried, an old gardener carried on with his weeding. The hum of the buses came from beyond the walls. King Haakon looked at King George. King George looked at an equerry, who hurried away. He returned with the news that the guard had been told by a policeman that there was no raid, otherwise he would have heard about it. After a few short naval expressions there was seen, entering from the wings at the double, a number of guardsmen, who proceeded to make exaggerated passes at, and glances into, handy shrubs and bushes. The Queen burst into fits of laughter. As a result of this practical Norwegian experiment, various amendments to the regulations were made.

After Dunkirk and the fall of France, and with German air attacks on coastal shipping and airfields heating up, security and self-defence became matters of utmost urgency with the Royal Family. Aggression was there too. Shooting ranges were built both at Buckingham Palace and Windsor, and there the Queen practised regularly, recapturing the skill that she had achieved on her safaris in East Africa. Mr. Churchill sent along an American automatic weapon of particular efficiency. When the King travelled in his splinter- and bullet-proof car, he was always armed, as were those who travelled with him. He had already decided that, if invasion took place and matters went badly, he would offer himself as the leader of the Resistance movement.

When it was suggested to the Queen that it might be a wise step for the Princesses to be moved to safety on the other side of the Atlantic, she made the position crystal clear. She answered: 'The children won't go without me. I won't leave the King. And the King will never leave.' At Windsor the Princesses joined with their parents to make up a stirrup pump squad, and during practice they referred to one another by numbers instead of names.

The Government had drawn up a detailed plan for the whisking away of the Royal Family should an emergency arise. Cars, specially marked to give them top priority, would take them to secluded houses in the West country. The safety of the King and Queen was entrusted to selected men from the Brigade of Guards and the Household Cavalry, whose armoured cars were ready to move at a moment's notice.

Early in September the bombs began to fall on the terraces and factories, churches and hospitals, of south and east London. Time after time the figures of the King and Queen were to be seen among the rescue squads as they searched through the debris. There was still not an air raid shelter at Buckingham Palace. Then their turn came to be target.

On the 9th a bomb fell on the north of the Palace, below the King's study. It did not explode. The King went on working. By this time the King and Queen were spending the nights at Windsor, driving up to 'the office' in the morning. In the early hours the bomb went off. As the danger area had been evacuated, there were no casualties, but everywhere windows were broken. A new study was found and work continued.

The 13th of September was a Friday—a day of ill omen. In the morning the King and Queen drove up from Windsor. It was raining and the clouds hung low. In London the sirens were moaning their warning. The two went up to their new sitting-room, overlooking the courtyard. They began to prepare for another day's work. Then, through the open window, came the fierce, fast crescendo of an aircraft's engines and propellors screaming in a dive. From out of the clouds above Trafalgar Square rocketed a machine of the *Luftwaffe*. It flattened out and roared above its run-in of the tree-lined Mall.

For a fraction of time the King and Queen saw two bombs falling from the sky. Before they could move came the ear-shattering thunder of explosions, almost coincident. Then it was that their eyes met, and in a trice they were through the door and into the passage. They were filled with wonderment that they were still alive.

In the thick silence after the tumult they looked at the damage. In the Quadrangle, not a stone's throw from where they had been standing by their sitting-room window, were two great craters. A burst water main was playing its jet through a shattered window, turning a passage into a stream. The windows on the opposite side had all gone. Four workmen in the plumber's shop were casualties.

Six bombs had been dropped. Two had landed in the fore-court, two in the courtyard, one had wrecked the Chapel and the other had ended in the garden. 'What had been the Chapel,' wrote Princess Marie Louise, 'was nothing but a huge aching void, and the only thing saved from it was the old family Bible in which the births, marriages, and deaths of the Royal Family over many generations were recorded.'

The King and Queen went off on their tour of inspection. They marvelled that the workmen had not all been killed in the shambles which had so shortly before been the plumber's shop, and relief at their escape helped to lighten the tragedy of the Chapel. They went among the staff who had sheltered in the basement, and found them calm. Then a shaft of Cockney sunlight lit that morning of Friday the 13th. The Queen paused to speak to a policeman. He grinned at her, and said: 'A magnificent piece of bombing, Ma'am, if you'll pardon my saying so.'

One of the bombs in the fore-court was believed to be of delayed action type, so all windows were left open and the King and Queen lunched in the shelter which had been hastily prepared for them. It was, in fact, a maid's sitting room. But this experience had been enough. Plans were now made for the erection of a permanent shelter, with full protection and eating and washing facilities.

It was strange indeed how this near miss from death of the King and Queen was hushed up and kept quiet until after the war was over. Not even Ministers knew. Yet it was typical of the man and the woman, to make light of danger. Sir Winston Churchill, in *Their Finest Hour*, the second volume of his history of the Second World War, wrote: 'I must confess that at the time neither I nor any of my colleagues were aware of the peril of this particular incident. Had the windows been closed instead of open the whole of the glass would have splintered into the faces of the King and Queen, causing terrible injuries. So little did they make of it that even I, who saw them and their entourage so frequently, only realized long afterwards . . . what had actually happened.'

Queen Elizabeth's comment on the day was: 'I'm glad we've been bombed. It makes me feel I can look the East End in the face.'

In all Buckingham Palace was hit nine times by aerial weapons of various kinds. Every window in Marlborough House was broken and the doors stove in. Queen Mary bewailed: 'The old House cannot stand much more of this.' 145, Piccadilly was totally destroyed.

After the war, when genial Mr. George Tomlinson was Minister of Works and responsible for the Palace, the King asked him, 'What about my windows, George?' 'It'll come your turn, Sir,' was the reply. 'It's come our turn,' said the King to his wife, in the presence of Mr. Tomlinson, when he saw the workmen arrive.

Yet, despite their outward imperturbability, inside themselves the King and Queen were paying a price. Their constant visits to devastated areas, the uncertainty as to whether live bombs lay hid among the debris, their experiences at Buckingham Palace, the suffering that was all about them, the broken hearts they tried to cheer, all these combined to make a burden that was indeed hard to carry. Now, when the sound of a strange aircraft came from the sky, followed the moments of mental separation from the world around, the mask of expectancy, the tenseness of body, the racing of the heart. The Queen admitted to Queen Mary that at times she felt quite exhausted. There were tears in her eyes, day after day, as she listened to the heart-rending tales of suffering and bereavement that came to her amid the fire-scarred skeletons of London's murdered streets.

But, for their constancy, there was a great reward. Never before in British history had a Sovereign and his Consort been so close in spirit and understanding to their people. For him, there was the deepest appreciation and admiration, because he went to the scene of devastation and did what he could to help. An Equerry told Princess Marie Louise that, as the royal car was leaving a badly blitzed area in the East End, a man seized his arm and, pointing at the King, said: 'You see him? That's why we sing, *There'll always be an*

England! God bless him.' For the Queen there was a feeling transcending adoration. For red-eyed women, searching among the bricks for remnants of their possessions, some meaning to the day was born when she walked among them. A flower grew from out the dust of death. One afternoon they gave their verdict. From among a knot of Cockney women came the words: 'Oh, ain't she luverley! Ain't she bloody luverley!'

The Queen was on occasions able to be of practical assistance. She saw a woman crying and walked over to comfort her. She learned that the woman's terrier, terrified by the bombs, had hidden under a pile of rubble, and that nothing would induce it to come out. 'Perhaps I can help,' said the Queen. 'I am rather good with dogs.'[1] She crouched down in the roadway and talked her particular language into a hole in the bricks. After a considerable time a shaking terrier came back into the light.

The Queen made certain that, should the eventuality arise, she would be fully capable of herself dealing with casualties. Her duties at Glamis in the First World War, and her subsequent close association with hospitals as the Duchess of York and Queen, had given her considerable experience. To complete her knowledge, and also to indoctrinate the staff, Major Alexander White Knox, one of the leading experts on first aid in the country, was called to the Palace. When he had finished his course of instruction he was asked to leave his kit behind so that the Princesses could practice.

The Queen's frequent visits to bomb-damaged areas, and her deep concern with welfare, led to her being able to make a number of practical suggestions for the alleviation of the lot of the homeless and injured. These she discussed in conversations with the Minister of Health.

The King encouraged the Queen to take an interest and a share in his duties. He had no illusions about the immortality of Kings. He knew full well that in places such as Coventry, where unexploded bombs lay by their score beneath the rubble, his reign could end abruptly. And he had learned, from the case of his father, the fallacy

[1] Before the war the King, Queen and Princesses had eight dogs at the Royal Lodge: two Pembrokeshire Corgis, Dookie and Jane; three yellow Labradors, Mimsy, Stiffy and Scrummy; a Tibetan Lion Dog, Choo-Choo; a golden retriever, Judy; and a black cocker-spaniel, Ben.

of only letting one pair of hands know how to handle the reins. His policy was shared by his Prime Minister.

There were many who wondered what the relations would be between the King and Queen and Mr. Churchill as a result of the latter's spirited championship of the cause of King Edward VIII prior to the abdication. In truth, the King had grieved at the passing of Mr. Neville Chamberlain and looked upon Lord Halifax as his natural successor. When the nation's choice fell upon Winston Churchill, after a few minutes of jocular sparring, there was complete unanimity between the two men. There was the knot of the British Navy to hold them securely together, and the message— 'Winston is back'—had had a peculiar meaning for the naval officer who had served at Jutland.

During his first two months in office Mr. Churchill attended the Palace once a week for a formal meeting. Then the ice began to crack. The talks took place over lunch on Tuesdays, very often the Queen being present. When the sirens went they would totter off to the basement carrying their plates and glasses. Next it was decided to dispense with servants and that they should serve themselves, which meant, when the one-track mind of the Premier was fixed on a problem, he was administered to by the Queen of England. This is like Marlborough and Queen Anne, thought Winston Churchill. To begin with he was addressed as 'Mr. Churchill'. Soon it was 'Winston' or 'P.M.'

To the Queen, Winston Churchill became both an institution and a loyal friend. She admired his talents, particularly painting, and later she shared with him a love for the Turf. Yet, when the mood was upon him, he was proof against her charms. Obsessed with thoughts and plans, he could so remove himself from the goings on around him that on one occasion a young woman seated next to him at dinner got up and ate her meal at the sideboard. The Queen tried to make him play charades at Windsor, a game loved since her childhood. He sat, cigar in hand, eyes unmoving above his Orders. She attempted, by little asides, to draw him in. She pleaded for advice. No answer came. She tried the smile. With no avail. Not for the ghost of little Elizabeth Bowes-Lyon, not for the Queen of England in her castle, was Winston Spencer Churchill going to play charades.

22 *Wife and Mother in Time of War*

TWO Royalties, crouched low, crawled through a hole in a hedge at Windsor. It was the year that America went to war. It was a Sunday. Old Lord Clive Wigram[1] had asked the King if he could show two high-ranking United States officers over the Castle, although visitors were officially excluded. The request had been granted, and the King and Queen had decided to keep to their own apartments to avoid causing embarrassment to Lord Wigram and his guests. But the sun came out, the garden called, and the royal prisoners broke their parole and lay basking on the sward, forgetful of all but the soothing sun. There came to them, from along a path, the accents of Winchester, Washington and West Point. They looked at one another guiltily and then, with one accord, made for the hole in the hedge. No ripple of their passing disturbed the smooth flow of the tale of ancient Windsor.

Six weeks later General Eisenhower met the King and Queen for the first time. The King dearly loved a story and now he recounted how he and his wife had retreated before the American invasion. A slow smile lit the General's face. When the story was finished he revealed that the American invaders had been himself and General Mark Clark.

Now the deep importance of the Royal visit to the United States began to show, and, in particular, the friendship which had been forged with the Roosevelts. In the informality of Court life in the

---

[1] 1st Baron Wigram, cr. 1935, G.C.B., G.C.V.O. Born 1873. Assistant Private Secretary and Equerry to King George V, 1910–1931; Private Secretary and Extra Equerry to the King, 1931–1935; Permanent Lord-in-Waiting to King George VI throughout his reign; Deputy Constable and Lieut.-Governor, Windsor Castle, and Keeper of the King's Archives.

war years U.S. leaders found a welcome contrast with the impregnable fortress of nineteenth-century imperialism that had been associated with Windsor in the reign of George V. George V was insular, he admitted so himself. He was not in tune with the ways of Americans. Irregularities in dress when they appeared at Court, riled him. He never really recovered from the newspaper headlines that greeted the visit of the Prince of Wales to America in 1924. 'Oh! Who'll ask H.R.H. what he wears when he is asleep?' and 'Prince of Wales has 'em guessing in the wee hours!' were altogether too much for him, and thereafter he did his best to keep his children away from the levity of the New World. In his last years the friendship of the Prince of Wales with Mrs. Simpson strengthened his attitude.

In Washington and New York George VI, as the son of his father, had had to endure certain peerings at him as if he was a waxwork model of Ludwig of Bavaria, but he was too plain and unassuming a man for the apparition to endure long in the course of conversation. The Queen was a very different kettle of regality. In the beginning, she was a commoner, and had no part in the fantasy of Grand Ducal palaces, and the Coburg climb to fame. It was in the nature of her to invite confidences. An ideally-married woman with children, she became a new image.

Now she sat in the air raid shelter at Buckingham Palace, serving tea, while her husband and Mr. Harry Hopkins, Special Adviser of the President, discussed measures for the safety of the world, and the bombs rained down above.

Mrs. Eleanor Roosevelt came to stay at Buckingham Palace in October 1942. The King and Queen met her at the station, and the President's wife noticed with surprise that there were apparently no more security arrangements than if she was Mrs. Smith out shopping. Living conditions in the Palace ranged from the sublime to the ration. In her lofty, grandiose bedroom the windows were rough wooden frames containing translucent plastic material, a grim warning that bombs were shared by all. A little electric fire fought a losing battle with cubic feet, and she shuddered to think of the damp.

Mrs. Roosevelt's three-week visit coincided with one of the most important military operations in British history. On 23rd/24th

October the Eighth Army's offensive at El Alamein began. By 2nd November destruction of Rommel's armour was complete and pursuit of the Axis was on. By the 11th the enemy had been cleared finally from Egypt. Tobruk was entered two days later. Thereafter the advance of General Montgomery read like a time-table. He said: 'This time, having reached Benghazi and beyond, we shall not come back.'

As the thunder of the guns rolled over the desert, chilly Mrs. Roosevelt came down to dinner. She was impressed by the fact that small helpings of food, restricted by rationing, were served on solid gold plates. The Churchills were there, General Smuts, and the Louis Mountbattens. Mr. Churchill was definitely in one of his moods. But, having been apprised of the latest score from General Montgomery, he began to sing 'Roll out the barrel'.

The Queen took Mrs. Roosevelt to see the bomb damage in the City and East End of London and initiated her into the ways of life in deep shelters. By the time she returned home she had a clear picture in her mind of the rigours of life in wartime Britain, and an even deeper respect than before for the House of Windsor.

Other Roosevelts became royal guests. The President's son, James, had his moments of minor crisis. He became lost in the maze of corridors at Windsor. Found, and brought before the King and Queen, he forgot all about the instruction given to him to bow low. He held out his hand. Without a sign on her face that the porcelain of etiquette was being shattered, the Queen took the hand and shook it. James also forgot, in the midst of discussion, that plates at Palaces are not taken away until they are empty. He woke to find himself looking down at cold soup while other guests were busy on the fish. The Queen sized up the situation and, at her signal, the soup was whisked away.

One of the sacrifices that the Queen made in the war years was that, on account of her many duties and journeys, she was unable to spend as long as she would have liked with her daughters. The short weekends came and went so quickly, and even then there were often guests to be entertained at Windsor. Education posed no problem. Princess Margaret was still much in the care of a governess, and there were ample learned instructors available to care for Princess

Elizabeth. In the sphere of schooling the Queen was modern in her thinking, too modern for some of the elder brethren around the Castle. But she had learned wisdom from the methods of her mother.

On the side of personal relationship matters were not so easy. The elder girl was serious, studious but not brilliant, intensely loyal and bound to duty, and a trier. There was much of Queen Mary in her, with a dash of the Empress Frederick. And just as 'Pussy', Princess Royal, had sat for hour after hour imbibing the creeds and beliefs of Prince Albert, so now Princess Elizabeth walked beside George VI in the Park, hanging on to his every word. Again the bond between father and first-born daughter was strong indeed, and was vastly to influence the Queen-to-be in the years ahead.

The younger girl was gifted, impish, overflowing with the personal, striving always to bridge the gap between 1926 and 1930. There was about her the flavour of Louise of Argyll and Louise of Fife. There was an echo of Queen Victoria's youngest daughter who, at the age of four, told a lady-in-waiting: 'I was very naughty last night. I would not speak to Papa, but it doesn't signify much!' Now there came tales of salt found in 'Lilibet's' tea and tapioca in her bath.

Princess Elizabeth received religious instruction from Canon Crawley, a member of the Chapter of St. George's Chapel. Sir Henry Kennett Marten, then Vice-Provost of Eton, taught her history. This was her most important subject, the coverage was wide, and she learned from both sides.

In March 1942 Princess Elizabeth was confirmed at Windsor by the Archbishop of Canterbury, Dr. Cosmo Lang. It was to be the last official act of his career and Queen Mary motored up from Badminton for the occasion. The previous month the Princess had been appointed Colonel of the Grenadier Guards, and on her sixteenth birthday she carried out an inspection with somewhat terrifying efficiency. She then went to the Windsor Employment Exchange to register for National Service. She began to plague her father to be allowed to join one of the women's Services. For once, considering her too young, he resisted her. It was her mother who at last persuaded the King to change his mind. In March 1945 she went into the records of the Auxiliary Territorial Service as: 'No. 230873 Second Subaltern Elizabeth Alexandra Mary Windsor. Age 18.

Eyes, blue. Hair, brown. Height 5 ft. 3 in.' At the Mechanical Transport Training Centre near Camberley she got oil in her hair, grease in her finger-nails. She learned how to drive and to change lorry wheels. A high-ranking A.T.S. officer enquired of the Queen if her daughter talked of her training at home. 'Well,' answered the Queen, 'last night we had sparking plugs during the whole of dinner!'

In the Princess's room was a photograph of a young naval officer with a beard. Letters were passing between Prince Philip and herself. During his leaves they met on a number of occasions. They danced at a party given by the Duchess of Kent at 'Coppins'. At Christmas 1943 he was among the guests at Windsor. 'Philip thinks this and that' began to drift into the family conversations.

As in the First World War, the Queen had personal losses and worries to face. Her nephew, John Patrick, Master of Glamis, a captain in the Scots guards, was killed in action in 1941. Another nephew, Andrew Elphinstone, was a prisoner of war.

In August 1942 the King and Queen took a short holiday at Balmoral. The Duke and Duchess of Gloucester were with them. During dinner on the 25th the King was called from the table to take an urgent telephone call. He returned with the news that his brother, the Duke of Kent, had been killed in an air crash.

It was at one o'clock that afternoon that a tender had taken the Duke, his secretary, his equerry and his batman[1] out to the Sunderland lying on the smooth waters of Cromarty Firth. The rear gunner, Flight-Sergeant[2] Andrew Jack, was in his place in the turret and the heavily-laden flying boat took off on its long haul to Iceland.

What happened shortly afterwards was described by Andrew Jack[3]: 'About 25 minutes after take-off we ran into heavy cloud. It was rather low, and I remember thinking to myself, as I sat there with cloud all around me: "What a silly day to fly." I could feel the aircraft going down and I said to myself "We're going to see the coastline again." If you're not flying a compass course you've got to be able to see the coast to follow it. Looking back now, I think we must have been drifting inland without realizing it, and that the

[1] Lieutenant J. A. Lowther, R.N.V.R., Pilot Officer the Hon. M. Strutt, and L.A.C. J. W. Hales.
[2] Later Flight-Lieutenant.
[3] In an article in the *Daily Express*, 18th May 1961.

captain, trying to get below the cloud, came down over land instead of out to sea. I didn't know any more until I woke up and found myself on the ground.'

How long he was unconscious Flight-Sergeant Jack never knew. Nor did he realize that his face and arms were badly burned and his hand was broken. When his brain started working again he saw that the aircraft was in little pieces, and he realized that the rest of the passengers and crew must be dead. He recognized the Duke's body by his uniform of Air Commodore. He staggered off along a shepherd's path by a burn. When darkness fell he lay down in the ferns. In the brilliant light of a sunny dawn he struggled to a hill top. Eventually he reached a cottage.

This tragedy, which shattered the life of the Duchess of Kent, had a deep and lasting effect on the King and Queen. For her, it meant an added strain when her husband was away on overseas visits to the Forces. Such an occasion came in June 1943 when the King flew to North Africa, the Queen being one of the Counsellors of State during his absence. On the day before he left the King was visited by his solicitor as he wished to ensure that, should disaster overtake him, his house was in order.

The York aircraft in which he travelled was due to land at Gibraltar for refuelling. The Queen was kept in touch with the plane's progress. She was told that it was near the Rock and would be landing soon. Then silence, absolute and utter. For an hour and a half she paced her room, back and forth, back and forth, eyes focused on the telephone, never leaving it, as she prayed and begged that it would ring. And when it did, the message was that there was thick fog over Gibraltar and that the York had circled and droned on south. Silence again, and the gamut of fears continued. The vision of a long scar on a hillside in Caithness. Then at long last, the overwhelming relief of being told that the York had landed safely in Africa and taken off again.

The war years took a heavy toll among the older royalties. Of the remaining children of Queen Victoria Princess Louise died in 1939, the Duke of Connaught in 1942 and Princess Beatrice in October 1944. Her funeral was at St. George's Chapel, Windsor, and Queen Elizabeth led the Princess's daughter, Queen Victoria Eugenia of

Spain, to the open vault, and there the two curtseyed. Behind, in the choir stalls, stood a slim figure in black, Princess Elizabeth. Princess Beatrice had been born before the advent of Bismarck, weaned on the rise of Germany's power and lived to see the decline before the fall.

In the same year the Queen lost her father, at the age of eighty-nine. He was succeeded, as fifteenth Earl of Strathmore, by her eldest brother, Patrick, born in 1884. As the new Earl's elder son had been killed in action, the younger, Timothy, serving in the Black Watch, became Lord Glamis.

It was in March 1944 that the first royal wedding of the war took place. It was of particular interest for the Queen, and brought back many memories, for she had cradled the bridegroom in her arms at his christening in Belgrade in 1923, the first time she and her husband had been abroad together. King Peter of Yugoslavia had found refuge in Britain in 1941. Now, at twenty, he was marrying twenty-three-year-old Princess Alexandra of Greece. Four Monarchs were at the ceremony at the Yugoslav Legation. The King and Queen, mindful of the promise made at the baptism, cared well for the godson whose father had been assassinated in Marseilles in 1934.

D-Day approached. On 30th May Mr. Churchill drove to the Palace for his customary weekly lunch. At the back of the minds of both the King and himself was a common thought. Where would they be on the day of the invasion of the bastion of Europe? Both had the same ambition, to be off the beaches of Normandy. They had not as yet discussed it. Now the King put the question to the Prime Minister as to his planned whereabouts on that eventual night. Casually, glibly, Mr. Churchill revealed that he intended to watch the bombardment from one of the cruiser squadrons, and that he had begun the arrangements a month before.

Although the King had been thinking about the idea for some time, he had not got as far as making plans. Now he drew level with the Prime Minister by suggesting that they should go together. Mr. Churchill's reactions appeared favourable.

Apart from the obvious advantages of leaders seeing for themselves what actually happened, and the cheering effect of their

Prince Charles and Princess Anne greet their grandmother on the
completion of her tour of the United States and Canada, 1954

With Mr. Robert Menzies at the State Ball, Canberra, 1958

presence among the fighting men, both King and Prime Minister had more personal reasons. They were both tired out after the paper-work of planning and they needed 'the refreshment of adventure'. Also they wished to savour again the days of youth, the thunder of the Lancers as they charged at Omdurman, the smell of cordite as Jutland unfolded on the grey North Sea. Whilst the Prime Minister only had to have the blessing of the King, the King had to consult many people before he sailed away on his adventure, Number One on the list being his wife.

One might have expected the Queen to put the kibosh on the idea, smartly and finally. Not at all. She was, as the King said, wonderful about it, 'as always'. Not only was she wonderful about it, but she even encouraged him to go. Then the Queen knew her husband very well.

The royal advisers took a very different view. The adventurous scheme filled them with something approaching consternation. Sir Alan Lascelles, the King's Private Secretary, had a very long face. It was presumed, of course, that the departing Monarch would leave instructions for Queen Elizabeth II as to the appointing of a new Prime Minister. By the next day the King had surrendered. It was then his task to prevent Mr. Churchill going, and this he only managed to do at the last moment. Yet not many days were to pass after D before both men were walking the beaches of Normandy.

No sooner was the King back than the V-1 bombs began diving down on London. The Queen called them 'inhuman'. Once again all her windows went, and a large slice of her garden wall. She went to an Anti-Aircraft site and watched the A.T.S. girls operating their predictors.

Meantime, every night, the Queen had to listen to her husband bewailing the fact that he was not in the firing line. He certainly did his best. In July he visited his troops on the Italian front and in October he was with the 21st Army Group, the guest of General Montgomery.

In March 1945, when the V-1s had changed to V-2s, the Queen began to think of arrangements for a most important guest who had been asked to stay at Buckingham Palace, none other than the President of the United States. It was not to be. On 12th April

President Roosevelt was taken ill while at lunch in Warm Springs, Georgia, and died shortly afterwards. He was buried at his home at Hyde Park, in the gardens which the Queen knew well.

The Court went into mourning and, when the Memorial Service at St. Paul's was over, the King and Queen snatched a short rest at Appleton House, Sandringham. It was there that they received a message from Mr. Churchill that the war was nearing its close.

VE-Day, 8th May 1945. The lights came on again all over the land, flooding the towers and turrets with a loveliness that children had never seen. The newspapers carried weather reports for the first time since 1st September 1939. Outside Buckingham Palace a mighty concourse was shouting for the King and Queen. Eight times in all they came out on to the balcony. They came out with Mr. Churchill in their midst. The Queen stood on his right, a smiling radiant figure in an off-the-face hat. Princess Elizabeth was in uniform.

The Queen had another reason for happiness that day. Staying with her at the Palace was her nephew, the Master of Elphinstone. He and Lord Lascelles, Grenadier son of the Princess Royal, had just been repatriated after the Nazis had tried to hold them as hostages. The young men had been flown from Germany, met at the airfield by the King's Equerry and taken direct to the Palace. The Master of Elphinstone, a lieutenant in the Black Watch, had been captured five years before. He was able to go out and sample the VE-Day sights.

Shortly after eleven o'clock that night the two Princesses slipped unnoticed through a side door and joined the quarter of a million people who were milling round the Palace. They had an escort of Guards officers. Their mother had said they might go, as they had had so little fun in their lives. Searchlights were swinging their long fingers across the sky and bombers were dropping flares and coloured lights. The two girls were deep in the crowds, almost unrecognized, when the King and Queen came out on to the balcony for the last time just before midnight.

23   A Daughter in Love

AT the end of the war with Germany Queen Elizabeth and Mrs.
Churchill found themselves with the same problem on their
hands—the care of tired husbands. The Prime Minister was
on occasions so worn out that he had to be carried up the stairs of the
Cabinet Office. But for him there was to be a respite, bitter and
unwelcome as it was, for the Labour Party swept into power. For the
King's part, the demands on him were to increase and, once the
Victory celebrations were over, the worries that came in the train of
war were to sear more deeply into his soul than had the sole aim of
bringing hostilities to a successful conclusion.

The programme that the Queen shared with the King after VE-
Day was non-stop and relentless. There were State drives through
South and East London. Each night demanding and vociferous
crowds summoned them to appear on the Palace balcony. On the
13th they drove to St. Paul's for the National Service of Thanksgiving. Three days later they were in Edinburgh for a similar Service
at St. Giles' Cathedral. Back again, and, with the two Princesses,
they went to Westminster. There the two Houses of Parliament were
assembled in the Royal Gallery. Never before had they addressed a
Monarch in this intimate way. When the addresses of congratulation
had been made, the King had replied, and the Royal Family were
leaving, Mr. Churchill stood up. Waving his top hat, he cried 'Three
cheers for his Majesty!'

There were visits to the Channel Islands and Northern Ireland.
With the victory over Japan, the celebrations started all over again.
Now the Queen noticed that her husband could no longer relax in
the evenings. Problems ahead loomed so large that he could not fully

savour the sweetness of triumph. On all sides the old order was changing, yielding place to new. It was the same for both of them. They missed the weekly lunches with 'Winston' and the complete confidence that five years of partnership had brought. They missed the friendly letters from President Roosevelt. Now there were the ways of a new Prime Minister and a new President to learn.

Perhaps the greatest change that came to them was in the rebirth of Party politics. Since their accession the nation had been concerned with one aim—the destruction of the menace of Nazism and Fascism. The Government had been truly national, and Party aims shelved. Now the aims were revealed, and the people took their sides.

To the Queen the innovations of the Labour Party came more lightly than they did to her husband. It was only natural that this should be so. Brought up in the country at the tail-end of a large family, indoctrinated in her teens into the care of wounded men, now with an almost unrivalled knowledge of welfare and medical services, she could see much that was important and essential in the advent of the Welfare State. On the other hand the King, although he had himself admitted that he had no time for 'the damned red carpet', had been successively bullied and branded by Queen Victoria, King Edward VII and King George V. Protocol was part of him. He could not tolerate incorrect dress or wrongly-worn Orders. Yet he had to endure politicians standing about him with their hands in their pockets and wearing lounge suits when they should have been in evening dress. And he found it hard to acclimatize himself to the speed in which changes in the national life were being made.

The state of the King's mind is best judged by his own words. Sir John Wheeler-Bennett quotes from a letter which the King wrote to the Duke of Gloucester, then Governor-General of Australia, in January 1946, while the Royal Family were at Sandringham for the Christmas vacation: '. . . I have been suffering from an awful reaction from the strain of war I suppose & have felt very tired especially down here but I hope I shall soon start to feel well again. Medicine, not even Weir's, is of any use as I really want a rest, away from people & papers but that of course is impossible. I am perfectly well really but feel that I cannot cope competently with all the varied & many questions which come up. My new Government is not too easy & the people are rather difficult to talk to. Bevin is very good & tells me everything that is going on. The others are still learning how to run their departments, & their efforts have not made life any easier so far. Food, clothes & fuel are the main subjects of conversation with us all.'

Sir John explained the King had absorbed from his physician, Sir J. Weir, a belief in homoeopathy—the system which aims at curing diseases by administering small doses of medicines which produce in healthy persons symptoms similar to those they are designed to remove.

In fact, the King was not perfectly well, and, for the first time, a Sovereign had found that the wide acres of Sandringham did not provide sufficient cover against the demands of statesmen. He wanted to be left alone for a while, to be allowed to enjoy the privacy of his home. He wanted to concentrate on his Southdown sheep and Red Poll cattle. He wanted to garden with his wife, and browse through his collection of medals. He lacked the 'Great I am' assuredness of his great-grandmother, or the ego of his grandfather. No one could trespass along the lochside track when Queen Victoria was in retreat at the Glassalt Shiel. And anyone who approached King Edward on political matters while his mind was engaged with pheasants would probably have been peppered. They were both great believers in 'time off'.

Queen Elizabeth had then, and has continued to have, a very different approach to the worries and duties of this world. There was no fretting over rocks that might lie on the path ahead. There was a stoic acceptance of the inevitable. When, thick with a cold, she had finally learned that she was to move into Buckingham Palace, she had merely remarked, 'Well, we must make the most of it.' She has, since a child, always been able to lose herself in another world, as she had done when she lay with a book on the nursery floor at St. Paul's or played Red Indians with her brother David at Glamis. Games she had taken with her into adult life, in particular charades, recalling the 'dressing up box' of schoolroom days. She was able to relax on stages of imagination at times of crisis. She could recharge her strength by music, among paintings, at art exhibitions, safety valves denied to her husband. She could lose herself in games of cards, patience, children's games of Snap and Racing Demon, and Canasta, at which she was brilliant. And she could dance all night, and know that there were few on the floor better than she. Probably her greatest art in peaceful living was her gift of making a home, and being complete in that home stamped by herself. Within a few weeks of her husband's accession the Palace began to look like a lived-in house instead of the London vault of Queen Victoria. 'Elizabeth could make a home anywhere,' commented her husband.

This was the Queen of England in 1946. Ten years of crisis had left little mark upon her. A happy little woman who might easily break into 'Lily of Laguna' at breakfast time or while away a motor drive with 'Daisy, Daisy'. Non-smoking, light drinking, with a partiality for champagne. Eating what she liked, regardless of her figure. A lover of sweets. A woman who liked tweeds and an old felt hat, and who referred to her Hartnell creations as 'my props'. A woman who knew loveliness was asked of her, and so saw that it was created, in the spirit of Winterhalter. A non-photogenic woman whose likenesses were now a joy for ever. A woman whose courage and love had helped to cure the King's impediment. A woman with a dog. Not smart, not sporty. A woman who weighed up what she said. A woman who knew that change was coming, and went with the tide. The woman who knew, when she married 'Bertie', that a wife could make or mar him. The woman who had made 'Bertie'.

Mabell, Countess of Airlie, gives a picture of her as she was at Sandringham in the New Year of 1946. It was the first time the Royal Family had stayed at the 'Big House' for five years and in its resurrection it was a new abode indeed. Everywhere was stamped upon it the Elizabethan mark, and only in the immediate environs of Queen Mary could traces of the old ownership be found. The change came strange to Lady Airlie, but then it dawned upon her that the place was now more like a home and that with the easing of formality friendliness had entered. Jig-saw puzzles were strewn over a baize table. Princess Elizabeth was playing the radio. Young officers were teasing Princess Margaret. 'You must ask Mummy', was the King's reply when his daughters asked permission to do this or that. 'Mummy' told Margaret to put on a thicker coat, and was rewarded with a pout that would have meant an evening visit to father's study if it had happened forty years before. How the Queen was helping the King in his work became clear when Lady Airlie congratulated the King on his Christmas broadcast. He looked lovingly across at his wife and said with pride, 'She helps me.'

Yet the King was eating little, and obviously finding conversation a strain. He was working at his dispatch boxes before dinner, and when the meal was over, he went back to them. They danced that night, through to the early hours, the Queen in the forefront of the fun, Queen Mary joining in, through the fox-trots and 'The Lambeth Walk' and into country measures. Was Lady Airlie the only one in that gay throng to guess that the reign of King George VI would not endure long?

There was one source from which the King could draw on the nectar of relaxation, and that source was his younger daughter. It was because the Queen knew this that her hands were lighter on the reins than they might otherwise have been. He adored 'Meg' but regarded her as an *enfant terrible*. From where, he wondered, does she get this satirical impishness? Certainly not from him. Maybe it was the same strain as had showed in his sister Mary, who had once had a fried tadpole served as a savoury for her French tutor. His own humour was of the ribald breed and savoured of the sea. This quick repartee and mime and imitation was new to him. Did it stem from her mother? There was little outward evidence of this. Yet perhaps there were incidents at St. Paul's in the early nineteen hundreds of which he was not aware. But in those days elder brothers quickly poured cold water over signs of bumptiousness and elderly parents thought that little girls should be seen and not heard.

In character the two Princesses appeared far apart. Elizabeth was her father's shadow. Always she wanted to be with him, and, for that matter, he with her. He adored her, but about the love there was a touch of sadness at the thought of losing her in marriage and at the heavy duties that would one day be hers. She strove for his smile and there were occasions when, thinking that she was outshone, she cried.

Many and strange were the stories circulating about sixteen-year-old Princess Margaret. It was said that, when her father had told her to go steady with the sherry, she had replied that, if she could not have another, she would not launch any ships for him. When asked where she had picked up a slang expression she had retaliated with: 'Oh, at my mother's knee—or some such low joint.'

Queen Mary described her as *espiègle* and 'so outrageously amusing that one can't help encouraging her'. So the balance of power became the problem of her mother. And there certainly were problems. The Queen had decided that Margaret was too young to attend the first post-war Ascot meeting. So she was left behind. But not for long. Quickly changing into suitable clothes, she called up a royal car and set off in pursuit. As their Majesties and Princess Elizabeth acknowledged the cheers of the racegoers from the royal box, the younger daughter slipped in and took her place behind them.

Margaret was going to a fancy-dress party. She was supposed to represent an angel. Her mother looked at her and commented: 'You don't look very angelic, darling!' In a flash came the reply: 'All right, then I'll be a holy terror.'

Yet it was with Princess Elizabeth that many of the Queen's thoughts were concerned in 1946. The Princess had been in love with Prince Philip of Greece since he had spent his Christmas leave at Windsor two years before. And she was obviously very one-track about her attachment.

For the Queen, there were two sides to consider, the personal and the political. The former was obviously of more private interest to her. The Princess was only in her twentieth year. She had met few eligible young men, in the strict confines allowed to her. Prince Philip was probably the only one. Was it then feasible that she should fall finally in love with the first eligible suitor that she met? Would time, and quickly changing times, bring to her a change of heart? Peace and war were vastly different settings for a love affair. The welfare reports from all branches of the Services were telling of the aberrations of separated hearts, and the tragic total of marriages made in haste was piling up. Heroes of the Seven Seas were apt to appear in a different light when they donned a utility suit and caught the morning train. So, on the personal count, time was obviously an essential element. As Queen Mary pointed out, look how long the King had had to wait and see how successful his marriage had been.

There then came to be considered the political aspects and the reactions of the public. The Labour Party firmly backed the members of the People's Liberation Army in Greece, who had been supplied with arms to enable them to resist the Germans. Many Conservatives, Mr. Churchill among them, considered that these guerilla bands, under their Communist leaders, were aiming to bring chaos to the country and then set up a totalitarian state. So they backed the Government of King George of Greece, which was in Cairo.

Workers on the Clyde struck when they were told that British soldiers were being used against the Communists. But in 1946 a plebiscite brought King George back to his country. King George was an ill and tired man, and in the event he had but a year to live. His heir was Prince Paul, married to the Kaiser's granddaughter, Frederica. Obviously there would be objections from the public at the idea that the Heir to the British Throne should marry a member of the Royal House of Greece.

Another disadvantage was the fact that Prince Philip was a member of the house of Schleswig-Holstein-Sonderburg-Glucksburg, with its connections with the former Court in Berlin. When rumours of an engagement began a politican wrote in the Press that the British nation would never tolerate a member of the House of Glucksburg beside the Throne.

The love affairs of her daughters were, from different directions, to cause considerable headaches to the royal mother. Now she decided for the present to ignore the obvious attachment, and Prince Philip was advised, indirectly, to put aside all thoughts of a matrimonial arrangement.

He came back from the Far East at the war's end with the fixed determination to continue his naval career. To achieve this end he had to become a British citizen. Here, to offset the obvious difficulties, he had an ally in Lord Louis Mountbatten. He had already achieved the first step by renouncing all rights to the Greek Throne.

In 1946 Prince Philip became a 'salt horse'—a non-specialist instructor—at H.M.S. *Royal Arthur*, a training establishment for petty officers. The 'ship' was a bleak collection of stone huts built over an underground ammunition dump at Corsham in Wiltshire. He lectured on sea warfare, morale and self-expression. He played skittles at the Methuen Arms and, according to a 'regular', was 'just one of the lads'. He owned a black M.G. sports car. There was competition among the instructors as to the time taken to cover the ninety-eight miles to London. The M.G. was driven hard. The Queen heard about this. She told her daughter: 'Darling, he mustn't kill himself coming to see you.'

The Prince would beg a bed and a bite at the Mountbattens' in Chester Street. The housekeeper would greet him with: 'Well, you old tinker, I suppose you want a bed for the night', and then cut him sandwiches. He had few civilian clothes and little money, but he was careful with that which he had. The arrival of the M.G., driven by the tall fair young man, at Buckingham Palace was noted, and talk began.

The Queen and her husband were both fond of their daughter's boy friend. They appreciated his intelligence and straight way of thinking. They liked his sense of humour, though there is a tale that there were long faces when, on the first occasion that he wore the kilt, he curtseyed to their Majesties. The King had known his naval grandfather and now liked to swap sea yarns of an evening. The Queen was no stranger to the Greek Royal Family. She had been hostess to King George of Greece at Balmoral when she was Duchess of York. He was very good with children. Princess Elizabeth was then four. She began to call him 'Georgie'. Her mother had remonstrated with her. 'You must call him Uncle George,' she said. 'But I like him,' said the young Elizabeth, 'and I am going to call him Georgie.'

It had been hoped that Prince Philip would become a British citizen after the plebiscite in Greece of March 1946, but it was now considered that it would not be diplomatic for one who had been in line of succession to change his nationality so soon after the return of King George. So the papers remained tied up with red tape in Whitehall, along with the many other applications for the same aim.

8th June was a day that the Queen was always to treasure and remember. It was the day of the Victory Parade, the end-piece of the Second World War. She drove with the King to the saluting base in the Mall. She was dressed in mauve, and she was chatting with

Earl Alexander of Tunis when the moment of fulfilment came—
with the pipe music of the 51st Highland Division. In their thousands
the men and women of the war marched past their Sovereign and
their Queen. Eleven million people crammed into London to glimpse
the scene.

That evening there flared up from the River Thames the greatest
display of illuminations and fireworks that the capital had ever seen.
The King and Queen went by royal barge from Chelsea to the
Terrace of the Houses of Parliament. Massed searchlights dipped in
salute. They watched the extravaganza of lights in the sky from the
shelter of the Lord Chancellor's flat. Mr. Churchill was there. As a
salvo of rockets went up, he jumped on a chair, waved his cigar and
shouted, 'London can take it!'

It was at half past twelve that night that the volume of shouting
outside the Palace became undeniable. The King and Queen came
out on to the balcony.

From one great moment to another. It was in August at Balmoral
that the Queen was told by Princess Elizabeth that Prince Philip had
asked her to marry him, and that she had accepted. Out there in the
solitude, among the burns and the heather, with the autumn tinting
the trees, her only love had found its answer. The engagement was
unofficial. Her parents said that the announcement must wait until
she was twenty-one, until the forthcoming trip to South Africa was
over, and until Prince Philip became a British citizen. But it did not
need a rubber stamp or a newspaper headline to make the engagement sunshine perfect.

It was fitting that the words should be spoken on Deeside. The
parents knew this. Perhaps they even helped to set the stage. Balmoral
has often been a trysting-place for royal lovers. On 29th September
1855 Queen Victoria had written in her Highland Journal: 'Our dear
Victoria was this day engaged to Prince Frederick William of Prussia
... during our ride up Craig-na-Ban this afternoon, he picked a
piece of white heather (the emblem of "good luck"), which he gave
to her; and this enabled him to make an allusion to his hopes and
wishes, as they rode down Glen Girnoch, which led to this happy
conclusion.' On 3rd October 1870 Princess Louise walked alone with
the Marquess of Lorne from the Glassalt Shiel to the Dhu Loch and

came back to the Castle with the news that she was engaged. And, most reminiscent for Prince Philip, his great-grandmother, Princess Alice, and Prince Louis of Hesse had been together at Balmoral in the autumn days of 1860, and at the time they too were unofficially engaged.

24 South African Sunshine

FIELD Marshal Smuts had suggested to the King on several occasions, both during and after the war, that he, with the Queen and Princesses, should visit South Africa and while there open Parliament in Cape Town. It was at length decided that the Royal party should leave early in February 1947, sailing aboard *Vanguard*, the battleship which Princess Elizabeth had launched in 1944.

It was a busy autumn for the Queen. She had not only to arrange for her own wardrobe, to cover the sea journey and six thousand miles on land when she reached Cape Town, but also she had to supervise the clothes for her two daughters, neither of whom had been abroad before. This time there was no falling back on outfits made for previous trips, for eight years had passed since she had visited Canada and America. The dresses of 1939 seemed now to be of another age. In addition she had to learn about South Africa. To this end she and the King talked with many people who knew the Union well, and the Governor-General, Mr. Brand van Zyl, and his wife were guests at Balmoral. Then there were books to read, endless books, about South Africa, the Rhodesias and the Protectorates. A few essential words of the various native tongues had to be mastered, and the pronunciation learned of strange, far-sounding places. The Queen had also to help the King with the selection of many gifts for local dignitaries and native chiefs.

The sailing date was fixed for 1st February. Two evenings before Lord and Lady Louis Mountbatten gave an intimate little dinner party for the departing travellers at their home in Chester Street. Not a sumptuous affair, for the housekeeper did the cooking on an old gas stove. This was Princess Elizabeth's *au revoir* date with Prince Philip.

By now the steel fingers of frost had closed hard on that terrible, never-to-be-forgotten, winter of 1947. The lights were low and coal became a jewel. Yet Queen Mary, in her eightieth year, travelled to Portsmouth to wave good-bye to her son and daughter-in-law, as she had done when they sailed for Canada. Again she cast her expert eye over the cabins. She found them of particular interest, as some of the fittings had been taken from the old *Victoria and Albert*, the royal yacht which had so many memories for her.

· There were memories for Queen Elizabeth too. The date of *Vanguard*'s sailing was, to within a month, the twentieth anniversary of the departure of the Duke and Duchess of York, aboard *Renown*, at the beginning of their world tour. Now, as far as the Canaries, they were to sail over the same waters, a sea of memories for her. Then Princess Elizabeth had been an infant, left in the care of her grandparents. Now she was approaching both adult age and marriage.

The royal entourage numbered thirty-seven. The Queen's Ladies-in-Waiting were Lady Harlech and Lady Delia Peel. Her Private Secretary was Major T. Harvey, D.S.O. One of the King's Equerries was Wing-Commander Peter Townsend.

When the sun had warmed the waters, *Vanguard* life became gay. Despite Princess Margaret's tinkling on the piano and her sister's choruses, the officers were adamant that it was the Queen who was the brightest light on board. On one memorable evening she led a conga line around the decks. It was very necessary for her to be cheerful and in high spirits, for her husband was fussing. He felt that people at home would be saying (and a few did) that the Royal Family was lazing in the sun of southern climes whilst they were crouching round a candle for light and warmth. The King, in fact, suggested that he flew back. What he intended to do about the snow and ice remained somewhat of a mystery. Fortunately Mr. Attlee was firm that he stayed where he was.

The three days in Cape Town were crammed full with reception after reception. The Queen early made her mark. On landing she and the King stood for three-quarters of an hour shaking hands in the blazing sun. At the end, as they moved towards their car, the

Queen was seen to turn and speak to her husband. They changed
course and walked across the road to where a group of men,
wounded in the war, were sitting in their invalid chairs. As they
chatted the crowd closed round them and, once again, as had happened on other overseas tours, King George and Queen Elizabeth
were lost to their official party. Fifteen minutes later they emerged.
Already she had written 'Success' firmly at the head of the South
African story.

There were dense crowds outside the City Hall where the great
banquet was to be held. Mr. Dermot Morrah, in his vivid book on
the royal tour, 'The Royal Family in Africa', thus described the
scene: 'It was a long slow process to clear a way for the royal car to
the door, and even when they arrived the King and Queen were
reluctant to go in to dinner until they had stood for some minutes
on the balcony, waving smiling acknowledgements of the enthusiasm
below. This again was to be a frequent experience all over the
country; conscientious officials might work out their programme to
the minute, almost to the second, but they reckoned without the
King and especially the Queen. . . .'

The Queen had an errand to carry out in Cape Town. Before she
left London the widow of General Sir Horace Smith-Dorrien had
handed into her keeping the family bible of President Kruger, which
had come into the possession of her husband during the Boer War.
Now, after nearly half a century, the Queen was able to return it to
the Kruger family.

The saga of the White Train began. For the next two months this
caravanserai in ivory and gold, a third of a mile long, was to be the
home of the Royal Family. Eight of its coaches had been shipped
out from England and six were borrowed from the Johannesburg–
Cape Town express. The King, Queen and Princesses each had their
own bedroom, with bathroom attached. It was the longest train ever
to travel the South African tracks, and yet even it could not cope
with the demand for seats. Ahead of it went the Pilot Train, carrying
railway officials, newspaper and camera men. Behind it came 'the
Ghost Train', carrying railway spares and equipment. In addition
there was a fleet of cars, whose drivers had to keep pace with the
White Train, always ready to take the Royal Party to places of interest

away from the railway track, and four Viking aircraft of the King's Flight, ready for long hops when speed was essential. This South African tour was 'the greatest'.

One of the first stops was at Swellendam, well known for its Nationalist leanings. Yet the Mayor sent a telegram asking that the train should halt and the station was crowded. It was with the Afrikanders that the Queen's tact showed at its best. An old farmer told her, that much as he was delighted at meeting the Royal Family, he did not like the overseeing from Westminster. To the Queen was attributed the classic reply: 'I understand perfectly. We feel the same in Scotland.'

It was the Queen's constant consideration for the young and the old, the ill and the wounded, that won her honours throughout the tour. At Camper a request came from a father that Princess Elizabeth should look towards his son, immobile in an invalid chair. The Queen read the message, asked an official to lower the crush barrier, and led her daughters over to chat with the boy.

For the two days at Port Elizabeth the White Train was in a siding by the sea, and every spare moment was spent in the water. Here the Queen nearly became a hero's wife. The King was playing about in the waves. He pretended to save a lady-in-waiting from drowning, and then to revive her. They played their parts so well that an observing newspaper man thought that he was observing true life. He was enlightened before the story raced round the world.

After East London the White Train headed north and the Orange Free State and Bloemfontein were reached on 7th March. Here some of the Voortrekkers had expected figures from Ruritania to step on to their platform. Instead they met a simple family from London, England. The Queen went down particularly well. A prominent citizen puzzled about this, until he realized that the Trekkers who had passed before him, and the Presbyterian ancestors of Lady Elizabeth Bowes-Lyon, had had very much in common.

They reached Basutoland, where sixty thousand horsemen had ridden in to see them. As they cantered behind the royal cars the dust they raised lay thick as the smoke from a factory chimney. In the evening there was a firework display, amid great enthusiasm and

rriving with Princess Margaret at Royal Ascot

The winning owner

At the Castle of Mey

some excitement for the watchers. Princess Elizabeth had a hole burned in her dress. The next day she stole the limelight. She was reviewing four hundred Girl Guides. She asked if she had reviewed them all. She was told that there was one bus-load that she had not seen. She walked over to the bus, and slowly round it. The girls in it were lepers.

Ladysmith, four days' rest in the Natal National Park, Pietermaritzburg, Durban. Here there was a touching moment at the opening of the Gate of Remembrance which had been added to the War Memorial in memory of the men of Natal who had died in the Second World War. The Last Post sounded. The King opened the door with a golden key and passed through with his wife. Then the Queen turned and stepped back. She had noticed that the other half of the door was still shut. Gently, she pushed it open.

The sentiment of this moment was in marked contrast with her visit to the races. Fortunately, the incident happened just after the Royal party had left. There was a very close finish. The judges decided that one horse had won, and the public decided another. Those in majority did not like the decision one little bit. They were so forceful about it that the meeting had to be abandoned.

On to the Kruger National Park, where the King himself drove his wife around to see the animals. There was some family competition as to who had seen what, the Princesses claiming victory by one wart hog. In contrast with the Park's emptiness came the multitudinous welcomes in the great cities of Pretoria and Johannesburg. The crowds were tremendous, slowing up the tightly arranged programme of events. On the East Rand came the only disturbing moment of the whole tour. The people were so thick that the Queen's car had been brought down to walking pace. Suddenly she saw a giant Zulu lunging his way towards her. The excitement on his face appeared to predict imminent attack. The smile never left her face, but there was Highland determination in her eyes. Her parasol became a skene dhu. She fenced and she parried. But looks can be deceptive. The poor man only wished to press a ten shilling note into the hand of Princess Elizabeth.

On Easter Monday the Royal Family flew the six hundred miles from Pretoria to Salisbury, Southern Rhodesia, the White Train in pursuit. At Salisbury the great event was the State opening of Parliament. The Queen had attended so many like ceremonies and always, however far away, there was the traditional memory of London. Mr. Dermot Morrah thus described it: 'Every punctilio of Westminster that can be adapted was scrupulously observed. Sir Alan Welsh, the Speaker, wore the same black and gold state robe as his elder brother at St. Stephen's; the Sergeant-at-Arms led in the procession of members in English court dress with a mace copied from that of the House of Commons; and when all were assembled came the familiar simple cortège, the King handing the Queen to her throne with the same forms of courtesy as in every Parliament, large or small, in which he has had the opportunity to preside.'

Three days later the White Train carried the Royal Party to the Victoria Falls. The Queen had seen the geysers of Rotorua, the might of Niagara, and now she added the showpiece of Africa. She saw the Falls by daylight and then returned at night to see their magic under the light of the moon. They walked through the 'Rain Forest', the King remarking that he had never been so wet in his life. As Livingstone had said less than a century before: 'Scenes so lovely must have been gazed upon by angels in their flight.'

After a short visit to Livingstone, in Northern Rhodesia, they journeyed back down the line to Bulawayo. From there they drove out into Matabeleland. The cars stopped by a rough and stony path in the Matopo hills. The King, Queen and their daughters dismounted and began their climb. The Queen was wearing high-heeled shoes. They slipped and twisted on the stones. Princess Elizabeth's light shoes were flat. She took them off and gave them to her mother, who, gratefully, put them on. The Princess strode on bare-foot.

They came to the summit, crowned with boulders twenty feet high. Here were the graves of 'those who have deserved well of their country'. They stood by the granite slab beneath which, at his own request, Cecil Rhodes had been laid in 1902, before the Boer war was over. Rhodes had named this lonely spot in the bush country, 'World's View'. Princess Elizabeth wandered away on her own, standing, a still slight figure, looking out over the emptiness. The King's eyes followed her. Turning to his wife and the few who stood about him, he said: 'Poor Elizabeth. Already she is realizing that she will be alone and lonely all her life; that no matter who she has by her side, only she can make the final decisions.'

The going now became hard. 1350 miles lay between them and Cape Town, and the allotted time was four days. The White Train snaked its way across the Kalahari Desert to the little town of Mafeking. Besieged by the Boers from autumn 1899 to the spring of 1900, the scene of dire suffering and superb courage, the visit of the King and Queen was a moment of pure history. Yet there was nothing of the sombre or recriminatory about the royal arrival. The opposite was the case, and the reception was more than boisterous. The underlying reason was that, to celebrate the occasion, the bars had opened early and the inhabitants were all set to write another 'Mafeking Night' into their story.

On 20th April the Royal party came back to Cape Town, in time to prepare for the morrow, a great day in the life of a mother and a daughter. It was the twenty-first birthday of Princess Elizabeth. By right, it was her day, and Cape Town saw that she would never forget it. There was a march-past in the morning and a youth rally in the afternoon. In the evening the Princess broadcast to the Empire: 'I declare before you all that my whole life, whether it be long or short, shall be devoted to your service and the service of our great Imperial Commonwealth to which we all belong. . . .' At a ball at Government House she danced her way into adult life, packing her parents off to bed at midnight and twirling on towards the dawn.

The next day was the Queen's. She appeared before Field Marshal Smuts, Chancellor of the University of Cape Town, in order that there should be conferred upon her the honorary degree of Doctor of Law. The Chancellor dwelt on the associations of the University with the Royal House, and their enrichment now that they were enrolling among their graduates one who had exercised such an inspiring and harmonizing influence throughout the Union. Then he thrice tapped the Queen on her already capped head with another inverted cap, and bade the Vice-Chancellor invest her with the hood of the degree. Arrayed now in the full robes of the doctorate, the Queen addressed to Congregation the only formal speech she made throughout the tour. It was one of the most eloquent that South Africa heard from any member of the Royal Family. Speaking with deep conviction of the supreme mission of a university to inform and inspire a nation's life at the highest levels of its aspiration, the Queen defined the four cardinal virtues of the academic faith. They were, she said, honesty, courage, justice, and resolve; but beyond all these, she reminded her audience with grave simplicity, religious faith was the indispensable foundation of the learned life.[1]

She spoke once more. It was at the farewell State luncheon, the last meal with the people of South Africa. The luncheon was the counterpart of that given for the Royal party on their arrival two months before, but how different was the atmosphere. Now everybody knew everybody. In those nine weeks and six thousand miles many firm friendships had been forged among the army of officials connected with the tour, visitors and hosts. Christian names were freely used and personal visits were being planned. The King ended his speech with the words '*Tot Siens*', which, being interpreted, meant that he intended to come back. When the applause died down, the Queen stood up. Her few words were unrehearsed, simple, and came from her heart. She ended the tour as she had begun it.

Vanguard eased out into Table Bay. Four figures stood, waving, on the high platform above the guns. There came to them, across the water, the sound of thousands singing *Auld Lang Syne*.

[1] *The Royal Family in Africa.*

25 'Granny Royal'

ON 9th July 1947 Queen Elizabeth was suffering from a summer cold. She was due to go to the International Horse Show at the White City, but her daughters went without her. Just before five o'clock a black M.G. passed through the south gate of Buckingham Palace. The driver was Lieutenant Mountbatten, R.N., formerly Prince Philip of Greece. He dined at the Palace and spent the night there. Princess Elizabeth drove to a private dinner party at the Dorchester Hotel, and then on to a dance at Apsley House. A crowd outside watched the candlelight scene through the war-scarred windows. The Princess sparkled. She danced until two.

In the morning the newspapers headlined a typewritten addition to the Court Circular: 'It is with the greatest pleasure that the King and Queen announce the betrothal of their dearly beloved daughter The Princess Elizabeth to Lieutenant Philip Mountbatten, R.N., son of the late Prince Andrew of Greece and Princess Andrew (Princess Alice of Battenburg), to which union the King has gladly given his consent.'

The Princess put on her engagement ring, of platinum, with one large diamond and two smaller stones set at the side as baguettes. She showed it off at the Royal Garden Party that afternoon. There nineteen American Navy officers were introduced and offered their congratulations. Among the top-hatted guests stood out the bowler-hatted Mayor of Shoreditch. The Queen sought him out and shook hands with him.

That evening the Queen stood between her daughters on the Palace balcony as the crowd chanted for a sight of the engaged couple. Then, without delay, she got down to work. As the wedding was to be in November, there was no time to lose. The task of top priority was dresses, for the bride, for the Queen herself, and for the eight bridesmaids, among whom was Princess Margaret. The Queen summoned Mr. Hartnell. He came, he listened, he cancelled a trip to America, and raced round London after inspiration. For herself the Queen had decided on a draped and trailing dress of apricot and golden brocade. For Princess Elizabeth's train she wanted a particular rich and stiff satin. The material to match it was to be made in Scotland. Then there came a snag, and a waste of precious days. It was said in certain circles that the silkworms were of ex-belligerent origin. It was at length proved that they were 'one of us', and work proceeded. Mr. Hartnell wanted ten thousand pearls for the bride's dress. His manager brought them back from America. There was quite a stir in the Customs' shed when he mysteriously revealed that he had those ten thousand pearls.

Then there came the question of presents. The King and Queen remembered well the endless hours that they spent before their own wedding, sorting out which presents could be accepted and which had to be sent back. Now gifts flooded in from all over the world. The parents were deeply touched, and also mindful of the work of sorting them. So they decided to make an exception in this case, and send none back. It was the Princess's idea to ask all those who had sent gifts to a reception and view at St. James's Palace.

The wedding-ring was made from the same gold nugget, mined in the Welsh hills, from which had come Queen Elizabeth's ring.

On 19th November Lieutenant Mountbatten was created a Royal Highness and Baron Greenwich, Earl of Merioneth and Duke of Edinburgh. On the same day he was made a Knight of the Garter. Next morning he had his last gin and tonic as a bachelor, and drove to Westminster Abbey.

The King and Princess Elizabeth were alone in Buckingham Palace, except for one dresser. The Queen had left for the Abbey. The staff were all in the fore-court, ready to cheer the Princess as she left. It was discovered that the bridal bouquet was missing. The Princess had no idea where it was. Neither had her father, who had some outspoken comments on the subject. After a few minutes of wild searching it was discovered in a cupboard, where someone had put it to keep it cool. The bride was sixty seconds late at Westminster.

The Queen Mother and the Queen had been the last to take their places. In Queen Mary was depicted all the majesty of the centuries. Of Queen Elizabeth an observer said: 'Gallant she looked, and trim and small—and nervous. I thought she was anxious for her daughter.'

When the King knelt beside her, he touched her arm. She smiled up at him, and he smiled back, with the unspoken message that all was well. Both knew, from their Coronation day, that things could go wrong at Westminster. But on that great day for Elizabeth and Philip there were no hitches, except the minor ones belonging to small boys. The hair of young Prince William of Gloucester fell over his forehead and began to tickle. He dropped the train to deal with it. At the close, as the King and Queen came from the Abbey, they found one visiting King in the care of a policeman. Twelve-year-old Feisal had left his place to have a look at the bridal coach and the horses. A policeman, thinking that he was just another inquisitive boy, had taken him into his care. An Equerry rescued the young King.

On that day which belonged so wholly to the bride and groom, the role that Queen Elizabeth had played as mother, and the work that she had done behind the scenes, did not pass without laudation. Anne Edwards wrote in the *Daily Express*: 'Not every mother, though, who makes her daughter a star can see the star shine so brightly. . . . For, of course, yesterday—as at most weddings—was a great day for the bride's mother. You could detect the imprint of her personality everywhere. It was the Queen's personality which had shaped the entire wedding. She was the one, it seems, on whom everyone relied to make the tedious decisions. She was the one who knew just where to stop the list of invitations, knew how to welcome delightedly people she did not know very well and had not seen for years. It was the Queen who (present at every fitting) finally decided the details of the wedding gown, who asked also for the details of the clothes to be kept a secret because she meant this to be her daughter's day. How like each other the two are! Their voices are almost the same; their mannerisms, as the wave from the royal cars, their knack of perking up interest at the right thing; most of all, perhaps, their clothes . . . you can see so clearly the mother's influence at work. Twice yesterday I watched the Queen on the balcony of Buckingham Palace. The first time was just after the official photographs had been taken. I am told that the Queen took charge of this business as she has taken charge for 21 years. Were the right relatives in the right places? Were the photographers certain they had got the best pose? (In the middle of all this Prince William, the Duchess of Gloucester's six-year-old son, got lost. The Queen found him.) But when she stepped out there on the balcony—taking second place for the first time in ten years—someone near me said: "She must be very proud." '

And happy. As the honeymoon couple left for Broadlands, the Hampshire home of Lord and Lady Louis Mountbatten, there was a roar from the crowd. Out from the Palace came a posse of Royalties, headed by the King and Queen. They raced across the quadrangle, caught up with the open carriage as it turned into the Mall, and deluged it with rose petals. Four times that evening did the King and Queen come out on to the red and gold balcony.

The festive spirit ran right on until Christmas. Sandringham was packed. There were three Households there, those of the King and Queen, Queen Mary, and the Edinburghs. After the King's broadcast there was an abundance of present giving. A woman cleaner said to the Queen: 'Thank you, Your Majesty, for all your kindness. You are the sort of person I would like for a neighbour and we all love you.' The Queen rated this the nicest compliment that she had ever been paid.

Big moments for the staff was when their turn came to dance with members of the Royal Family. When Mr. John Dean, the Duke of Edinburgh's valet, was told that he was to have the Queen as his partner, he crossed his fingers and prayed for a waltz, his only accomplished step. Into his shoes went his heart when the band leader announced a samba. He confessed his incompetence. Her smile returned his heart to the proper place and she said: 'Never mind, we'll just go round.' Her crinoline dress was so lovely that he scarce liked to touch it. Her feet were so light that he managed to avoid treading on them. He thought that she danced even better than the Princesses.

Mr. Dean was a great admirer of the Queen. In his memoirs he wrote of her: 'The most charming of all the Royal ladies, it seemed to me, was the Queen, now the Queen Mother. She has a great gift for putting everyone at ease, as I found at once when my initial shyness left me tongue-tied in her presence. She is the motherly type. She is very fond of chocolates, but like other people with similar tastes, all centres do not appeal to her. Her maid used to tell me that sometimes she found bitten chocolates in the wastepaper baskets, discarded by the Queen because she did not like their centres.'

In the spring the Queen played hostess to a very particular guest. Mrs. Eleanor Roosevelt had come over for the unveiling in Grosvenor Square of Sir William Reid Dick's twelve-foot-high statue in bronze of her husband. She stayed at Windsor, the other members of the week-end party being Mr. and Mrs. Churchill. Mr. Churchill commented on the fact there were no Labour politicians present. 'This is a private family party,' said the King firmly. It was the family atmosphere amid the tradition that Mrs. Roosevelt liked—the way that the King and Queen wore tweeds, casually, and said, 'Meg, please turn the radio down.' The three came away wiser people. The King took them on a two-hour conducted tour of the state apartments, with a non-stop running commentary throughout. In a chair by the fire Princess Elizabeth chatted and planned with the late President's wife about the trip that she hoped to make to America, in the footsteps of her parents.

Public life came easier now for the King and Queen. Princess Elizabeth and her energetic husband bounded through a full engagement programme with youthful zest. Princess Margaret was coming up to her eighteenth birthday, was advanced for her age and blossomed in regal duties. Yet there was one day that was particularly theirs—the 26th of April 1948. King George VI and Elizabeth, his wife, had been married for five and twenty years.

On this, their Silver Wedding Day, they drove, in gleaming sunshine, to St. Paul's Cathedral, to give thanks and re-dedicate themselves to the service of their people. Their landau moved through a channel banked solid with humanity. The surging swell of the ovation was an echo, just as loud but deeper now, of the cheers that had greeted them as they drove away from Westminster in 1923.

Loyal addresses of congratulations came to them from the Lords and the Commons. In the afternoon they drove over twenty miles through packed London streets. In the evening both the King and Queen spoke on the radio and then, as a curtain call, they were called out time and again on to the balcony of the Palace.

As the floodlights went out and they turned towards one another at the close of the day, the climax came in the story of George and Elizabeth. They were riding high. She was forty-seven; he was fifty-two. They were still in their prime. They had seen a daughter happily married, but still had not the advancing label of grandparent about them. They had taken over the Throne at a few days' notice and had been a shining example through war and its troubled aftermath. They had been the first British King and Queen to visit Canada, the United States of America, and South Africa. Now they looked forward to a visit to Australia and New Zealand in 1949. They stood at the zenith of a nation's esteem. They could have turned to one another that night and truly said, 'Partner, well done.'

Yet neither of them knew the extent of their success. The King wrote to his mother that they were both dumbfounded, at the acclamation of the people and at the thousands of letters that poured into them from all over the world. He, like his father, always underestimated the public feeling for him. There was a tendency in him, when he heard the cheering, to push someone else forward and then, from behind, join in the applause himself. He had loved the moment in New Zealand when he had jumped from the train, joined the crowds at a station and enthusiastically cheered his wife in to the platform. As for her, she had simply never looked for a harvest. She has always done whatever jobs she has to do to the best of her ability. There has never been thought of cream buns at the end. 'Your work is the rent you pay for the room you occupy on earth.' But now the two knew, beyond any doubt, that the Nation and the Commonwealth considered that they had been very good tenants of Buckingham Palace.

The climax over, they moved towards the milestone of grandparenthood. Princess Elizabeth was expecting a baby in November. For the mother there flooded back all the memories of Bruton

234

Street in 1926. In the new nursery was placed the cot that had been Princess Elizabeth's when she was born. In the wickerwork Moses basket she had been carried from her nursery to her mother's room. Another reminiscence was that the new nursery in Buckingham Palace was the room in which Princess Elizabeth had slept while the Duke and Duchess of York were away on their tour of New Zealand and Australia.

On 10th November Princess Elizabeth went to the pictures. On the evening of the 14th the news flashed round the world that a son had been born. The birth had taken place in her own room. The King picked up the telephone and informed the Home Secretary. He had previously instructed him that his presence would not be necessary. Thus the King and Queen broke with a custom that had been handed down from the days of James II and 'the warming pan plot'. The days when the likelihood existed of another baby being substituted, had gone.

That which had finally decided the King and Queen to break with the tradition had been their experience at the birth of Princess Margaret. Then Mr. J. R. Clynes and Mr. H. Boyd, the Ceremonial Secretary at the Home Office, had arrived at Glamis on 5th August, although the baby was not born until the 21st. They had stayed with Lady Airlie. Throughout the long wait Mr. Boyd had appeared obsessed with the fear that some fearful plot was being hatched behind the battlements of Glamis. He studied a book telling the story of the birth of the son of James II and Mary of Modena, and certain passages were heavily marked. 'We must not risk anything of that sort,' he said. He appeared at breakfast, haggard after sitting up all night waiting for the telephone to ring. It was an experience that the mother was determined should not come to her daughter, at the birth of her first child.

On the 15th of the next month, in the Music Room at Buckingham Palace, the baby Prince was christened. The names chosen were Charles Philip Arthur George. The reasons for Philip and George were obvious. Arthur was a reminiscence of the Duke of Connaught and, before him, his godfather, 'the Iron Duke'. Charles breathed of Scotland. As a girl at Glamis the Queen's favourite man from history had been 'Bonnie Prince Charlie'. He had slept at Glamis and left his

235

watch still ticking under the pillow when the English surprised him there. She would stare at his picture.

It did not seem long ago, yet now little Elizabeth of Glamis had graduated to the sobriquet of 'Granny Royal'.

26   Brave Spirit

D EATH'S emissary tapped upon the doors of both King
George VI and Sir Winston Churchill in 1948. The taps
were light, but they were heard and recognized. In both
cases the root cause behind the message was war-weariness.

From that time until the dawning of 1952 Queen Elizabeth's life
was devoted entirely, selflessly, to the care of her husband's health,
to supporting him in his duties, to ensuring the happiness of her
daughters, and to concealing the probable seriousness of the King's
illnesses.

Both of them had lost weight in the rigours of the South African
journey. The King had lost over a stone and, for a man with his
medical history, that was a great deal to recover. He began to get
cramp in both legs and, while at Balmoral in the autumn, consulted
his doctor there. They came back to a full programme. On 24th
October the King and Queen of Denmark arrived on a visit. Two
days later Parliament was opened in full state. On the 31st there was
a review of the Territorial Army in Hyde Park. On 7th November
there was the Remembrance Service at the Cenotaph. The King's
doctors had advised him not to attend. But it was a case of his
father all over again. Just as King George V had defied his doctors
by going to the Cenotaph in 1928, so did his son now do.

On 12th November the Queen was told that her husband was
suffering from incipient arteriosclerosis, with the threat of gangrene
setting in. There was a danger that he might lose his right leg. This
bombshell arrived at the moment when, in another wing of the Palace,
Princess Elizabeth was awaiting the arrival of her first baby. Adoring
her father as she did, it was vital that the news be kept from her.

The Queen moved from one bed to another, the balance in her hands. If, in the next few days, medical complications came either to husband or daughter, the effect on the other might prove tragic. The King had to be assured that the Princess knew nothing about the seriousness of his illness. He was not an easy patient and soon became bored with bed. He was fussing too, about their forthcoming tour of Australia and New Zealand, for which preparations were well advanced. He tried to persuade his doctors to let him go provided the programme was curtailed. They talked with the Queen and they were adamant. The answer was no. The King gave in. He decided that he would go later. Now he realized that rest would be the only cure and he set about his convalescence with good spirit. By early in December the risk of his losing a leg had gone.

The Christmas broadcast was one of the most moving that the King ever made. It was clear that the moment when he had knelt with his wife at the High Altar in St. Paul's on their Silver Wedding Day was a many-splendoured page in his life. In January the Queen took him to Sandringham and, after seven weeks of recuperation there, he returned to London in good spirits and apparently his old self again.

A few days later came the first of the set-backs which were to demand of the Queen all of her courage and sympathy, understanding and tact. The doctors announced that, if the King was to lead a life beyond the boundaries of an invalid, an operation was necessary. The whole character of the man, and his job, forbade a contented surveillance of affairs from an invalid chair, as his wife knew only too well. But when he was told of the ordeal that he had to pass through, there was a burst of Teck temper, as he considered his long rest had been a waste of time. He was mollified when he was reminded that at least he still had his right leg. On 12th March an incision was made in his back to cut the nerve controlling the blood flow to his foot. Throughout the summer he carried out a number of engagements and, after a short holiday at Balmoral, he thought that he was out of the wood.

There was to be other sadness and worry for the Queen in 1949. Her brother, the Earl of Strathmore, died. As his heir, John Patrick, had been killed in action in 1941, he was succeeded by his younger son, Timothy, one of twins, born in 1918. The Countess had died in 1946. The heir of the sixteenth Earl now became the Queen's brother, Michael.

Of the Queen's brothers now only Michael and David remained. The Hon. David Bowes-Lyon and his wife, a niece of Lord Astor, lived at St. Paul's Walden Bury. The King and Queen saw much of them. It was here, probably more than anywhere else, that they could most easily put aside the mantle of sovereignty. For her, childhood memories lay deep in every tree and flower-bed, out-building and hedge. For both of them there was the treasured memory of a walk in the wood on a Sunday morning more than quarter of a century before. Here they had found oases of peace in the desert of worry and work during the war.

The brothers-in-law had shared interests. Chief among these was gardening. Here the royal one bowed to his master. The squire of St. Paul's not only knew, but he practised. Attempts to get him on the telephone at week-ends always met with the same reply. 'Mr. Bowes-Lyon is in the garden. You might catch him at lunch time— or tea time.' His love of flowers was said to be the secret of his constant and charming imperturbability. He was also a crack shot and often acted as host to the King. He was a regular guest at Balmoral for the grouse shooting, and was a member of the well-remembered party in 1945, which also included the Queen, when at least one of all the nineteen varieties of game which Deeside can boast, was on the card.

From 1942–1944 Mr. Bowes-Lyon had been head of the Political Warfare Mission in Washington, and had been used unofficially to carry messages between the King and President Roosevelt. He had made many friends while in the United States, and in the post-war years the King and Queen were often among the guests at small parties given for visiting Americans at his London home. One of the marked differences between George VI and his father was his liking for Americans, a feeling shared by the Queen and born out of their visit to Washington and New York in 1939.

The friendship that had been forged with the Roosevelts blossomed into others; with President Truman, whose autograph the King obtained for the Queen; with General Eisenhower who, with his wife, was a guest at Balmoral in 1946; and Mr. Lewis Douglas, U.S. Ambassador to Britain from 1947–1950. It was from Mr. and Mrs. Douglas that the King and Queen learned more about American ways and thoughts than had any previous occupiers of Buckingham Palace, and their delightful daughter, Sharman, became a close friend of the Princesses. Now Americans were more frequently seen at royal functions, and the Queen became deeply interested in the activities of the English-Speaking Union and the exchange of schoolteachers between the two countries.

By the autumn of 1949 the Queen knew that, if her husband was to live more than a few years, the tempo of his life would have to slow. The King knew it too. He tried hard to do what his wife told him, but he could not bring himself to give up his duties and his pleasures. Instead he tried to cut down the worry and the energy that they demanded. Out shooting, he used a Land Rover as much as possible, and a pony to tow him up the hills. He struggled not to worry over political matters, but in those troubled days the monetary crisis, the General Election and the war in Korea all took their toll of him. He wanted so much to ensure that, should he die, the house was in order for Queen Elizabeth II.

Meantime the Queen had been busy helping the Princess move into her own home—Clarence House. There had been certain criticism over the finances of the restoration of this residence. This was upsetting to the Queen and the Princess, as nothing worried the King more than insinuations that public money was being wasted. The Government had allotted £50,000 for the work, but it was now being said, quite wrongly, that as much as £250,000 had been spent. It was not generally appreciated that many of the fittings installed, and some of the materials used, had been wedding presents.

The Princess needed a mother's support—and she got it—when she told two thousand young wives at a Mothers' Union Rally at the Central Hall, Westminster, in October: 'When we see around us the havoc which has been wrought, above all among the children, by the break-up of homes, we can have no doubt that divorce and separation are responsible for some of the darkest evil in our society today.' Criticism was inevitable, but the Queen was well satisfied, because that was precisely what she thought.

The big event for the Queen in 1950 was the birth of Princess Anne. Both she and the parents wished for a girl. In the Houses of Kent, Harewood and Gloucester boys preponderated, and it was now hoped that the feminine team would be strengthened. The baby was late in arriving. The Queen had, fortunately as it proved, packed the King off to Balmoral, as she knew that if he was in London he would sit by the telephone, fretting as he waited for the news to come. She herself arrived at Clarence House just before noon on 15th August. Shortly afterwards the child was born. She was six pounds in weight and had a mass of dark hair. As the Clarence House staff celebrated with champagne, the news was telephoned to the King. He was out on the moors, and it took a ghillie an hour to find him.

The Duke of Edinburgh went off to register the birth. Having completed the form, he was handed an identity card, a ration book, and bottles of orange juice and cod liver oil. Thus was the Princess dated with the Second World War.

On 21st October the Princess was christened by the Archbishop of York in the Music Room at Buckingham Palace. The Queen was a godmother and her nephew, the Hon. Andrew Elphinstone, was a godfather. On the christening cake was a silver cradle holding a baby doll dressed in ivory lace.

There was an incident during the photographing of the family group. Prince Charles, apparently inheriting his father's alertness in the presence of cameramen, bolted for safety behind a settee. He was pursued by 'Granny Royal' and firmly placed in the position that she had allotted him.

In the months ahead, with the Princess visiting the Duke at Malta, the Queen found herself playing the same role to her grandchildren as Queen Mary had to Lilibet in the nineteen-twenties. Charles and Anne proved the best antidote for the King against worry.

Under the tender care of the Queen, the King's health continued to improve. But it was noticed that he sat down whenever possible. There were streaks of silver now in his thinning hair, and the strain of his life showed clear in his face. In March 1951 a feverish cold kept him to his bed for a week, yet he still held firmly to his determination to visit Australia and New Zealand with the Queen and Princess Margaret during the following year.

May was a busy month for the King and Queen. On 3rd May they drove to St. Paul's for the declaration of the opening of the Festival of Britain, a century after Prince Albert's Great Exhibition in Hyde Park had dazzled the world. The next day they toured the South Bank Exhibition, the buildings of which Queen Mary described as 'really extraordinary and very ugly'. The King was noticed to be in a somewhat impatient mood. It was his last important public appearance.

At the end of the month he developed influenza. He had to cancel his trip to Northern Ireland, and the Queen went alone. In the evenings she rang up to find out how he was progressing. The news that she heard decided her to postpone a visit she was due to pay to Scotland. Throughout June and July the King rested at Buckingham Palace and in his beloved garden at the Royal Lodge. On 3rd August the Royal Family travelled to Balmoral.

The King found that he could still put in a day's shooting without feeling unduly tired. The sun and the breezes out on the hills tanned his face, and his eyes shone with pleasure as he followed the sport that he loved best. Then the weather changed and cold wind and rain chilled the heather. He developed a sore throat.

It was the Queen who first suspected that this was something beyond a minor ailment. She was worried because her husband was still losing weight. The doctor was consulted. It was the Queen who insisted that two specialists should be called from London. Dr. George Cordiner, radiologist, and Dr. Geoffrey Marshall, chest specialist, duly arrived. It was announced that they were on 'a purely routine visit'. On 7th September the King travelled by train to London and next day went to Dr. Cordiner's consulting room in Upper Wimpole Street. X-rays were taken, and he flew back to Balmoral. On arrival he said: 'Now they say there's something wrong with me blowers!' Two days later he heard the verdict. A sample of tissue from his lung had to be removed for examination. Dreading as he did a further cut from a surgeon's knife, he found comfort in taking his gun once more into the mist on the hills. All about him were the cairns of those of his family who had loved this place before him. King George and Queen Elizabeth were at the moment that had come for Queen Victoria and Albert, on the same stage, ninety years before. Then, about to depart, Victoria had written in her journal that she feared that she had made her last great expedition with her husband. Later she was to write, in capital letters, 'IT WAS OUR LAST ONE!' The same words were destined for the diary of Queen Elizabeth.

On the 18th a Palace bulletin, signed by nine doctors, said that structural changes had taken place in the King's lung. The King was told that a removal of a lung was necessary owing to the blockage of one of his bronchial tubes. He was not told that he had cancer. He never knew, though his wife did. She worked with him on the wording of the bulletins, to ensure that the public were not unduly disturbed. But many of them knew more than the King and Queen thought they did, and they stood in silence before the Palace.

Mr. Price Thomas carried out the operation on the 23rd. There were two immediate dangers. That coronary thrombosis would bring a sudden end to the King's life, or that the operation would hush the King's voice to a whisper for as long as he lived. He survived it well. Four days later he signed a warrant authorizing five Counsellors of State, the first of whom was the Queen. By the middle of October he could make his own way to the bathroom. On the 24th the Queen, in opening an extension to a London hospital, paid tribute to the marvellous work carried out by his doctors. But his health was such that the ardours of a lengthy trip to New Zealand and Australia were obviously beyond him, and it was arranged that Princess Elizabeth and the Duke should undertake it. Instead the King and Queen planned to travel to South Africa in March, staying at a house which had been offered by Dr. Malan.

Meantime the Queen's days were crammed with duties, State and domestic. Not only was she now doing much of a Sovereign's work, but she was nurse as well. Her constant presence near to the King was as vital to him as that of Queen Mary had been to George V. In addition she had charge of Prince Charles and Princess Anne while their parents were away on their long tour of Canada and America. The King perked up. The lightening of the load, the fun of his grandchildren, the return to power of Mr. Churchill at the head of a Conservative Government, and the enthusiastic reports that were coming back across the Atlantic about Princess Elizabeth and her husband, combined to set him on the road to apparent recovery. On 10th December he took over the reins again from the Counsellors of State and on the 21st the Royal Family made their annual pilgrimage to Sandringham for Christmas.

There were lighted trees on Wolferton station to greet the largest gathering since pre-war days. Queen Mary was there, the Edinburghs with their two children, the Gloucesters with two, and the Duchess of Kent with three. The Queen gave the presents to the staff. They grieved at the obvious weariness of the man who sat beside her. It had been suggested that she should make the Christmas broadcast in his place, but these were moments that he was determined to handle himself.

Yet the fun of Christmas and the peace of Norfolk brought a revival of his spirits. Each day he was out with the guns. He wore electrically heated waistcoat and boots, and his cartridges were so designed that there was less kick to his shoulder when he fired. He forecast that he would spite his doctors by outliving them, and threatened that he would go out over the saltings again after duck. He told them: 'You have had your fun. Now I will have mine.' The Queen was satisfied with his progress. On 17th January she flew with Princess Elizabeth to Hurst Park to watch one of her horses run. It came in second.

The doctors, too, were satisfied, when they examined the King at Buckingham Palace on the 29th. This called for a celebration. To mark the good news the Family went to see *South Pacific* at Drury Lane the following evening. It was also a good-bye party, for Princess Elizabeth and her husband were off to East Africa on the morrow, on the first leg of their journey to Australia.

The King and Queen waved goodbye to their beloved Elizabeth at London Airport. Slower he waved, until his arm fell limp by his side. Still he stood on the tarmac, until the aircraft was swallowed by the sky. Then the Queen touched his arm, as a signal that it was time to go. They fulfilled a series of engagements, had a chuckle with Mr. Churchill, tea with Queen Mary and returned to Sandringham.

On 5th February the Queen and Princess Margaret went on a cruise on the Norfolk Broads. The King shot for six hours. A halt for lunch was made at the village hall at Flitcham. He bagged nine hares that sunny day.

Prince Charles and Princess Anne were put to bed. After a quiet dinner, the Queen sat by the fireside. The King was worried about his golden retriever, whose paw had been cut by a thorn. He walked down to the kennels, looked at the dog, and strolled back through the gardens. Princess Margaret played the piano for half an hour. Then came the important moment—the ten o'clock news. They heard that all was well with Elizabeth and Philip. They made their way to bed.

At eleven a footman took a cup of cocoa up to the King. He was sitting up, reading about guns and dogs. Sandringham slept. But for a solitary policeman, it keeps its own guard over its Squires. At around midnight the King was seen at his window, fixing the latch. All was well.

At half past seven next morning James Macdonald, the valet, took up a cup of tea. He pulled the curtain but the King did not stir. He discovered that he was dead. The love story of George and Elizabeth was over.

27 Lonely Heart

QUEEN Elizabeth II flew back from Africa. She reached Sandringham in the afternoon of 8th February. At five o'clock a waggon carrying the coffin of George VI left on its short journey across the park to the Church of St. Mary Magdalene. Behind it walked his wife and daughters.

The gates were closed, and the paths and the lawns were empty. The chill, steel light of the setting sun cast thin shadows from the sleeping trees. The pipes wailed, and the pheasants called from the woods.

The coffin lay before the altar. There were three wreaths upon it. One carried the words: 'Darling Bertie from his always loving Elizabeth.'

Of all the grief that has come to Sandringham[1] none has rivalled the poignancy of the emotions which swept over the woman who was now Queen Mother. For over three years she had nursed a sick husband. Then, when tired herself, he had been snatched from her when she least expected it, when she was not by his side. The shock to her was tremendous. Lady Cynthia Colville wrote: 'What surprised people who knew the Royal Family well was that, whereas everybody realized how much the King had owed to his wonderful consort, how she had given him not only deep affection but just that support and encouragement that enabled him to overcome his natural shyness and inclination to stammer, few people realized how much she had relied on *him*—on his capacity for wise and detached judgement, for sound advice, and how lost she now felt without him.'

[1] Prince Alexander Charles died at Sandringham in 1871; Prince Albert Victor, Duke of Clarence, in 1892; Prince John in 1919; Queen Alexandra in 1925; and King George V in 1936.

246

'Lord, now lettest Thou Thy servant depart in peace.' The heavy doors of the church opened and the King began his last journey to London. Behind him followed his wife and daughters, his Pipe-Major and his valets, his gamekeepers, through lines of those who loved him. Slowly now. Fifty years before he had raced down the same hill on his bicycle with Mary and David to see the trains come in to Wolferton. Only a week before he had shot through the wide woods that were filled now with the piper's lament for his passing. Only the flowers of Elizabeth his wife lay on the flag that covered him.

Soon his coffin lay in state on a high catafalque in Westminster Hall. There was a brief service, and then the Royal mourners left. After a brief silence, the first of many thousands of his people began to file by.

There was to be little rest for the Queen Mother in the next four days. Kings and Queens, Princes and Heads of State arrived in London for the funeral, and she played her part in receiving them. In this she was helped by Queen Mary, who, although eighty-four, received in one day twelve Royalties and a President. In truth, for the old Queen the news of the passing of her son was near to a death sentence. She had lost three sons and been at the deathbed of none of them. Yet still she held her head high and carried on with her duties. From the time that she became the Duchess of York until the first year of her daughter's reign, Queen Elizabeth had always the example of her mother-in-law to follow, her advice to lean on, her courage to imitate.

Now she showed her training in the love and strength that she gave to her own daughters. When the new Queen landed at the end of her flight from Kenya, the first thing that was handed to her was a letter in her mother's writing.

On 15th February the Queen Mother's standard flew over Buckingham Palace. Incorporating the Royal Arms of England with quarterings of the Bowes-Lyon family and the Garter, it had been designed at the Herald's Office after the abdication and was first flown over the Palace in November 1937 when the King went to Sandringham and his consort was alone in London.

On that day, in the dark tent of her sorrow, she followed the gun

247

carriage that bore her husband's coffin from Westminster to Paddington. The stoicism of her was almost past belief. *In te Domine speravi.*

At a first floor window in Marlborough House Queen Mary sat below a half-drawn blind. As the procession came in sight, dry-eyed she whispered, 'Here *he* is!' and held her Lady's hand. It was as if she was a child again and waiting for the cortège of some great King to pass. Then she stood and, from the coach below, her daughter-in-law, her daughter and her granddaughters bowed to her. The Dukes saluted her, and slowly she turned and went inside.

Many people that day studied the Duke of Windsor, and pondered on the twist of events that had placed him where he was. James A. Jones wrote in the *Evening News*: 'Our eyes went at once to the Duke of Windsor, for his is a story that will be told from generation to generation as a man who gave up a throne for the woman he loved. He wore the blue of the Navy. His face was pale, thin, and a little drawn. His eyes gazed steadily before him. What thoughts passed through his mind as he saw the shine of the Crown—the Crown he put aside? His face was unrevealing. He must have been aware of the multitudes of the people on each side of him as he walked, the people that were once his own people, the people behind the lines of soldiers that were once his soldiers. But he walked steadfastly on behind his brother the King. And if he said to himself, "This is the first procession I have walked in since a grey destroyer took me in the darkness from my own land," if he thought that he gave no sign of it.'

As the gun carriage lumbered by there was born in many minds the poignant probability that, when the Duke of York had consented to become King, he had thrown away a slice of his years, that his wife had been robbed of the sunset days together among the roses at Windsor. If Edward VIII had continued to reign and his brother become a Governor-General of a Dominion, whose body would now be in the coffin? The ultimate appearance of certain weaknesses point to the possibility of their earlier arrival if Edward VIII had undergone the terrific strain of monarchy in wartime. If he had a wife's comforting presence beside him, could those weaknesses have been staved off?

Certain it is that events between 1937 and 1946 so tired the King, mentally and physically, that he became ill and old before his time.

He had burned his lamp too high, as Prince Albert had done before him. King George had never really understood his brother's attitude towards the abdication. For him loyalty and duty transcended death. When he met the Duke in 1939 he wrote to the Prime Minister: 'He seems very well, & not a bit worried as to the effects he left on people's minds as to his behaviour in 1936. He has forgotten all about it.' There were no recriminations, except over the point that the Duchess had not been granted the rank of Royal Highness. So the King had ruled in May 1937, and on the point both he and the Queen had remained adamant.

The attitude towards the Duke and Duchess seemed to harden rather than soften after 1945. The Duke has written: 'I was having a talk with my brother, on my second or third visit to London after the war. By then I had decided that the chances of a reconciliation with the family, let alone a job for me, were hopeless. "Perhaps it would be best," I finally said, getting up to leave, "if I were to give up all thought of ever living in Britain." My brother looked me straight in the eye. Without emotion he said: "Yes, I believe that would be the best thing." '

Yet King George's last instruction before he underwent his operation of September 1951, was that three brace of grouse should be sent round to his elder brother who was then visiting London.

'The chances of a reconciliation within the family . . . were hopeless.' The King was heeding somebody 'within the family'. Queen Mary, the Princess Royal, the Duke and Duchess of Gloucester,[1] the widowed Duchess of Kent.[2] More and more it came to be said that it was the Queen and her elder daughter who found that reconcilia-

---

[1] The Duke and Duchess of Gloucester met the Duke and Duchess of Windsor in Paris in November 1938, and brought back a request from the Duke of Windsor that he should be allowed to return home early in 1939 to see his mother. In the event Queen Mary did not see her eldest son until 5th October 1945, when the King joined them for dinner. On their way back from Kenya by air, the Duke and Duchess of Gloucester landed at Le Bourget. They drove to the Hotel Meurice, where they lunched with the Windsors and were together three hours. They then drove, the two brothers in the first car, the wives in the second, to see the Windsors' new home in the Bois de Boulogne. Deterred by cameramen, they went on to tea with Baron Eugene de Rothschild. Later, driving to Larue's restaurant for dinner, the positions in the cars were reversed, the brothers sitting with their sisters-in-law. The Gloucesters slept in a suite above the Windsors, and flew back to London next morning.

[2] The Duchess of Kent was at Balmoral in the autumn of 1936, when Mrs. Simpson was among the guests. The Duchess visited the Duke and Duchess of Windsor during the Duke's illness in London in March 1965, as did the Queen and the Princess Royal.

tion impossible. No woman who rates loyalty the highest cares to see that loyalty down-graded. No elder daughter who has leaned upon and hero-worshipped a father can avoid the ice cold terror of the thought of his passing, or ever fill the gap when he has gone. No woman can conquer the loneliness of sitting among the roses in a sunset garden, a garden that two have made, and, putting out her hand, find the chair beside her empty.

The gun carriage halted. Gently the strong shoulders bore the King to the train that was to carry him to Windsor for the last time. There had always been such excitement in going to Windsor, to see what the gardeners had done at the Royal Lodge. Always, when they left, there had been last moment instructions about planting this or that. This garden was made by George and Elizabeth, 1931-1951.

They came to the Chapel of St. George perched upon the hill. A bosun's whistle was piping the Admiral 'over the side'. His friends saw him go, Mr. Churchill, Mr. Attlee, General Eisenhower. Only the Sovereign's stall was empty. The King was swallowed by the vault below. The Queen turned to her mother and her sister, and the three walked slowly round that open vault. They left by a side door. Outside the stones and turf were thick with flowers.

The widowed Queen sent her message of thanks to the British people everywhere: 'Throughout our married life we have tried, the King and I, to fulfil with all our hearts and all our strength the great task of service that was laid upon us. My only wish is now that I may be allowed to continue the work we sought to do together.' A visitor came to see her at Buckingham Palace—the Duke of Windsor.

In the strain of the last months she had lost a stone in weight. There were many who said that the smile that had won her the title of 'The Smiling Duchess', would never be the same again. She went out into her loneliness, away from the eyes of men. Alone with her memories and her dreams. Alone with the echoes of words and sounds of long ago. Back to her second honeymoon, in Africa, a quarter of a century before.

'I have seen him in the watch fires of a hundred circling camps;
They have builded him an altar in the evening dews and damps . . .'

The lamp goes out and the moon shows through the tent flap.
A lion roars and the zebras gallop by.

It took Queen Victoria a full twenty years to recover from the
death of Prince Albert. Eventually Lord Beaconsfield came to the
conclusion that, on the matter of her black-edged gloom, she had
her tongue in her cheek. Queen Elizabeth the Queen Mother was
back in the ring of life after ninety-six days. Her first engagement
was an inspection of a battalion of the Black Watch, a regiment which
meant so much to her and her family. In May, with Princess Margaret, she was airborne in a Comet, the new British jet airliner that
was the talk of the world. They were up for four hours, covering a
nineteen-hundred-mile circuit of France and Italy. She asked if she
could take the controls, and she did so, with the test pilot in the seat
beside her. Then she radioed her speed back to her squadron at
Biggin Hill.

Her face was still unlined, and there were no streaks of grey in her
thick, dark hair. But she knew that she was past the half-century
mark, and made no pretence about it. When she was shown the proof
of a photograph in which she considered the touching up process
made her look too young, she asked that some of the gilding be
removed. Her comment was that, as she had been in the battle of
life for fifty years, she could not have passed through quite unscathed.

One of the reasons why the years had, and have, left her so untouched is her great belief in being comfortable. When she opened a
new building at London University she was seen to be bouncing up
and down in the armchairs. She told Sir Mortimer Wheeler: 'I
always think it is most important to be comfortable when one is
sitting down. Sitting here is very comfortable. One might even be
able to have a snooze!'

One of the Queen Mother's safety valves during her early widow-
hood was her grandchildren, Charles and Anne. She adored them,
and they her. They had been with her when the King died, not
understanding why suddenly everyone was so sad. She spoiled them,
of course she did. What grandmother in like circumstances would
not have done. She took them out alone, on drives and rambles in the
park, their constant queries and wonderings keeping her mind off
other things. She tried the experiment of taking her grandson to an

afternoon concert. But he became bored, started to fidget, and had to be led out. In church it was always 'Granny Royal' whom he insisted on sitting next to, smiling up at her as he left before the sermon. He insisted on being present at her arrivals. In Scotland he climbed into an aircraft to greet her and, in his excitement, left a bag of sweets behind. Discovering his loss, he told her to stand still while he went back to get them.

There was much domestic business to occupy the Queen Mother's days. There were the arrangements to be made for the swapping of homes with her elder daughter, Balmoral to Birkhall, Buckingham Palace to Clarence House. The Queen and the Duke moved into the Palace in May, occupying the Belgian suite on the ground floor. Alterations began at Clarence House, one point on which the Queen Mother was most insistent being that the staff quarters should be comfortable and up to date. Meantime she stayed in the rooms that she had known since 1937. On the first floor, they had first been used by William IV and Queen Adelaide, and since that date occupied by the Sovereign. But as reluctantly the new Queen Elizabeth had moved into Buckingham Palace from 145, Piccadilly in 1937, so it was now also with reluctance that she faced leaving the suite that was so rich in memories for her. It was not until 1953 that she and Princess Margaret moved down the Mall to Clarence House.

A worry for the Queen Mother as 1952 ended was the declining health of Queen Mary. At Christmas time, at Sandringham, the old Queen stayed in bed until the afternoon and spent much of her time in her own rooms. The shadow of death lay over the 'Big House', as it had done the year before. Sad beyond telling would it be if yet another coffin were to cross the park to the Church of St. Mary Magdalene. Queen Mary had known the house almost from the days of its building. The Prince of Wales had been sponsor at her christening in 1867 and in her young days she had seen much of the Wales children. But she seemed to recover some of her strength and returned to Marlborough House a few days before the anniversary of her son's death. She was seen again driving in the London streets. She saw the preparations beginning for the Coronation stands. 'Go it, old girl,' people murmured in the streets. But the race to see another crowning was too long for her. At three o'clock on the afternoon of 24th March the Queen Mother called at Marlborough House, and said her soft good-byes. At twenty minutes past ten Queen Mary died, and her flag came fluttering down.

On 2nd June the Queen Mother drove from Clarence House in the glass coach to attend the crowning of her daughter at Westminster. The deep sympathy for her could be sensed among the milling, jubilant crowds. Smiling, Princess Margaret beside her, she reached the Abbey.

'In she came glittering from top to toe, diamonds everywhere, a two-foot hem of solid gold on her open dress—the Queen Mother playing second lead as beautifully as she played the first. On she came up the aisle with a bow here to Prince Bernhard, a bow there to the row of ambassadors, and up those tricky steps with no looking down like the Duke of Gloucester—no half turn to check on her train like the Duchess of Kent, no hesitation at the top like Princess Margaret, no nervous nods of her head like Princess Mary. She is the only woman I ever saw who can always slow up naturally when she sees a camera.'[1]

The Queen Mother arrived at the Abbey just after half past ten.

Most of the chosen assembly of eight thousand had by this time been there for three hours. The Duke of Portland, a relation of the Queen Mother through her mother, was on the scene at twenty minutes past seven. 'How long did it take you to dress?' asked the Duke of Norfolk. 'About an hour,' answered sixty-year-old Portland. The Duke of Wellington entered and he and Portland began fussing about with one another's ruffles. 'It's a bit draughty in these breeches,' complained Portland, walking about to keep warm. 'I've got nothing on underneath.' Field Marshal Montgomery pulled out a newspaper, apparently oblivious of the chatterings of the peacock peerage about him. An hour later the Duke of Portland was still on the subject of his dress. 'My breeches are tied on to my shirt. I have nothing on underneath.' Lord Montgomery folded his newspaper and began talking with the Lord Chancellor.

In the Abbey procession the Queen Mother was preceded by the Earl of Airlie, Lord Chamberlain of her Household. The four pages, Jonathan Peel, Viscount Carlow, Michael Anson and the Earl of

[1] Anne Edwards in the *Daily Express*.

Erne, were followed by the Mistress of the Robes, the Dowager Duchess of Northumberland, whose page was Lord James Douglas-Hamilton. The Queen Mother sat with Princess Margaret in the front row of the Royal Gallery. To begin with there was a vacant place between them.

As the Queen was joined by her husband at the altar and they knelt to receive Holy Communion, the vacant place became occupied. The brilliantined head of Prince Charles, Duke of Cornwall, appeared. He could scarce see over the rail. Someone brought him a stool. He covered his face with his hands and, through his fingers, stared at the scene in bewilderment. Then began a battery of questions, fired at his grandmother and his aunt, that continued almost unchecked for an hour. He was in ivory shirt and shorts. It was the day that he got his first medal.

Soon the wonders of the gold plate caught his eye. He leaned far out over the Gallery to have a look at it. The Queen Mother pulled him back. Then he disappeared. His grandmother and aunt began talking towards the floor. The Queen Mother appeared to be moving her feet. She was talking more urgently now. Up shot the head of the Heir to the Throne. There was triumph on his face. In his hand he clasped his grandmother's handbag.

Back at the Palace, before six, the Queen and her husband and her children came out on to the balcony. The tide of the people piled up before the gates, the thunder of them clashing with the roar of the aircraft racing by overhead. Suddenly the Queen and her husband moved apart, leaving a space between. Prince Philip turned, and led out Queen Elizabeth the Queen Mother. A proud and gracious little woman, she stood radiant with her family and her grandchildren about her.

28 A Mother's Problem

WHEN the Coronation festivities were over the Queen Mother, with Princess Margaret, flew to Southern Rhodesia for a sixteen-day visit. They travelled in a Comet. The Queen Mother's heart was heavy with worry. An event had taken place in the Royal Household which had aroused a public interest unrivalled since Queen Victoria accused Lady Flora Hastings of being in the family way in 1839. Her younger daughter was in love with an Equerry of the Queen.

Royalty owes much to the men and women, often invisible, who circle in the orbit of the Throne. The foundation of their dynasty was laid by Prince Albert. He pointed the way to Queen Victoria, as to how to select those who were to be close to her, and her recipe has been followed in the twentieth century. The result has been men of the calibre of General Grey, Sir Henry Ponsonby, Lord Stamfordham and Sir Alan Lascelles.

Queen Victoria demanded of those who served her that they should have but one God. Even Death should fit in with the convenience of the Throne. When members of her Household passed on at awkward moments, Sir Henry Ponsonby always anticipated the order to write a sharp note to the Almighty about it. She regarded the men about her in the light of very junior brothers, almost, perhaps, as neuters. Sexual activities, either by them, or her Ladies, was bound to distract their attention and cause her inconvenience. She was displeased with the Duke of Argyll when he married a Woman of her Bedchamber, the Hon. Ina McNeill, and angry when her physician, Sir James Reid, announced his engagement. She only forgave him when he solemnly promised that he would never do it again.

The way of the men behind the Throne did not alter appreciably under the rule of Edward VII and George V. There was a thick dividing line between Royalty and Household, and each stayed their own side.

In the days of King Edward VIII certain changes in the structure of the Household began to show. But they were short lived, as his younger brother quickly restored the old order, as he did on the estates of Sandringham and Balmoral. But a few years later he was to make a change. Overflowing with admiration for the exploits of young men on the battlefields, at sea and in the air, he decided to break with tradition and appoint 'Equerries of Honour'. The War Office, the Admiralty and the Air Ministry selected candidates. The Air Ministry put forward the name of a man who had shot down a number of enemy aircraft, won the D.F.C. and bar in 1940 and the D.S.O. in 1941, for 'outstanding leadership and organization, and determination in aerial combat'. During that summer he was wounded and shot down. After his convalescence, he married. His name was Wing-Commander Peter Townsend. His age was twenty-nine. The King sent for him, and what he saw he liked. On 16th March he appointed Townsend a Temporary Equerry.

The Equerry and his wife were given a house at Windsor, Adelaide Cottage, where once the sweet Queen had taken her ladies of a summer afternoon to sew and chatter and play their games. Two sons were born, the King being godfather to the second. Peter Townsend became a full Equerry.

The struggle of wars, the uncertainty of wars, even the economies of wars, can shatter in a week a wall of tradition built up over a hundred years. The firm ritual of Windsor in the peaceful days ensured that its children kept their rightful seats, and walked not in forbidden corridors. Now there was a sense of urgency. Things had to be done quickly, and forget that damned red carpet. The King found the speed and organizational capabilities of Wing-Commander Townsend of the greatest assistance to him. So did the Queen. He oiled the wheels for her. He was always there. He was with them on their South African tour. Together aboard *Vanguard*, out and back. Together for nine weeks and six thousand miles in the narrow confines of the White Train. Ever watchful of the two Princesses on their first tour abroad. Ever ready with a helping hand for the Queen. 'I don't know what we'd do without you, Peter,' said the King.

Of natural course, the marriage of Princess Elizabeth brought a feeling of loneliness to seventeen-year-old Princess Margaret. More and more she turned for conversation to her father's Equerry. She wanted to know more about the life outside. One evening they went for a stroll together, alone, along the Strand.

For a Queen, a mother's task is made exceedingly difficult owing to the demands on her time. The Queen always fulfilled a heavy programme, and from the time of Princess Elizabeth's wedding she became increasingly concerned with her husband's health. This reached an hiatus when there was little room for other thoughts in her mind.

Neither she, nor the King, nor for that matter the Household, took seriously the Press coverage that soon surrounded the evening excursions of Princess Margaret. Her name was coupled with that of so many eligible bachelors that, in truth, there was safety in numbers. Trying to look serious, the King said to one young man, 'I hear that you want to marry my daughter,' to the considerable discomfiture of the latter.

One by one the sons of the great Houses were photographed with her in the small hours. One by one *The Times* announced their engagement to somebody else. New ones took their place. 'Do you know,' she said to one, 'that you are looking into the most beautiful eyes in the world?' She had been reading a magazine. They were entrancing eyes, as were her mother's, showing clear the emotion in her, and the changing lights in them portrayed the changing moods.

Strangely enough there has been no marriage between a member of the Establishment of English landed gentry and a Princess of the Blood since the advent of the Georges, except for that of Princess Mary to Lord Lascelles in 1922. There have been five unions with Scottish houses; the Marquess of Lorne and Princess Louise in 1871; Princess Louise of Wales and 'Macduff', Duke of Fife, in 1889; Princess Patricia of Connaught and the Hon. Alexander

Ramsay in 1919; Princess Maud and Lord Carnegie in 1923; and Princess Alexandra and Mr. Angus Ogilvy in 1963.

There was little thought of such marriages until Bismarck precipitated the German wars in the 1860s. Thereafter, owing to the danger of divided loyalties, Queen Victoria decided to seek an alternative to the Continent as a source of husbands for her daughters, and she scanned the parks of Britain.

But the Queen was not as yet fully accepted by the Establishment of the landed gentry. Many still drunk the royal toast over their finger bowls. There was loyalty to the Throne, but little close friendship with the Houses of Coburg and Hanover. The question had been exacerbated by Prince Albert. Frankly, the gentry did not like him. They had doubts about his birth and his ambitions. They disapproved of his business acumen. He did not like racing and only hunted if he had to. His habit of having deer driven before the front door and then picking them off to show what a good shot he was, was deplored. There was little masculinity in his approach to pretty women. And their sons did not like the Prince of Wales. The idea of bringing Eton boys to Windsor to commune with H.R.H. came abruptly to an end as both sides immediately attacked one another.

The Queen had imagined that the scions of the great houses would fall over one another at the chance of marrying a Princess. She was very wrong. These young men wanted to be free to fight wars, run their estates, govern colonies. They did not relish the Sovereign as a mother-in-law, to be tied to the Palaces and told what they could do by John Brown.

The first attempts to so ensnare one came as a considerable jolt to the Queen. She asked a likely young man to be a guest at Balmoral. Unsuspecting, he arrived. On the first evening a member of the Household quietly asked him if he knew why he was there. When he learned the truth, sheer terror seized him. Next morning he borrowed a pony and rode fast to a neighbouring house where he knew a girl friend of his sister was staying. He had never met the girl, but he introduced himself and asked her to marry him. When he announced the news that he was engaged, his visit to Balmoral came to an abrupt end.

The Queen sent an emissary to the estate of a very rich young man to sound of his possibilities as a husband. The emissary found him seated by a newly dug grave, staring dismally into it. The ruse worked, and the emissary returned.

Then into the breach stepped a Campbell, once again to support the English Sovereign at a time of need. The Marquess of Lorne, eldest son of the Duke of Argyll, was talented, artistic, handsome, fey. Princess Louise fell in love with him with the immense violence that is sometimes evinced by members of the Royal Family. She threatened that she would enter a convent if her wishes were thwarted. As the Queen had the awful suspicion that a delay in the wedding date might have dire results, she was given extra power in her decision that the practice that royalties should be reserved for royalties should end. The Princess married for love, but in the words of James Pope-Hennessy she 'lived to regret it'.

The forties ended and the fifties began. Princess Margaret remained unattached. Townsend, a Group Captain now, was divorced. George VI died. The death of the King hit the Princess hard. It was her first encounter, except for childhood memories of the passing of her grandparents and the fatal crash of the Duke of Kent. Although she had played the role of *enfant terrible* to her father, she had leaned upon him completely. She wrote: 'Life seemed to stand still when Papa died. I cannot believe that I will grow old without seeing him again.' Now, in the nights, sleep was hard to find and her appetite, always slight, decreased. In her suite, at the opposite end of Buckingham Palace to that of her mother, feelings of loneliness and emptiness encompassed the young Princess.

There was emptiness also for the Equerry, who had lost both his wife and his master. He had known Princess Margaret since she was thirteen. There was ample reason, on grounds of propinquity and emotion, why the two should be drawn together now. There were also very good reasons why the drawing together should not attract attention. The Queen Mother was prostrated by her husband's death and needed time in her own chamber to recover. She had had little experience of the kind of love that turns life upside down. She had entered into her own marriage after careful consideration, fearful that, as royalty, she would never again be able to think or speak or act as she really ought to think or speak or act. The marriage of her elder daughter had been a romance from childhood and developed naturally with the years.

Another reason was that Princess Margaret, from her earliest days, had been averse to interference with her plans and doings. It is attributed to her that she once told her sister to look after her Empire, and leave her to look after her life.

A third reason was that, in recent times, the exigency of a member of the Household falling in love with a member of the Royal house whom he served, had not arisen. Abroad there had been the case of Prince Alexander of Hesse bolting with Countess Julia von Hauke, a lady-in-waiting of his sister, the Empress Marie of Russia, an adventure which, after entailing a sojourn in the wilderness, ended happily in the founding of the Battenburg family.

Yet in the servants' hall, where observation and surmise are keen, there was an atmosphere of anxiety. The Princess and the Equerry were so much together. At shooting parties she would move over to the place that he had been allotted. At Balmoral they would ramble off into the hills. Both were liked by the staff. For the happiness of both, they hoped that the thick dividing line would stay between them.

In the new reign Group Captain Townsend became Deputy Master of the Queen's Household, caring for the administration of the Palace, the employment of domestic staff, the payment of internal expenses, and organization of state banquets and entertainment. But it was arranged that he should accompany the Queen Mother and Princess Margaret on their visit to Southern Rhodesia, where they were to attend the Rhodes Centenary Exhibition at Bulawayo.

Then there came a change in the arrangement. It was now announced that Captain Lord Plunket would go to Southern Rhodesia, and that the Group Captain would accompany the Queen and the Duke of Edinburgh to Northern Ireland, a visit timed to start on 1st July.

On 29th June the Queen ended her Coronation visit to Scotland and travelled back overnight to London. In the afternoon she went to London Airport to see her mother and sister off to Rhodesia.

The Queen Mother and Princess Margaret were at Umtali, on the eastern border, when the news reached them that Group Captain Townsend had been appointed Air Attaché at Brussels, the appointment dating from 15th July. This meant that he would have left the country before the royal travellers returned to London. From Salisbury Princess Margaret spoke on the telephone to the Queen. Ill, she retired to bed for three days.

If ever a daughter needed a mother, she did then. How much the Queen Mother knew of the attachment can only be surmised, but to her has been attributed the comment: 'I never thought.' Now the agony was not only for Princess Margaret, and the world was peering through the window. The Princess had early said of her royal estate, 'Not even your love is your own.' She had known, but at the time of the equinoctial gales in life, tides sweep high.

The character of a woman, even a Queen, is formed on the experiences of life. This was a new kind of experience, a new form of emotion for the mother. The discoveries in it broadened the human vista. It helped to change the public image of her from H.M. Queen Elizabeth, Queen of George VI, Empress of India, into the simple sobriquet of 'Queen Mum', a title that she alone can ever bear.

For two years the Princess and Group Captain Townsend did not meet. Then, in August 1955, came a date of importance—the twenty-fifth birthday of Princess Margaret. The Royal Marriage Act of 1772 laid down that no descendant of King George II could marry under the age of twenty-five without the Sovereign's consent. But it added that 'in case any descendant of George II, being above twenty-five years old, shall persist to contract a marriage disapproved of by his Majesty, such descendant, after giving twelve months notice to the Privy Council, may contract such marriage, and the same may be duly solemnized without the consent of His Majesty. . . .' Thus on 21st August the Princess was free to do as she pleased.

There were three main considerations to be faced by the Queen Mother when weighing up the inadvisability of her daughter marrying the former Equerry. It was upon the mother that the main onus of guidance and advice rested, for a mother's advice will always transcend that of a sister, even if that sister is a Queen. The first, and foremost, consideration was that Group Captain Townsend was divorced.

The Queen Mother had backed up her elder daughter when, as Princess Elizabeth, she had told the Mothers' Union that 'divorce and separation are responsible for some of the darkest evil in our society today'. She has always believed in the sanctity of marriage. It was the issue of divorce that had cost Edward VIII the Throne. On the other hand there had been a number of cases of divorce and separation in the Royal Family. In Georgian days those whom God had bound together were quickly separated when the urgency came to find an heir to the Throne. Prince Albert's mother was divorced from his father, and his father had married again. Three of Queen Victoria's grandchildren, Princess Victoria Melita, the Grand Duke of Hesse and Princess Marie Louise, were divorced, the former two remarrying. Yet, in 1936, the Church and the State had made their views abundantly clear. The possibility that the demands of Royal Service might have contributed to the causes leading to the divorce, was outside the issue.

The second point to be considered was the danger that a precedent would be set of a Royal Servant marrying the daughter of a Sovereign. Here the issues were far more complex than seen by a public evaluating the love in two people's hearts.

The third point was that of finance. If she married, Princess Margaret would forfeit her six thousand pounds a year paid from the Civil List. Group Captain Townsend's income was limited. The income, fully liable to tax, on the monies that the Princess had inherited, would not allow her to continue living in a state approaching that to which she had become accustomed.

Affairs moved towards their climax. On 12th October Group Captain Townsend returned to London, staying with the Marquess of Abergavenny in Lowndes Square. At half past five that afternoon the Queen Mother arrived back at Clarence House from Scotland. At six o'clock the Group Captain called on Princess Margaret there. It had been a long time apart since those gay Coronation days. The Queen Mother left them to themselves. But he had used the Household door for the last time. In future his Renault was to pass through the main gate. He had crossed the line.

Princess Margaret and Group Captain Townsend spent the week-end with the Queen Mother's niece[1] at Allanbay Park in Berkshire. On Sunday morning the Princess attended morning service at Windsor. Her mother was there, and the two talked together.

The next four days were happy days for the couple. There were parties in friends' houses. There were quiet hours at Clarence House—but for him no invitation to dinner. Meantime the matter had been discussed by the members of the Cabinet. Sir Anthony Eden, the Prime Minister, saw the Queen. It became clear that Members of Parliament would be hostile to any suggestion that the Princess should retain her title on marriage. In fact, the terms that attended her marriage were onerous. Not only would she lose her rank and her allowance, but in all probability she would have to live abroad for a time. It was generally considered that the marriage would weaken the link with Commonwealth countries and that, at home, it would create a difficult position between the Crown, the Church and the Government.

Then came two engagements for the Princess. On the evening of the 19th she went with her sister and her mother to Lambeth Palace. The occasion was the re-dedication of the thirteenth-century Chapel, which had been devastated by a German bomb. Afterwards they dined with the Archbishop of Canterbury and some fifty bishops. Two days later, as the rain poured down on Carlton Gardens, the Queen unveiled the national memorial statue of her father. She said: 'Much was asked of my father in personal sacrifice and endeavour, often in the face of illness; his courage in overcoming it endeared him to everybody. He shirked no task, however difficult, and to the end he never faltered in his duty to his peoples.'

Thus was the seal put on the envelope of the married life of the Queen Mother. If ever she missed his clear way of seeing to the heart of a problem, his balance and commonsense, she missed it now.

The Queen Mother was definitely against the marriage and she was more rigid in her attitude than the Queen. She had been trained by Queen Mary, and just as her mother-in-law, at the time of the Abdication, had put duty above love, so did the Queen Mother now.

[1] The Queen Mother's sister, Lady Mary Frances Bowes-Lyon, married Lord Elphinstone in 1910. Their daughter, the Hon. Jean Constance, born 1915, married Captain John Lycett Wills in 1936.

She asked a question. Would King George VI have approved of such a marriage? The answer was clear. No. Therefore she could point out to her daughter in which direction her duty lay. The Queen Mother had seen her husband die because of the high grading he put on duty. She did not wish to see it down-graded.

The Princess decided that she would not marry Group Captain Townsend, and to him she paid great tribute. She drove once more to Lambeth and there she spoke words that were to ring around the world: 'Archbishop, you may put your books away. I have made up my mind.'

She said her sad good-byes and her message went through the air: 'Mindful of the Church's teaching that Christian marriage is indissoluble, and conscious of my duty to the Commonwealth, I have resolved to put these considerations before any others. . . .'

And the smile that was part of a mother's face was washed away.

29 Wings Across the World

IN the years that she has been mother of the Queen, the Queen Mother has winged frequently across the world. Gone are the days when it took three months to prepare for a royal trip, when the King and Queen came to the station to say good-bye, when three Princes waved farewell from the quayside at Portsmouth. Now the Queen Mother flies back across the Atlantic and three hours later is at Sandown or Lingfield to watch one of her horses come home.

In 1953 she was in Southern Rhodesia. In 1954 she was in New York. They dubbed her 'the Queen Mum' and fell in love with her all over again. This was one of her days. In the morning she drove to the north end of Manhattan Island, to the Cloisters, one of the most beautiful museums in the world. It is an annexe to the Metropolitan Museum of Art. Its five cloisters are part of France. Into their construction went pieces of the monasteries of St. Guilhem Le Desert, Trie, Bonnefont, Forville and St. Michel de Cuxa. She saw the Romanesque chapel constructed from parts of a former church at Langon, and the chapter house of the twelfth century, complete from Pontaut. Prying among the treasures on view, the paintings and the iron work, the sculpture and the furniture dating from the Middle Ages and beyond, it was the beautiful tapestries that drew her attention most.

From Manhattan she drove to the contrast of East 98th Street, to see the Lexington Houses children's centre. Most of the children here were Puerto Ricans, being cared for while their mothers were at work.

She dined that evening with the British Consul-General and his wife, Mr. and Mrs. F. A. Rundall. From their flat, high in a block overlooking the East River, she looked out over the fantastic skyline of New York. She saw another side of life.

From there she went to the most colourful occasion of her American visit, the Commonwealth Ball at the Armoury of the U.S. Seventh Regiment, in Park Avenue. There was a guard of honour for her of ex-Servicemen from the countries of the Commonwealth, and the flags of over fifty Commonwealth Societies were carried into the hall. The regimental band played *Colonel Bogey* as she went to the royal box with Sir Roger Makins and Sir Pierson Dixon and Lady Dixon, her host and hostess.

Mr. Hector Bolitho tells a story about the Queen Mother on this trip to America. He had driven out by taxi to Mount Vernon, George Washington's house above the Potomac river. 'When the cab driver heard me speak, he asked, "You from England?" "Yes," I answered. "Have you ever seen Queen Elizabeth the Queen Mother?" (He gave her her full title.) When I said, "Yes," he answered: "Well, so have I. I was at Mount Vernon, inside the gates, on the day she went there. As she stepped out of the car, just beside me, there was a shower of rain. She opened her parasol and, as she did it, she looked at me, smiled, and said, 'Excuse me.' What do you think of that! My! She's a very lovely lady." '

Her evening dresses were greatly admired and helped to swing the fashion back to long formal dresses for American women. There was one, back-swept, in smoke blue, with Alençon lace embroidered over satin, that held everyone's eye. And just as on her pre-war visit she had, by her example, emptied the shops of parasols, now she did the same for long white gloves. She did something for American women of her own generation—she gave them a very good reason why they should stop banting.

The Queen Mother was the first member of the Royal Family to complete the circumnavigation of the world exclusively by air.

She went back to old familiar bases in 1958, to New Zealand, where the ghosts of the Duke and Duchess of York still walked. In Wellington, where thirty-one years before the crowd to greet them had been so lively that the Duke could scarcely make himself heard, she visited a children's hospital. Over one bed were pictures of Prince Charles and Princess Anne. A doctor asked her if they were as nice as they looked. She answered: 'I think so. Prince Charles is particularly nice. He is a very gentle boy and has a kind heart, which I think is the essence of everything.' Then she went to the races. It was a good day for her, for she was presented with one of the winners, a four-year-old gelding named Bali Hai. It had just won the £4,000 St. James's Cup for its owner, eighty-two-year-old Sir Ernest Davis.

In the garden of Government House in Auckland she sat beside Queen Salote of Tonga, whose smiling face had won her a million friends when she drove in the Coronation procession of Queen Elizabeth II. It was a boiling hot day. They only had one fan between them, so they shared it. For days afterwards Queen Salote could talk of nothing but the Queen Mother's charm and sense of humour.

But in the accomplishment of one feat in the Pacific the mother has to give pride of place to her daughter. In Fiji Queen Elizabeth II, bravely and as etiquette calls, downed in one draught the contents of the cup of *Kava*, scooped from the ceremonial bowl. The warriors squatted on the ground, the dirges were intoned, and the Queen sunk the lot, as her father had done before her. On the first visit the Duke of York had excused his wife. Next time there the Queen Mother excused herself.

Everywhere the Queen Mother has been, her first thought has been for the children. She adopted a little Ibo girl from Eastern Nigeria, who was suffering from leprosy. When the Queen and Prince Philip were in Africa in 1956 they visited the Settlement where she was being treated. A tidy little girl in a checked dress was led up to them—the adopted daughter of the Queen Mother, well on the way to recovery.

On her way back from Australia in 1958 the Queen Mother had planned to visit Kenya and Uganda, but delays to her aircraft caused her to cancel the arrangement. She went the following year, and the crowds that greeted her as she drove in an open car with Sir Evelyn Baring through the Nairobi streets, rivalled the receptions of the South African tour. But much had changed in Nairobi since she had arrived there with her husband at the beginning 'of their 'safari' in 1924.

It was on this tour that many Africans had been instructed by their leaders to boycott the royal occasions and processions. It was a political gesture that failed completely. Those who remembered the visit of the 'Smiling Duchess', or who had been told of it by their parents, raced to the roadside to see her, and the flags that they waved were Union Jacks.

The Queen Mother always considers the crews of the transport which serves her. She always thanks them with a smile. In South Africa, when a railwayman was killed in an accident, she immediately sent her condolences to his family. And just as she had won all hearts on the Union railways, so she did now on the Kenyan Royal Train. She was a ray of sunshine in the boredom of the railroad. On St. Valentine's Day her crew excelled themselves. They presented her with a card, gay with frills and ribbons. On it was written:

> 'We railwaymen are deadly dull,
> Our lives run straighter than our line.
> Today our cup is more than full,
> For you provide our Valentine.'

In the same year the Queen Mother was in Rome and had audience of the Pope. There was a certain amount of comment, particularly from religious circles in Scotland. Yet in recent years such calls have become more frequent. The Queen, Prince Philip, Princess Margaret and the Duke of Gloucester have all been to the Vatican. The Duke of Windsor went when he was Prince of Wales, as did Queen Mary on the last occasion that she left British shores. Edward VII visited the Pope several times. His first audience, when he was eighteen, lit a flame of anti-Roman hate which spread across the country. But then it must be remembered that, not since Henry VIII broke relations with Rome four hundred years before, had a member of the British Royal Family trod Vatican ground.

As the Queen Mother was preparing to leave for Italy, she became uncertain as to what she should wear at the audience. So a message was sent asking for guidance on the point. The answer came back from the Pope himself. He would be pleased if she would wear plenty of jewels. He said that he had seen, and admired, so many photographs of her so garbed that he would like her to come that way. She did, complete with tiara and the insignia of the Garter.

On 10th May 1960 the Queen Mother left London for Rhodesia and Nyasaland—her objective to open the Kariba dam on the Zambesi river, one of the great engineering projects of the world, holding back a lake covering two thousand square miles. This she did on the 17th.

On this visit one little thing about the Queen Mother worried the Earl of Dalhousie, Governor-General of the Federation of Rhodesia and Nyasaland. Why did she insist on being alone on long car drives? Eventually he discovered. As soon as the car was clear of the crowds she was slipping off her shoes, putting her feet up on the occasional seat, opening her handbag and bringing out a bag of butterscotch.

She was in high spirits, full of memories of the wedding of Princess Margaret to Mr. Anthony Armstrong-Jones, who at this moment were on their honeymoon and had reached Trinidad. She spoke to them on the telephone. She went to a dance, radiant in white with a veil drooped over her tiara. She looked twenty years younger than her fifty-nine. Then trouble broke out. An American newspaper headlined her forthcoming wedding. The news was said to have come from 'sources close to royal circles'. The man involved was Sir Arthur Penn, her seventy-four-year-old Treasurer.

The following statement came quick from the Press Officer for the royal tour:

'Through Lt.-Col. Martin Gilliat, private secretary to Queen Elizabeth the Queen Mother, her Majesty stated that a report in an American newspaper that she and Sir Arthur Penn were contemplating marriage was "complete and absolute nonsense".'

The Press Officer added: 'These were her Majesty's last words. In fact, her Majesty used a stronger word.' The word remained a secret, but as an example of how to scotch rumours, this sample was unique in its efficiency.

A bouquet came from Scotland. The loyal address of the General Assembly of the Free Church of Scotland praised the Queen Mother for her 'courage in visiting Africa in present circumstances'. It added that the visit 'was in keeping with the best traditions of the Royal House'.

The next time that the Queen Mother went to Africa, in April 1961, she sailed in the Royal yacht *Britannia*. With her went a private guest, Brigadier Bernard Fergusson. The man whose eyeglass had flashed in the sun in battles from the Western Desert to Burma, whose name had become a legend in the Wingate expeditions, shared a common bond with the Queen Mother—the Black Watch. He had joined the regiment thirty years before and commanded the first Battalion from 1948–1951. Now he travelled with the Colonel-in-Chief.

The Queen Mother has always welcomed a spice of adventure in her travels. This time, as she landed in Tunis, the French rebellion was flaring across the border. 'I am excited to be here. I love Africa,' she said. She took a wreath of carnations and red roses to the Commonwealth war cemetery at Medjez el Bab and laid it at the Cross of Sacrifice, which commemorates two thousand men of the Commonwealth who fell in Tunisia and have no known graves. When she went to the Grand Mosque at Kairouan, veiled women ran into the streets to cheer her, forgetting about their purdah. She took off her shoes and entered the mosque in stockinged feet. The country so loved her, and she the country, that she told President Bourguiba that she would like to spend a private holiday there.

Britannia then took her to Cagliari, in Sardinia, where she had a rendezvous with the Queen and Prince Philip. She arrived first and although she was 'in transit' homebound, she asked to see something of the island. The Prefecture arranged to show here a Nuraghi village excavation and take her for a drive through the Arab quarter above the city. After a reunion with her daughter and son-in-law, she flew back in the Comet in which they had travelled from London, leaving them to board *Britannia*, which was to take them to Italy.

In June she made royal aviation history, when she flew the Atlantic in a commercial aircraft on a routine flight, with paying passengers aboard. An official of Trans-Canada Airlines said: 'People throughout Canada will be delighted that, for this "first time" occasion, the Queen Mother has chosen their national carrier.'

But the journey had an ignominious start. The royal car broke down in the tunnel at London airport, and had to be towed out.

Primarily the Queen Mother was bound for the centenary celebrations of the Black Watch (Royal Highland Regiment) of Canada, of which she is Colonel-in-Chief, in Montreal. But it was believed that there was another underlying object. This was that the visit of Britain's best Ambassador would patch up the relations between Canada and Britain after the trouble that had arisen over Britain's proposed entry into the Common Market.

The Queen Mother was due to visit New Zealand and Australia in 1964. In the period of preparation she received the All-Blacks Rugby team at Clarence House. She was talking to Mr. Ian Smith, the wing threequarter known as 'Spooky', and she told him that she would be going to his home area in New Zealand, Central Otago. She told him the time and date that she would be at certain places.

'Oh, no, Ma'am,' he said. 'Those are not your times. You'll be passing point A at 9.25 a.m., stopping at point B for morning tea from 10.27 7/8 to 10.39½ . . .'

'My goodness, Mr. Smith,' cut in the Queen Mother. 'You seem to know a good deal about my tour.'

'Ma'am,' he replied, 'I always keep up with the news.'[1]

The tour was to take her by air to Fiji via Vancouver, where she was to join the *Britannia* for the journey to Auckland. She was to fly on to Australia on 28th February. Her main engagement there was to be to attend the opening of the Adelaide Festival of Arts, of which she was patron. But at nine o'clock on the evening of 3rd February she was admitted to the King Edward VII Hospital for Officers in London for an emergency operation for appendicitis. The tour was, dramatically, off.

The Queen Mother had had little trouble with her health in recent years. The inconveniences that she had suffered had been connected with bones in her legs. In 1956 she fell and twisted her ankle at Clarence House. In February 1960 she made a quick recovery after knocking an injured leg. In June 1961 she cracked a small bone in her foot. And in September 1963 she stumbled at Birkhall and again fractured a small bone.

---

[1] *Willie Away*, by Terry Mclean.

Next morning the operation began at nine o'clock and was over in half an hour. 'Her Majesty's condition after the operation is satisfactory,' said the bulletin. Thirteen days later she stood on the steps of the hospital waving good-bye to the nurses at the windows. 'She was a model patient. Marvellous.' Such was the comment of Sister Astbury.

Exactly a year later the Queen Mother was airborne on a regular flight to Kingston via New York and Nassau. The wind in London was icy and she was changing it for West Indian sunshine. And in Jamaica she was to receive an honour from a still very active granddaughter of Queen Victoria.

On 25th February 1883 a daughter was born to the Duke and Duchess of Albany, and was named Alice Mary Victoria Augusta Pauline. When she was twenty-one Princess Alice married Prince Alexander of Teck, the younger brother of Queen Mary. In 1917 they became the Earl and Countess of Athlone. It has been the custom, in recent years, for this remarkable old lady, without making any special arrangements and accompanied only by a maid, to set off in a banana boat for Jamaica. There is special interest for her there, as she is Chancellor of the University College of the West Indies. Then on she has gone to New Zealand and Australia, to stay with her daughter, Lady May Abel Smith, wife of Sir Henry Abel Smith, Governor of Queensland. There is a strong bond of friendship between the Queen Mother and Princess Alice, as there is between her and Queen Victoria Eugenia of Spain.

So it was that Chancellor Princess Alice conferred upon the Queen Mother, in cap and gown, the honorary degree of Doctor of Letters, the first to be conferred by the West Indies University.

She opened a new thoroughfare, constructed in honour of her visit, and went by launch to look over the ancient buccaneer city of Port Royal. Then her aircraft rose again, high over the waters that she had sailed in *Renown* thirty-eight years before. Only a matter of hours after she landed she was at Lingfield races, watching Laffy win for her the Manifesto Handicap 'Chase.

30   The Lady of Clarence House

IN 1953 a rumour ran through Scotland that the Queen was about to sell Balmoral. John Brown's body turned in its grave in old Crathie churchyard. It was said that Prince Albert's Gothic castle was too cold on autumn evenings, as, indeed, Edward VIII had discovered. It was said that it was not private enough, and certainly the camouflage nets which hung along the banks of the Dee indicated an objection, and a very understandable one, to peerings into royal seclusion.

In fact the Queen had no intention of parting with Balmoral. The rumour was in parallel with the occasion when a royal doctor called at a Palace to look at a housemaid's throat, and the story began that a Princess was going to have a baby. There was a property deal in progress in Scotland, but it had no connection with Deeside. The Queen Mother was buying the Castle of Mey in Caithness.

Mey lies on the coast road some six miles west of John o'Groats, its bay nestling between Tang Head and St. John's Point. The land around is empty still. Evelyn Burnaby, on the last stage of his celebrated ride from Land's End to John o'Groats seventy-five years ago, wrote: 'We could see no signs of habitation until at last, on suddenly descending by a steep road, we caught a magnificent view, all in a moment, of Stroma Island, with the whole range of the Orkneys perfectly distinct. . . .'

The Queen Mother was feeling the reaction from the death of her husband. She was in a 'get away from it all' mood. She learned that Mey was for sale, and would be pulled down if a purchaser could not be found. She bought at the right time, for, owing to the web of

s   273

building restrictions, tumble-down castles were in little demand. A few years later the search for anything 'Scottish' began.

In choosing the north-easterly tip of Scotland as a spot to be alone, the Queen Mother was following in other footsteps. In the 1890s the area was seething with curiosity about 'a lady, well born and with a large fortune and house in London, alienating herself from her friends, spending her months in complete solitude there'. In the event she has spent much less time at Mey than was her original intention, mainly due to the fact that her family and her people have clearly said, 'We can't spare you.'

She now found herself with a far bigger home-making problem before her than she had faced at the Royal Lodge. The roof was falling in. The garden was a wilderness. There was no heating. The empty stone rooms were a challenge to her creative mind. She has spent some £40,000 on the place that she always calls 'my little castle'.

The result has thus been described. 'Today, the Castle is a delightfully feminine mixture of eighteenth-century console tables, Victorian needlepoint chairs, Queen Anne bureaux, and Regency and Empire lamps, clocks and candelabra. Mey's chatelaine has filled it with whimsies in startling contrast to the grim grey of its walls—bedrooms in pink, turquoise, coral and blue, crisp chintzes, a carved kneeling Regency blackamoor carrying a garden of greenness in a polychrome seashell on his back.'[1]

Outside, the Queen Mother has interests beyond her garden. As a patron of the Aberdeen Angus Cattle Society, she has had a long ambition to establish a herd of pedigree Angus cattle. At the Perth sales in 1964 she bought two heifers and two cows. They went to her one-hundred-and-twenty-acre Longgoe Farm at Mey, to join seventy North Country Cheviot sheep and sixteen commercial cows. Mr. G. Swanson, her farm manager, said: 'The Queen Mother has always wanted a herd of "blacks". She was brought up in the heart of the Aberdeen Angus country.'

In an area hitherto little touched by royalty, the Queen Mother is much in demand for local occasions. In 1962 she went west along the coast to Thurso, for its Lifeboat Week. She was presented with a

---

[1] *The House Wife*, 1960.

bouquet and then introduced to a French widow, Madame Cavigneaux, who had helped a Caithness man out of Occupied France and now came on visits to his family. Madame Cavigneaux told the Queen Mother that her husband, a member of the Resistance, had just died. The Queen Mother picked a flower from her bouquet, and handed it to the French widow so that she might lay it upon her husband's grave.

Fishing is another attraction of Mey, and she is prepared to spend hours in the chill waters of the River Thurso after salmon. She is an expert fisherman. That great enthusiast, Mr. Neville Chamberlain, was most impressed with her skill, and the two exchanged books on the subject.

Her other Scottish home is Birkhall, now with a new wing. She lent it to the Duke and Duchess of Kent for their honeymoon. She is as much loved at Balmoral as was Queen Victoria. She also likes to picnic. She was seen with Princess Margaret among the boulders by the Dee, boiling up the kettle on a fire of twigs.

She passes quietly on her way. A fisherman saw her coming along the river bank towards him. He was holding his cast. He tried the near impossible of trying to take off his cap at the same time. 'Don't do that,' the Queen Mother called out, in the tone that she had once used to the convalescent soldiers at Glamis. 'You will overbalance and drown.'

Her other home in the green and under the trees is the Royal Lodge at Windsor, now wholly hers. In the garden there memories of afternoons with George VI tumble over one another. He would plant for hours, while his wife contentedly carried to him the lilacs and the pyracanthas. They made it themselves, with a certain amount of personal competition. When Mr. Shewell-Cooper was writing his book, *The Royal Gardeners*, the Queen Mother sent him a note. It read: 'I planted the willow tortuosa myself; I stuck a tiny bit with a heel on it into the ground, and it grew like lightning.' Here she has so often played with her grandchildren, though not without attendant dangers. At the age of four Prince Charles pushed over the sun dial.

The home with which the Queen Mother will be indelibly connected is Clarence House. It has successively been the home of the

Duke of Clarence, who became William IV; Princess Augusta, his sister; the Duchess of Kent, mother of Queen Victoria; the Duke of Edinburgh; the Duke of Connaught; and the Duke of Edinburgh again. Here visitors congregate to watch the Changing of the Guard and stare at the black and gold top-hatted doorman. The duties of this official have puzzled many visitors from overseas. One giant who occupied the post was asked by an American what his occupation was. The doorman replied that he was an undertaker. The answer seemed to satisfy, and the visitor passed contentedly on his way.

It was to Clarence House that the Queen Mother and Princess Margaret moved in 1953. The house was under the control of the Queen Mother, and she paid the administrative and domestic staff. The Princess was responsible only for her personal maid and her lady-in-waiting. She had a suite on what used to be the nursery floor when Princess Elizabeth and the Duke of Edinburgh lived there. They dined together, in the big apple-green dining-room, under the gaze of long ago members of the House of Hanover, in their frames around the walls.

In the mornings, when lessons would allow, Prince Charles and Princess Anne would come over from the Palace with their corgis, Whiskey and Sherry. As there were six dogs at Clarence House, including Princess Margaret's sealyhams, the royal morning was apt to get away to a lively start.

Grandchildren, dogs and horses have been the great joys in the Queen Mother's life since her husband's death. Not being one who regards regular exercise in the light of a medicine, the Corgis are often the reason behind her walks. It has been guessed that she does not trust her staff to take them much beyond the front door. It was a filthy day at Windsor, wind howling and rain pouring down. A sentry cursed his fortune. Then through the 'Dog Door', so named as most of its traffic is canine, came two small ladies enveloped in sou'westers, mackintoshes, and Wellington boots. 'Hard luck,' the Guardsman said to them, 'having to exercise dogs on a day like this.' They passed silently on into the rain. Shortly afterwards the soldier was apprised of the identity of the walkers. He later admitted that, for the first time in his career, he nearly fainted on duty.

She has always been on the look out for tricks and games to amuse her grandchildren. At an official dinner she watched a conjurer very carefully to see how he did a particular trick. Afterwards she sent for him and asked to be shown how it was done. She admitted that she wanted to surprise Prince Charles. She perfected it, and did surprise him. The only trouble was that thereafter she was constantly being asked for more tricks. 'Granny Royal', the magician, became a family joke.

The Queen Mother has always got along well with her staff, of all grades. She is firm about the rules, but never forgets those who have worked for her, or helped her. When her chiropodist, Mr. Robert Sahli, was ill in 1960, she drove to Wanstead to see him. The comment from Clarence House was: 'It's the kind of thing she is always doing.' For thirty years the Queen Mother's personal maid was Miss Catherine Maclean. When sickness caused her to retire and her assistant, Miss Christine Wilcox, took her place, she took over an hotel on the shores of Loch Ness. In 1961 the Queen Mother drove one hundred and sixty miles to see her former 'dresser', and the deep curtsy of reception dropped by Miss Maclean became one of the most pleasing pictures of the year. It rivalled in chivalry the act of student Mike Steadman who, in the manner of Raleigh, laid his scarlet cloak across a puddle so that the royal visitor might keep her feet dry when she opened a new library block at Queen's College, Dundee.

Chauffeurs are important cogs in the royal machinery, combining, as they have to, the two essentials of safety and punctuality. The Queen Mother's cars[1] are kept in the mews behind Clarence House, the garages being former carriage houses. She is not fond of speed, but on one occasion she was in a hurry. She was late for an appointment and the chauffeur was driving faster than usual. He pulled out to pass a big lorry. 'Stop! Stop!' she shouted. Unmoved, the chauffeur proceeded to pass. He then politely informed his mistress of the great truth that there can only be one man at the wheel. She won another round. It was at a staff ball at Balmoral. A chauffeur was following the not unusual practice among British males of having a look at the dancers, then going to the bar for a drink and a

---

[1] A description of the cars of King George VI and the Queen Mother appears in *Royal Motoring*, by J. Dewar McLintock.

chat, and repeating the performance. The Queen Mother spotted him. He found the figure of Lord Plunket[1] beside him. He bore a message that the Queen Mother would dance with the chauffeur. In vain were his expostulations that he could not dance. There was no sympathy in Lord Plunket's reply: 'Now is your chance to learn.' A few seconds later he was repeating his deficiencies to the Queen Mother. 'Don't worry,' she said. 'I'll see you round.' This time she did the driving.

The Queen Mother always thinks of those who are away on business on her behalf, arranging forthcoming tours and the like. They have, to their astonishment, found a case of champagne waiting for them when they booked in at their hotel.

She is not a rich woman, judging by the standards of some Royalties, yet she is generous. At Christmas 1961 she gave £12,000 to an organization which helps the families of Servicemen. She learned 'canniness' as a child, when she had to make do with elder sisters' tennis rackets and shoes. She learned to shop carefully when she bought the tobacco and cigarettes for the wounded men at Glamis. Being at the tail end of a large family, there was little fortune to come from the Bowes-Lyons. When her father died in 1944 he left £94,000 in personal estate and land.

As a bachelor the Duke of York had received £10,000 a year, and as a married man, £25,000. Even so, when he took a cut in the financial depression, he was forced to sell his hunters. His allowance was increased on his father's death, but when he came to the Throne the Civil List was fixed at £410,000, £60,000 less than had been the case for George V. George VI was described as the most underpaid Monarch in the world, and in the last year of his reign Parliament relieved him of £40,000 of his expenses.

As his widow, the Queen Mother has been drawing an annuity of £70,000 from the State, the same figure as Queen Mary during her period as Queen Dowager. The huge expenses which are involved in her many official duties allow much of this to remain free of tax. Thus, despite all the tradition, etiquette and pomp to which she must conform, her yearly income is less than that of the highest paid men of business.

[1] Deputy Master of the Queen's Household.

A financial expert has estimated her fortune as being between three and four million pounds. This figure must be accounted for by the rising values in property and land, jewellery, furniture and paintings. It is in gifts that much of the royal wealth has come. In the imperial days of the 1890s a birthday might bring presents worth £10,000 at today's values, especially if the Czar of Russia was on friendly terms.

The Queen Mother's collection of jewellery is one of the finest and most valuable in Britain. Wedding presents formed the foundation and additions came at the time of her Coronation and as gifts on overseas tours. She was still able to say to Mr. Cecil Beaton in 1939, 'The choice isn't very great, you know.' But in 1943 died Mrs. Ronald Greville, the close friend of the Royal Family, at whose home the Duke and Duchess of York had spent their honeymoon. Her priceless collection of jewellery went to the then Queen. Items from among the Queen Mother's jewellery, including a massive diamond tiara, were seen at the International Exhibition of Modern Jewellery at Goldsmith's Hall in 1961. It was all done most casually. A selection of items were laid out on a table at Clarence House. Mrs. Mary Kruming, the American gem designer who helped to organize the exhibition, made her selection. The pieces were wrapped in brown paper and, with a fortune in her hands, Mrs. Kruming walked out and hailed a taxi. She said: 'It seemed the most unobtrusive way of taking it.'

In financial matters in the 1950s the Queen Mother was fortunate in being able to seek the advice of her brother, Sir David Bowes-Lyon,[1] the other half of 'the two Benjamins' in their childhood days. Sir David was managing director of the merchant banking business of Lazard Brothers and Company, and a director of Martin's Bank, the Cunard Steamship Company, the Dunlop Rubber Company and the Royal Exchange Assurance. He had travelled a long way across the financial field since the day that he and his sister collected every penny that they could lay hands on to save their pet pig from loss by raffle.

In the world of pictures the Queen Mother is advanced by royal standards. She collects modern paintings. It was a great bond that

[1] Mr. David Bowes-Lyon was created K.C.V.O. in 1959.

she shared with Sir Winston Churchill and she sent her friends copies of his work, *Painting as a Pastime*. She began her collection after she had moved into the Royal Lodge, buying an Augustus John and examples of Wilson Steer and Walter Sickert. When the war was over she purchased a seascape by Monet that had once belonged to 'Tiger' Clemenceau, Premier of France. She added paintings by Matthew Smith and Paul Nash. During her husband's life she asked John Piper to make water-colours and drawings of Windsor Castle. George VI was traditional in his taste. Noticing that the sky was stormy, he commented drily: 'What bad weather you must have had, Mr. Piper.'

As a subject, she is an artist's delight. Pietro Annigoni, talking to Clive Hirschhorn, has said of her: 'One of my best pictures is the one I did of the Queen Mother. And I'll tell you why this is so. It's because she has such an inner beauty. It is all very well to look glamorous on the surface, but without that personal quality your subject is nothing but a dummy. The Queen Mother is one of the loveliest people I have ever met. It is hard to imagine a kinder, warmer, more appealing human being. And she never interferes with the painting while it's in progress, or makes demands about how she would like to look. She is absolutely perfect.'

31 The Paddock and the Post

ON 31st July 1714 Queen Anne's Star, after running sixteen miles, won a £14 Plate. Early next morning Queen Anne died. Star was the last runner for a Queen until the wife of King George VI took an active part in steeplechasing in 1949.

In the years since, the Queen Mother has become the leading National Hunt owner. Her success is matched by her enthusiasm and her knowledge. She is in marked contrast with a former royal owner, William IV, the Sailor King, who, when asked what horses he wished to run in the Goodwood Cup, replied, 'Start the whole fleet.'

Clarence House is on the 'blower'. The Exchange Telegraph Company installed the service for the Queen Mother so that, when she cannot get to a meeting, she receives the same racecourse commentary as that relayed to the betting shops. She has bookshelves packed tight with form books. Her Secretary, Sir Martin Gilliatt, has kept a record of all her horses, with their photographs. She collects paintings and prints of famous racehorses of the past. Often, in the early light, she can be seen propped on her shooting stick, watching her horses at exercise.

She chooses her horses herself. She has a say in where they shall run. She decides if the going is right or wrong. In the evening, after a meeting, she telephones the stables to see that her horses are safely home. Her knowledge is respected. One of her trainers, Mr. Jack O'Donoghue, has said of her: 'She knows plenty, she does. By gosh she does. She won't run a horse if the going is not suitable. And she knows what courses suit them. By gosh, she knows as much, if not more, than any other owner.'

The love of racing is in both sides of the Queen Mother's blood.

281

She brought back to the paddock, after half a century, the famous Strathmore colours of her grandfather, the black cap with the gold tassel, and the blue and the buff. Through her mother she is related to Lord George Bentinck, the startling son of the Duke of Portland who dominated English racing in the early years of the reign of Queen Victoria. Unlike his distant cousin of today, who does not bet, Lord George could not resist a wager. He lost £26,000 on the St. Leger of 1826. Going into racing on a big scale, he decided to get his own back on the bookmakers. He had a horse, Elis, which he thought could win the St. Leger of 1836. In those days runners were walked to meetings, and a clear fortnight was needed to get Elis to Doncaster. A week before the race the scouts reported to the bookmakers that the horse was still in Hampshire. Out went the odds.

In deep secret Lord George had arranged to be constructed a horse-box, which, drawn by post horses, could cover eighty miles in a day. It took three days to reach the Town Moor. Elis stepped out fresh and in the peak of condition. He won easily, to the great financial advantage of his owner. But Lord George came near to losing his life in another betting venture, which ended in a duel with Squire Osbaldeston. The squabble was over the running of an Irish four-year-old named Rush. Lord George fired into the air, but the Squire put his round through the Bentinck hat.

In her wide travels the Queen Mother has attended race meetings all across the world. She was at a meeting in South Africa when the programme had to be abandoned because of the public's noisy objection to a declared result. In New Zealand she has been presented with the winner after the race. At Melbourne in 1927 she saw the King's Cup at the Flemington course. She is a little superstitious. Always has she touched the star inlaid into a post of the stairs leading to the Royal Box at Ascot. To do so brings luck, and so her fingers have caressed it.

Ascot has always meant much to the Queen Mother. There was a particular day in 1945. She was there with her husband. The King's horse, Rising Light, was running over a mile and a half. It won by a short head. This was the first time that they had watched one of their horses win, despite the fact that the King had headed the list of winning owners in 1942. His daughters would sometimes tease their father about his racing activities, yet in the seasons 1946–1949 he won over £37,000 in prizes. He had a sound knowledge of breeding and his patronage and interest in the post-war years did much for racing.

In 1949 Lord Mildmay of Flete was a guest at Windsor. Anthony Mildmay, known to the crowds as 'Lordie', lanky, the type of which legends are made, had been first past the post over a hundred times. In the 1946–1947 National Hunt season he had headed the list of amateur riders with thirty-two winners. He had ridden Cromwell into third place in the Grand National when he was suffering from a slipped disc and could not move his neck.

Lord Mildmay relived for the then Queen his thrilling, 'blind' ride round Aintree on his 33 to 1 chance. The magic of it enthralled her. She decided to see the Strathmore colours again and, at the same time, give a much needed boost to 'chasing. In partnership with Princess Elizabeth she bought Monaveen, a nine-year-old which cost them £1,000. Monaveen ran in the Grand National, won some £3,000 in prizes and then, tragically, was killed at Hurst Park. The £1,000 Monaveen 'Chase was named after the first steeple-chaser that the Queen Mother owned.

When Lord Mildmay was drowned off the Devon shore and, on a morning of sadness, 'chasing lost a figure and a friend that could never be replaced, the Queen Mother and her daughter purchased two of his horses. In their first four years the Royal owners saddled seven winners.

When George VI died, Queen Elizabeth II inherited his fourteen horses and continued to race them in his colours. The common interest of racing binds mother and daughter close. They are never happier than when wandering about the Sandringham stud with a basket of carrots and lumps of sugar. They love to drive out early along the straight, flat roads to Newmarket to watch the royal horses at work, and afterwards to breakfast there. It is the Queen's ambition to emulate the successes of her great-grandfather, who won the Grand National once and the Derby three times. He, too, loved to speed from Sandringham to Newmarket in his open car, arriving covered with dust and white as a miller. It was on the advice of Lord Marcus Beresford, King Edward VII's racing adviser, that thoroughbred breeding began at Sandringham, where previously the stud had been content with producing hackneys and hunters, and also that the royal horses should be trained at handy Newmarket.

The then Prince of Wales had little success until John Porter of Kingsclere bought the mare Perdita II for the Sandringham stud. She became the dam of Florizel II, Persimmon and Diamond Jubilee. Persimmon won the Derby and the St. Leger, bagging the Eclipse Stakes and the Gold Cup the following year. When his turn came, Diamond Jubilee won all the five classic races.[1] The Heir to the Throne went to the top of the list of winning owners. He estimated that the purchase of the mare Perdita II had brought him a quarter of a million pounds.

The Queen and the Queen Mother had high hopes of another royal Derby winner with Aureole in 1953, but Sir Gordon Richards on Pinza defeated them. Many people wondered what were the words that the Queen spoke to the famous, and somewhat shaken, jockey after the race. She was, in fact, assuring him that she was not going to send him to the Tower.

The royal turn came at the second Ascot meeting in July of the following year. Then Aureole won the greatest prize in racing, the King George VI and Queen Elizabeth Stakes. This put the Queen's winnings up to £35,799 and made her the leading owner.

The Queen Mother is most careful of her horses. If she considers that the going is too hard, they do not run. If there is a risk, there are long telephone talks with her trainers before she will give permission. Primarily, the Queen Mother is in racing for the love of it, and not the gain. She backs a noble British sport, and helps its stability. There is sweet music for her in the roar of the crowd in a race's closing stages, and thrilling suspense when her colours are concerned in a finish. She has wells of patience. She can wait for the right day and the right going. She takes every precaution to see that nothing goes wrong. Yet fate can play strange tricks in racing.

She ran Devon Loch in the Grand National of 1956. He was first over the last, and the crowds were wildly cheering home what appeared to be a certain winner, the first royal success since Ambush

[1] The Two-Thousand Guineas, the Newmarket Stakes, the Eclipse Stakes, the Derby and the St. Leger.

II in 1900. Then, a few yards from the post, the horse sprawled, legs outstretched. It was as if he thought that he saw yet another fence looming up before him. E.S.B. swept past to win. As the sigh of bewilderment came from the stands, she turned, moist-eyed to those around her, raised her hands and said: 'That's racing.' She won for herself a bigger cheer that day than if she had been the winning owner. Her sympathy turned immediately to Dick Francis the rider, and to all those who were concerned with Devon Loch, and to Devon Loch himself. She begged grief-stricken Francis not to be upset and told him that there would be another day. She went to the stable to comfort some very disconsolate lads. Seven years were to pass before the Queen Mother had another runner in the National, and Devon Loch went to the elysian fields at Sandringham, where royal ladies dish out lumps of sugar and carrots on Sunday afternoons.

Horses fare well in her hands. Rodney was bought for her as a potential steeplechaser. He was trained for a time by Major Eldred Wilson, a Sandringham tenant, but did not have the speed for racing. So he was given to the daughter of Crown Equerry Brigadier W. M. Sale, a friend of long standing. The Queen Mother is a good judge of a horse, and has conducted her inspections in odd places. It was in the yard behind a country public house that she decided to buy The Rip. She named him herself. He was by one of her favourite horses, Manicou, out of Easy Virtue. She made her decision on Super Fox in the garden of Clarence House. She had a heavy programme that day, so the box was sent up to the Mall.

On occasion the Queen Mother's luck has survived the omens of ill fortune. For example, the combination of Friday and the Thirteenth must always remind her of the day that she and the King narrowly escaped with their lives in the bombing of Buckingham Palace. In November 1957 she was at Sandown, enjoying the recent improvements to the Royal Box, above which was flying her personal standard, the Royal arms impaled with her own punning family arms of bows and lions. She was wearing green. It was a Friday. Her runner, Double Star, was No. 13 on the card. Despite all of this, she won the fourth race.

She had a moment of luck at the Badminton Horse Trials. She had been watching the progress from the platform of a truck, and was engaged in the somewhat precarious task of descent. A competitor coming in at the end of his ride suddenly saw a little woman in blue right before him. 'Look out,' he bawled. The Queen Mother stepped back and the horse missed her by a foot. Completely unruffled, she carried on as if nothing had happened.

The Kempton Park Saints and Sinners meeting of July 1961 was to be a memorable evening for her. She awarded the Aly Khan International Memorial Gold Cup. The winner was High Hat—the owner Sir Winston Churchill. Also the Queen's Augustine took the William Hill Diamond Handicap, the only saintly favourite of the evening. The Queen Mother had to make a choice. Mr. Hill asked her whether the Queen would like a very tempting diamond, or £2,000 in cash. The Queen Mother replied: 'It is a very nice diamond, but I think she would rather have the money!' Next month the Queen gave her winner, the four-year-old gelding Augustine, to her mother, and he went to Mr. Tom Masson at Lewes to be trained for hurdling.

The winter of 1961–1962 brought to the Queen Mother the best National Hunt season that she had ever enjoyed. She had eight horses with Cazalet, two with Masson, two with O'Donoghue and one with Boyd-Rochfort. Early in December Major Peter Cazalet pulled off a hat-trick for her at Lingfield, bringing her total of winners to that date up to twelve. The horses concerned were Laffy, Double Star and The Rip. Off to Kent went the Queen Mother for a celebration weekend with Major and Mrs. Cazalet at their home near Tonbridge, the trio beaming with smiles when they attended matins at St. Giles' Church, Shipbourne.

In March she made a sentimental journey to Hurst Park for the last steeplechase there. Full of memories of her first 'chaser, she had entered Laffy for the Monaveen Chase, but, sadly, he was cast in his box that morning. But Laffy was to go on to make his little bit of history. In April the Queen Mother entered him at Downpatrick. This brought great pleasure to Northern Ireland, as there had not been a royal runner there since King Edward VII sent Flaxman over in 1906. The Queen Mother flew to see the Ulster Harp National. On the historical side there was much to interest her, for the Downe Hunt Club is one of the oldest in the British Isles, the first mentions of it being some three hundred years ago and the records of the present club going back to 1757.

The Queen Mother's successes of that season—twenty-four, including a win for Laffy in Northern Ireland—were widely acknowledged. When, in May, she was a guest of the British Assurance Association at a dinner at the Guildhall, her table was decorated with an intricate, and beautifully executed, racing scene from Sandown, carried out in icing sugar. Three horses were concerned in a finish, the winner carrying the colours of the Queen Mother and the second and third those of owners from the Assurance world.

The Queen Mother's interest in racing peeps out all along the tapestry of her life. Her Christmas card for 1964 was 'The Thorough-breds', showing two mares and foals. It was taken from a painting in oils by Mr. Lionel Hamilton-Renwick, who has painted horses for the Queen and the late Princess Royal. If she is talking with friends or members of the Household at Clarence House, or San-dringham, or Windsor, and she very politely, but determinedly, says 'Excuse me,' it can be taken as a safe bet that there is 'chasing on one of the television programmes. When she slips out alone in the even-ing it is more than likely that her destination is the home of one of her many friends in the racing fraternity or people who share her interest.

It was during the 1964–1965 National Hunt season that the Queen Mother reaped the harvest of all her efforts and enthusiasm. Early she notched up her century of successes and then, on 27th November, came a milestone in her connection with the Fairlawne stable. She was at Lingfield to see Arch Point win Division I of the Caterham Novices' Hurdle. This horse, which, as a two-year-old had been a winner in the Dublin show ring and had made a miraculous recovery from stifle and back trouble, was the hundredth winner saddled for the Queen Mother by Major Cazalet. It brought her grand total to one hundred and nine, eight having been saddled by O'Donoghue and one by Masson. This called for a celebration, and the royal owner gave a private dinner at the Savoy Hotel a few weeks afterwards.

She continued to build up her total, although she gave her faithful band of followers some nasty moments. Lazy Makaldar, considered to be one of the best horses that she has ever owned, flattened the last flight at Windsor in December and did not appear concerned whether he won or not. Hearts beat fast in the run-in, but Bill Rees forced him home. It was Makaldar's seventh victory in nine outings.

There was one race that the Queen Mother was determined to see, and that was the Manifesto 'Chase at the end of February. She wanted to watch her favourite, Laffy, win at Lingfield as he had done in 1964. And she was sure that he would. She hurried from the plane that brought her back from Jamaica and within a few hours was in the unsaddling enclosure. Laffy came home in great style, bringing his owner's winning total for the season up to twenty and her prize money near to £9,000. Three weeks later she broke her own personal record when Antiar romped home in the Beech Open 'Chase at Sandown. With twenty-four winners the Queen Mother was way out in front of any other owner, but with prize money of £11,847 she stood second to Anne, Duchess of Westminster, who had captured £13,502 from the two outings of her wonder horse, Arkle. The issue now lay in the Grand National, with its prize of over £24,000. The royal runner, The Rip, was at the time joint favourite at 11 to 1.

The Queen Mother travelled to Liverpool on 26th March. Never has the nation been more united in its wish that a certain horse, her horse, should win a particular race, and that the greatest prize in the National Hunt calendar at the climax in its story. Once again, although The Rip ran gallantly, she had to face the disappointment of defeat. It did not rob her of her smile or make her congratulation to the winning owner any the less sincere.

For the men who ride the horses the First Lady of 'Chasing, the 'Queen Mum', is a figure apart, regarded almost as a treasured possession. She is deeply concerned with the safety of jockeys, and a strong supporter of funds to help those who have been injured, such as Paddy Farrell, who broke his back at Aintree in 1963, and the paralysed Tim Brookshaw. To help swell the contributions to the Injured National Hunt Jockeys' Fund the Queen Mother attended, in December 1964, a gala performance of *Our Man Crichton* at the Shaftesbury theatre. That night the racing world saw her in all her splendour of tiara and diamonds, in the star role that she has played impeccably on the royal stage for over forty years, contrasting with the familiar tweeded figure whom they know so well in the paddock.

F ROM the time of the Coronation to the end of the fifties, few family changes came to the Queen Mother. Princess Margaret continued to live with her. The number of grandchildren remained static at two. Then, when 1960 dawned, with her sixtieth birthday upon its calender, events began to crowd in upon her, some sad, most happy.

On 13th January she was at the Romsey Abbey wedding of Lady Pamela Mountbatten and Mr. David Hicks. It was her granddaughter's debut as a bridesmaid. The great crowd saved its biggest cheer for the Queen Mother, as the twelve hundred guests left the Abbey for the reception at Broadlands. There, in the arctic weather, the lights fused. Through the sudden darkness came a clear voice saying, 'Cor! It's dark in here.' It was that of Princess Anne.

On 8th February the Queen declared that her descendants, other than those entitled to style and title of Royal Highness and Prince or Princess, would bear the surname of Mountbatten-Windsor. On the 19th the Queen gave birth to a son[1] at Buckingham Palace, the first child born to a reigning British Sovereign for more than a century. On the night of the 20th–21st Countess Mountbatten of Burma died in North Borneo. On the 23rd the Marquess of Carisbrooke, the last surviving grandson of Queen Victoria, died at Kensington Palace. On the 26th the following announcement came from Clarence House: 'It is with the greatest pleasure that Queen Elizabeth the Queen Mother announces the betrothal of her beloved daughter the Princess Margaret to Mr. Antony Charles Robert Armstrong-Jones, son of Mr. R. O. L. Armstrong-Jones, Q.C., and

[1] Prince Andrew Albert Christian Edward.

the Countess of Rosse, to which the Queen has gladly given her consent.'

As the old order changed, yielding place to new, sorrow and sadness were sliced between jubilation and the beginnings of life. The body of Edwina Mountbatten slipped into the sea, the van from the men's outfitters came round to collect the uniforms of Prince 'Drino',[1] and the love of a Princess took over the headlines from a baby.

The engagement of Princess Margaret was one of the best kept royal secrets of all time, held back even from some members of the Royal Family. It was announced when it was, at a time of sadness, as it was suspected that the information might leak out from unofficial sources. The Queen Mother's Press Secretary revealed that the couple had first met at a party in London two years before and had seen one another continuously since that time. They had been together at both Sandringham and Balmoral.

Mr. Armstrong-Jones had taken a number of photographs of the Royal Family and thus had a ready-made alibi for visiting their residences. This had been thought to be the reason for his visit to Sandringham in January 1959. So as not to attract undue attention he was not asked for Christmas. Yet it was during these winter days on the Norfolk estate that friendship ripened into love. It was still thought that he was taking family photographs when he went to Balmoral in October. Yet, in the last five months before the engagement was announced, he was a frequent, and unnoticed, week-end visitor at the Royal Lodge, and was a number of times at Clarence House.

Only a small group of people were in the secret, the Queen Mother at their head. These were not easy times for her. She has never interfered with the plans of her children, but always been ready with advice should it be asked for. She could see that the engaged couple were made for one another. There were the same tastes, the same talents, the same quickness of mind. Princess Margaret was in her thirtieth year. Five years before she had undergone a severe emotional strain. Another set-back now might turn her into a

[1] Prior to 1917 the Marquess of Carisbrooke was titled Prince Alexander ('Drino') of Battenberg. He was the son of Princess Beatrice and Prince Henry of Battenberg.

changed woman. There was the example in recent years of Princess Victoria, who had been refused permission to marry a commoner and thereafter remained a spinster. Queen Mary had been a sufferer in that direction. So the mother's aim was to see her daughter happy. Yet she knew full well that a price would have to be paid, that the Crown and the camera would appear side by side in the Press. She knew that there was plenty of ammunition for those who wished to fire it, that on marriage Princess Margaret would have three mothers-in-law, that her first baby would put a Jones fifth in line for the Throne, that reminiscences of gay days would be resurrected. So she placed herself squarely behind the young couple. She did as Queen Mary had done at the time of the Abdication. She showed herself. She appeared in the engagement pictures. She let it be known that she was fully behind the marriage. She was all that a mother can be.

On the morning of 6th May the Queen, the Queen Mother and the Prince of Wales, in Queen Alexandra's State coach, drove from Buckingham Palace to Westminster Abbey, through greater crowds than had been seen in London since Coronation day. Fifteen minutes later the bride, Prince Philip beside her, followed into the peal of bells that heralded the greatest day of her life.

There was a moment during the service—a moment in the period of prayer. The flush of royal ladies bent their heads to the prescribed angle, watchful of their headwear, conscious of the ritual. One woman went right upon her knees. She was oblivious of the eyes upon her. Hers, and far away, was the moment, of prayers for happiness in the days to come, of dreams of Westminster in the long ago. It was the Queen Mother. And it was her smile to the bride, as she curtseyed to the Queen, that was the last memory for many of a joyful wedding day.

In June of the next year she was at another wedding, that of the Duke of Kent to Miss Katharine Worsley in York Minster. Some indication of the energy of the Queen Mother can be seen from her programme for that day: '10 a.m. Leaves Clarence House by car. 10.15. Leaves King's Cross by train. 1.45 p.m. Arrives York. 2.0. Arrives York Minster. 3.30. Drives to Hovingham. 4.45. Leaves by car. 5.50. Her plane takes off from Linton airfield. 7.11. Arrives

T*

London Airport. 7.13. Takes off by helicopter. 7.30. Arrives Buckingham Palace. 7.34. Arrives Clarence House. Dress: ice blue coat and feathered hat. 8.45. Leaves by car. Dress: crinoline, white furs. 8.58. Arrives Covent Garden for gala performance. 12.5 a.m. Leaves Covent Garden for home.'

Joy turned to sorrow. In September 1961 the Queen Mother's brother, Sir David Bowes-Lyon, died of a heart attack. He and his wife were on holiday at his sister's Deeside home of Birkhall. He was fifty-nine. Friends said that his death was brought on by 'sheer hard work'. 'We all begged him to ease up, but he would never listen. He was a staggering worker.' Thus it has been with both men closest to the Queen Mother. With the Queen and Prince Philip she attended a service at St. Kentigern's Church, Ballater, and then they travelled south for the committal service at the Church of All Saints at St. Paul's Walden Bury. The story of Elizabeth and David ended in a simple fifteen-minute ceremony, among their own people, many of whom could remember them romping round the garden half a century before.

Sorrow to joy again. On 3rd October Mr. Armstrong-Jones was created Earl of Snowdon, and on the evening of 2nd November he drove with his wife from Kensington Palace to Clarence House. Princess Margaret was going home to mother, to the apartments that she knew so well, to have her first baby. She was safely delivered of a son at 10.45 next morning. He became Viscount Linley. The important part that the Queen Mother plays in the lives of children had been clearly demonstrated once again.

The wedding of Princess Alexandra of Kent to the Hon. Angus Ogilvy in 1963 was of particular interest to the Queen Mother, on two counts. Firstly, it meant that the noble families of four castles in Angus, Glamis, Cortachy, Kinnaird and Brechin, lying in an area of only some seventy square miles, were now linked with the Royal House. Princess Patricia of Connaught had married the son of the Earl of Dalhousie, Princess Maud of Fife the son of the Earl of Southesk, the Duke of York the daughter of the Earl of Strathmore, and Princess Alexandra the son of the Earl of Airlie. Secondly, it linked in marriage a family which had long been in royal service. Mabell, Countess of Airlie, was for over fifty years lady-in-waiting to Queen Mary. It was while staying with her that Princess Mary had made one of her first visits to Glamis. The Countess was the first to know of the romance between the Duke of York and Lady Elizabeth Bowes-Lyon, and it was with her that the Home Secretary stayed in the weeks prior to the birth of Princess Margaret. Mr. Angus Ogilvy's father, the Earl of Airlie, had been appointed Lord Chamberlain to Queen Elizabeth in 1937, and by the time of the wedding he had completed over a quarter of a century in this capacity.

In the same year the Queen Mother gave herself a treat, something new, refreshing. She went off on holiday to France, to explore the Loire Valley. She stayed at an hotel, the Château d'Artigny, which had once been the home of the Coty family. At Tours, on her last day in France, she, with much acumen, dodged the Press and had dinner in a restaurant famed for its local dishes. Except for one occasion when she was in Italy, and once when she was in Manchester in 1959, she had not been in a public restaurant since becoming Queen.

1964 was the year of the babies. Not since the 'Royal Marriage Race' in 1819, when the sons of George III contested to provide an Heir to the Throne, have so many arrived. Then the Duchesses of Clarence and Kent gave birth to daughters, and the Duchesses of Cumberland and Cambridge, to sons. The Queen Mother now gained two grandchildren in Prince Edward and Lady Sarah Armstrong-Jones, and became great-aunt to James Robert Bruce Ogilvy and Lady Helen Windsor.

1965 began as a year of good-byes. She stood on the steps of St. Paul's, watching the coffin of Sir Winston Churchill moving through the City streets towards the last journey along London's river. She went to Harewood to see her girlhood friend, Mary, Princess Royal, laid to rest in the Yorkshire that she loved.

We leave her on a spring evening in the garden of the Château Legier in Provence, with her memories and with her plans, under the cypress trees, with the smell of mimosa on the still night air.

Bibliography

AGA KHAN, *The Memoirs of Aga Khan* (1954)

AIRLIE, Mabell, Countess of, *Thatched with Gold*, edited by Jennifer Ellis (1962)

ANON. *The Coronation of King George VI and Queen Elizabeth* (1937)

ANON. *Our King and Queen* (1937)

ARTHUR, Sir George. *King George V* (1934)

ASQUITH, Lady Cynthia. *The Married Life of the Duchess of York* (1933)

ASQUITH, Lady Cynthia. *Queen Elizabeth* (1937)

ASTON, Sir George. *H.R.H. The Duke of Connaught and Strathearn* (1929)

BEATON, Cecil. *The Candid Eye of Cecil Beaton* (1961)

BENSON, E. F. *Daughters of Queen Victoria* (1939)

BOLITHO, Hector. *A Biographer's Notebook* (1950)

BOLITHO, Hector. *A Century of British Monarchy* (1951)

BOLITHO, Hector. *Edward VIII* (1937)

BOLITHO, Hector. *George VI* (1937)

BROAD, Lewis. *The Abdication* (1961)

BROWN, Ivor. *Balmoral* (1955)

BUCHAN, John. *The King's Grace* (1935)

BUCHANAN, Meriel. *Queen Victoria's Relations* (1954)

CHANCE, Michael. *Our Princesses and their Dogs* (1937)

CHURCHILL, Sir Winston. *The Second World War*, 6 vols. (1948–1954)

COLVILLE, Lady Cynthia. *Crowded Life* (1963)

COZENS-HARDY, H. T. *The Glorious Years* (1953)

CRAWFORD, Marion. *The Little Princesses* (1950)

DARBYSHIRE, Taylor. *King George VI* (1937)
DEAN, John. *H.R.H. Prince Philip, Duke of Edinburgh* (n.d.)
DENNIS, Geoffrey. *Coronation Commentary* (1937)
DENT, H. C. *Milestones to the Silver Jubilee* (1935)
DIMBLEBY, Richard. *Elizabeth Our Queen* (1953)
ELLIS, Jennifer. *The Royal Mother* (1954)
EMDEN, Paul H. *Behind the Throne* (1934)
ESHER, Viscount. *Journals and Letters of Reginald Viscount Esher*, edited by Maurice V. Brett (Vol. 1) (1934)
GIBBS, Sir Philip. *The Book of the King's Jubilee* (1935)
GORE, John. *King George V: A Personal Memoir* (1941)
GORMAN, Major J. T. *George VI: King and Emperor* (1937)
GRAEME, Bruce. *The Story of Buckingham Palace* (1928)
GUNTHER, John. *Roosevelt in Retrospect* (1950)
HARTNELL, Norman. *Silver and Gold* (1955)
HOPE, W. H. St. John. *Windsor Castle* (2 vols.) (1913)
HOPKIRK, Mary. *Queen Adelaide* (1946)
HUNTLY, The Marquis of. *Auld Acquaintance* (n.d.)
LAIRD, Dorothy. *How the Queen Reigns* (1959)
LEE, Air Vice-Marshal Arthur S. Gould. *The Royal House of Greece* (1948)
LEE, Sir Sidney. *King Edward VII* (2 vols.) (1925)
MACKENZIE, Compton. *The Windsor Tapestry* (1938)
McLINTOCK, J. Dewar. *Royal Motoring* (1962)
MAINE, Basil. *Edward VIII: Duke of Windsor* (n.d.)
MARIE LOUISE, H.H. Princess. *My Memories of Six Reigns* (1956)
MASSON, Madeleine. *Edwina: The Biography of the Countess Mount-batten of Burma* (1958)
MICHIE, Allan A. *The Crown and the People* (1952)
MONTGOMERY, John. *Royal Dogs* (1962)
MORRAH, Dermot. *The Royal Family in Africa* (1947)
MORRAH, Dermot. *The Work of the Queen* (1958)
MURPHY, Ray. *Last Viceroy: The Life and Times of Rear-Admiral The Earl Mountbatten of Burma* (1948)
NICOLSON, Harold. *King George the Fifth* (1952)
NORWICH, Lord. *Old Men Forget: The Autobiography of Duff Cooper* (1953)

PETRIE, Sir Charles. *Monarchy in the Twentieth Century* (1952)
PONSONBY, Arthur. *Henry Ponsonby: His Life from his Letters* (1942)
PONSONBY, Sir Frederick. *Recollections of Three Reigns* (1951)
POPE-HENNESSY, James. *Queen Mary: 1867–1953* (1959)
ROOSEVELT, Eleanor. *On My Own* (1959)
ROWSE, A. L. *Royal Homes* (n.d.)
SENCOURT, Robert. *The Reign of King Edward VIII* (1962)
SHEWELL-COOPER, W. E. *The Royal Gardeners: King George VI and his Queen* (1962)
STANLEY CLARK, Brigadier. *Palace Diary* (1958)
STUART, Dorothy Margaret. *King George The Sixth* (1937)
TANGYE, Derek. *One King* (1944)
THOMPSON, Grace E. *The Patriot King: The Life of William IV* (1932)
THOMSON, Rev. Thomas. *A History of the Scottish People* (6 vols.) (1887)
TSCHUMI, Gabriel. *Royal Chef* (1954)
VICTORIA, Queen. *The Letters of Queen Victoria.* Edited by G. E. Buckle. (Third Series) (1932)
VICTORIA, Queen. *More Leaves from the Journal of a Life in the Highlands* (1885)
WATSON, Francis. *Dawson of Penn* (1951)
WINDSOR, Duchess of. *The Heart has its Reasons* (1956)
WINDSOR, Duke of. *A Family Album* (1960)
WINDSOR, Duke of. *A King's Story: The Memoirs of H.R.H. the Duke of Windsor, K.G.* (1951)

Magazines and Periodicals

Army Quarterly	*Queen*
The Field	*Sphere*
Homes and Gardens	*Sunday Express*
Housewife	*Sunday Telegraph*
Illustrated London News	*Sunday Times*
Past and Future	*Vogue*

Index

Baldwin, Rt. Hon. Stanley (Earl, of Bewdley), 64, 154, 159
Ballater, 292
Balmoral Castle, 77, 88, 116, 117, 151, 172, 176, 177–8, 192, 206, 237, 238, 242, 273
Bannerman, Mrs. Douglas, 122
Baring, Sir Evelyn, 267
Barrett, H. Roper, 94
Basutoland, 224
Bath, 139
Bath and Wells, Bishop of, 167
Batterbee, Sir Henry Fagg, 99
Beaconsfield, Earl of (Disraeli), 251
Beaton, Cecil, 189–90
Beatrice, Princess (Princess Henry of Battenberg), 123, 135, 168, 192, 207
Beaufort, Duchess of, (Lady Mary Cambridge), 62, 193
Beaufort, Duke of, 193
Belgrade, 77–8
Bennett, Sgt., 102
Bentinck, Lord George, 282
Beresford, Lord Marcus, 283
Berlin, 119
Bernhard, Prince of the Netherlands, 253
Bevin, Ernest, 213
Birkhall, 120, 122, 151, 193, 271, 275, 292
Black Watch, The, 37, 38, 41, 102, 251, 270
Black Watch (Royal Highland Regiment) of Canada, 271
Blacker, Sir G., 89
Bloemfontein, (S.A.), 224
Blondin, Charles, 185
Blunt, Rt. Rev., Bishop of Bradford, 154
Boleyn, Anne, 16
Bourguiba, President, 270
Bowes-Lyon, the family history, 28–32, 62, 179–80
Bowes-Lyon, The Hon. Alexander, 18, 37
Bowes-Lyon, Sir David, 18–30, 32–4 36–9, 119, 127, 213, 239, 279, 292
Bowes-Lyon, Captain, The Hon. Fergus, 18, 38, 41, 102
Bowes-Lyon, The Hon John Herbert, 18, 38, 119
Bowes-Lyon, John Patrick, (Master of Glamis), 206, 238
Bowes-Lyon, Lady Mary Frances, (see Lady Elphinstone)
Bowes-Lyon, Captain, the Hon. Michael, 18, 43, 44, 119, 239
Bowes-Lyon, The Hon, Patrick, (1863–1947), 33
Bowes-Lyon, Lady Rose, (Countess Granville), 18, 37, 38, 42
Bowes-Lyon, Timothy, Lord Glamis, (see 16th Earl of Strathmore)
Boyd, H., 235

Braemar, 117, 120
Brandon, 183
Brechin, 41, 292
Brechin, Bishop of, 41
Bridges, Sir Tom, 108
Britannia, R.Y., 270, 271
British Assurance Association, 287
British Broadcasting Corporation, 64
British Empire Exhibition, 87, 88, 94
Broadlands, Hampshire, 232, 289
Brooke, Rear-Admiral Sir Basil, 80, 193
Brookshaw, Tim, 288
Brown, 'Capability', 28
Brown, George, 124
Brown, Mrs. Gevina, 124
Brown, John, 34, 162, 258, 273
Bruce, of Melbourne, 1st Viscount, 92
Brussels, 141, 261
Bruton Street, No. 17, 46, 53–4, 71, 88–91
Buccleuch, Duke of, 142–3
Buchanan, President of U.S., 184
Buckingham Palace, 63, 64, 66–9, 73, 115, 126, 128, 142, 149, 162, 165–6, 169, 196, 197–8, 203, 241, 252, 254
Buist, Cmdr. Colin, 80, 99
Bulawayo, 226
Bull, Mr., 62
Burnaby, Evelyn, 273

Cagliari, 270
Caithness, 206–7
Caledonian Society of France, 141
Calgary, 183
Camberley, 206
Cambridge, Lady Mary (see Duchess of Beaufort)
Cambridge, Lady May, (Lady Abel Smith), 62, 131, 179, 272
Cambridge, Marquess of, 62, 193
Campbell, Archibald, 32
Canada, 13, 14, 127, 178–88, 189, 270, 271
Canary Islands, 99–100
Canberra, 92, 107–8
Cape Town, 221, 222–3, 227–8
Cape Town, University of, 227–8
Cardiff, 128, 138
Carlow, Viscount, 253
Carnegie, Lord, 78, 258
Carol, King of Rumania, 178
Carisbrooke, Marquis of, 191, 289
Cator, Elizabeth (Hon. Mrs. Michael Bowes-Lyon), 62, 119
Cavan, Earl of, 100
Cavan, Lady, 99
Cavendish-Bentinck, Rev. Charles, 2
Cavigneaux, Madame, 275
Cazalet, Major P., 286, 287